DELL RECOMMENDS WINDOWS VISTA® HOME PREMIUM.

studio

Your perfect combination of style and performance

PRICES START FROM £449
AT DELL.CO.UK

ALL NEW! With a 15.6" Form Factor - 16:9 - display and sub-woofer enhanced audio.

studio 15

- Intel® Pentium® processor T4200
- Genuine Windows Vista® Home Premium
- 2GB Memory & 160GB Hard Drive
- 15.6" WXGA LED Screen with True-Life™
- Dell 1397 Wireless Card
- Integrated 2.0MP Webcam

Price Incl. Savings¹, VAT & Delivery
E-Value Code: PCPUK05-N0553501

£449

Standard colour is black. Upgrade to a choice of 4 plain colours available for just £29. Or a Mike Ming graffiti-inspired cover for just £69.

Change your laptop cover to suit you – and change the world. Choose any Artist's (PRODUCT RED)™ design and you help fight AIDS in Africa for just £69.

With built-in Wi-Fi, for multimedia entertainment and everything else, anywhere.

studio 17

- Intel® Pentium® processor T4200
- Genuine Windows Vista® Home Premium
- 2GB Memory & 160GB Hard Drive
- 17" Screen with True-Life™
- Dell 1397 Wireless Card

Price Incl. Savings¹, VAT & Delivery
E-Value Code: PCPUK05-N0573501

£449

Standard colour is black. Upgrade to a choice of 7 plain colours available for just £29. Or a Mike Ming graffiti-inspired cover for just £69.

mini

Your ultra-portable internet companion

PRICES START FROM £199
AT DELL.CO.UK

Netbook portability and connectivity with an optional built-in tuner so you can also enjoy TV on its 10.1" edge-to-edge screen.

MINI 10

- Intel® Atom™ Processor N270
- Ubuntu Edition version 8.04
- 1GB Memory
- 8GB SSD hard drive
- 10.1" WSVGA Screen True-Life™
- Dell 1397 Wireless Card
- Integrated 1.3MP Webcam

Price Incl. Savings¹, VAT & Delivery
E-Value Code: PCPUK05-N05B1001

£199

Add a fun cover by Tristan Eaton, graffiti artist and toy designer for a cool £35.

You can choose to liven up your Mini 10 with a bright colour cover for just £19.

Click: dell.co.uk/deals | Call: 0844 444 3031

8am-9pm Weekdays, 9am-6pm Saturdays, 10am-5pm Sundays

Beginner's Photoshop

The easy way to getting started with Adobe Photoshop

Imagine Publishing Ltd
Richmond House
33 Richmond Hill
Bournemouth
Dorset BH2 6EZ
☎ +44 (0) 1202 586200
Website: www.imagine-publishing.co.uk

Designed by
Carly Barrett
Stacey Groves
Alison Innes
Katy Ledger
Kate Logsdon

Proofed by
Julie Easton, Colleen Johnson and Rosie Tanner

Editor in Chief
Jo Cole

Head of Design
Ross Andrews

Printed by
William Gibbons, 26 Planetary Road, Willenhall, West Midlands, WV13 3XT

ISBN 978-1-906078-29-4

IMAGINE PUBLISHING

Beginner's
Photoshop
The easy way to getting started with Adobe Photoshop

Welcome

Even if you have never used Photoshop before, you will find something to do in this book! We have gathered together tutorials and features that when combined, give you all you need to know in order to master the fundamental Photoshop skills.

We understand that Photoshop can seem intimidating, but you'll soon see how the same tools crop up in different situations. Once you get the hang of them you can use them for all sorts of image-editing jobs. That's not to say

that Photoshop doesn't have its tricky moments. It can be used to a very advanced level and there are some tools that are only called upon by professionals. But even if you are a complete beginner, you can use the program to create the images you want without getting bogged down.

To help you start your Photoshop journey, we have divided this book up into chapters. Each chapter deals with a 'part' of Photoshop – something that it is often used for. We begin each chapter

with an overview of the tools most commonly used for the task at hand. You'll start to see here how the same faces cross over into other chapters! You can also find a video tutorial for each chapter on the disc. for extra guidance .

Although we've targeted the tutorials to beginners, don't feel bad if you find one that's beyond your grasp. Leave it for now, work through the other tutorials and when you come back to it, you'll be surprised at how much your Photoshop skills have improved!

Chapters

Photo editing
Tutorials for editing photos to perfection

Restore photos
Bring your old print photos back to life

Photomanipulation
Vital advice for turning your photos into something unexpected!

Retouch your photos
Smooth skin, remove blemishes and more...

Creative projects
Easy ways to make digital art out of your photos

Like the tutorials in this book? They come from *Photoshop Creative* magazine – see how you can subscribe on page 151

contents

230

252

162

140

Over
70 toolbar tips

Get ready for the ultimate tour around the Photoshop toolbar, where
Tim Shelbourne uncovers some hidden gems and some insightful tips along the way

It's a fact that even if you were to spend the rest of your days studying Photoshop, you'd always find something new to learn about this super-powerful, highly intricate app.

Even Photoshop pros, who know more than most about the various tools and the way they work, are continually discovering shortcuts, workarounds and tricks. Over the next ten pages we're not only going to show you some of the basics about the Photoshop tools you know and love, but we'll also throw in lots of tips, hidden features and tricks.

Some of these tips will simply make your Photoshop workflow more efficient and seamless, but many of them will also reveal hidden gems about particular tools that can make a difference, not only to the way you work, but also to the quality of your output.

So, if you're in a pickle with the Pen tool or you've got trouble with Type, read on! There's something here for everyone, and you might just glimpse some hidden gems of Photoshop treasure along the way! Your toolbar education starts right here.

Losing the Lasso

If you've started making a selection with one of the Lasso tools and don't like the way it's going, just hit the ESC key on the keyboard to delete it and start over again.

Move tool: Quick transform

While using the Move tool (V), you can easily transform the current layer. With the Move tool active, simply check Show Transform in the Options bar. You can now use the transformation handles around the bounding box to transform the layer.

Marquee tools

As well as creating single selections in a predefined shape, with the Marquee tools you can combine multiple selections in many different ways. The key to doing this lies in Selection options in the top left of the Options bar. Once you have your first selection active, from these buttons, you can choose how your next selection will combine with the first. You can choose to add the second to the first selection, subtract it from the existing selection, or even specify that the final selection is the result of the intersecting area.

Lasso tools

Although the Freehand Lasso and Polygonal Lasso are two separate tools, you can use them both together via a keyboard shortcut. Simply choose the Freehand variety and hold down the Alt key whenever you want to use its Polygonal counterpart. As you can see in the illustration, this allows you to draw selections with both freehand and straight sections easily.

Magnetic Lasso Frequency

The Magnetic Lasso is a great way of making quick selections around complicated shapes. Photoshop will attempt to 'detect' the edges of the object and place anchor points along these edges, forming a selection. If you're trying to select a complicated, intricate shape, increase the Frequency value in the Options bar so that these anchor points are placed more closely together.

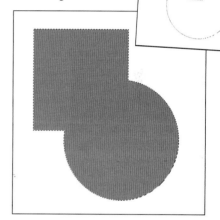

Stroking selections

To stroke a selection, for instance to create a key line over an image, once the selection is made, you can simply go to Edit>Stroke, enter the stroke width you want to use and choose Inside, Center or Outside for the location of the stroke. Choose a colour for the stroke from the colour swatch.

> "In order to close your final selection with the Lasso tools, click back on the point you started from"

Fixed Size In the Style Box in the Options bar, you can make Marquee selections a Fixed Size, Fixed Aspect Ratio or Normal, where you can drag to set the height/width.

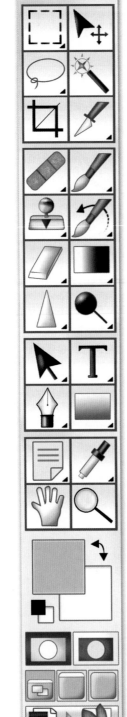

Smooth selections

With any of the Selection tools you can turn on Anti-aliasing. It's important to have it active to avoid any 'jaggies' around the edges of a selection.

Move tool: selecting layers

With the Move tool active, hold down Ctrl and click on a layer element to select that particular layer. To select more layers, hold down Shift as well.

Move tool: duplicating layers

To duplicate a layer with the Move tool, simply position the tool over an element on the layer, hold down the Alt key and drag!

A trusty shield

When you crop an image, areas outside the crop are overlaid with a translucent shield, To change its colour, click in the colour swatch; change Opacity using the slider.

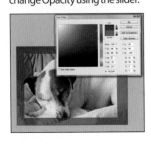

Selections made easy

Magic Wand tool Tolerance: The Magic Wand tool makes a selection of pixels based on colour. If you find there are too many areas of different colours included in your selection, try reducing the Tolerance value. At a value of Zero, the tool will select one single colour in the image; at the Maximum setting it will select every colour in the photograph.

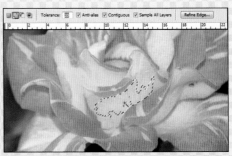

Quick Selection tool: With the Quick Selection tool you can simply paint your selection. Once the painted selection is active, you can remove areas from the selection by painting within it with the tool while holding down the Alt key on the keyboard. Control the Hardness of your brush by clicking in the Brush Picker as usual.

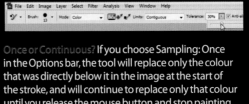

Color Replacement tool

Color Replacement tool Tolerance: The Tolerance is very important when using this tool. A low Tolerance value will only replace colour that's very similar, so increase the Tolerance setting to replace a wider range of colour either side of the original colour the tool sampled.

Once or Continuous? If you choose Sampling: Once in the Options bar, the tool will replace only the colour that was directly below it in the image at the start of the stroke, and will continue to replace only that colour until you release the mouse button and stop painting. Sampling: Continuous will replace the colour directly below it at any point within your stroke. To replace just a single colour in a certain area, choose Sampling: Once.

Adding extra canvas

Drag a crop around the image in the usual way. Now drag on the handles around the crop box to extend it outside the outer edges. Hit Return to add the extra canvas area using the current background colour. A great way to create simple borders!

Quick Selection tool brush sizing

You can change the size of the Selection brush you're painting with as you're actually painting the selection itself. Simply increase the size of the brush by hitting the right bracket on the keyboard, and make it smaller by hitting the left bracket.

Brush tool: Quick sizing

Rather than click in the Brush Picker each time, resize your brushes via the bracket keys on the keyboard. Use the right bracket key to make the brush bigger, and the left bracket to make it smaller.

Grid help When drawing from point to point with the Pencil tool, you'll find it easier to use the grid as a guide. Display this via View>Show>Grid.

Bedazzled by brushes

When it comes to using the Brush tool, it's vital to know your way around the Brushes palette. Here we'll look at the most important areas within this palette, for ultimate control of your brushes. You can display this indispensable palette via Window>Brushes.

Brush Tip Shape: From here you can choose your brush tip and change its size. Use the Angle and Roundness values to angle your brush and squeeze its shape. The Spacing slider determines how close the brush dabs are placed together.

Brushes galore: You're not limited to the standard Photoshop brushes – there are hundreds of others available. Just click on the small arrow in the top left of the palette to choose another brush library. Take time to experiment with the different varieties – they go on forever!

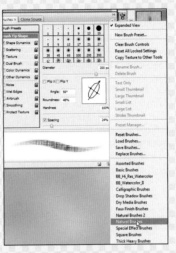

Texture: Here, you can click in the Pattern swatch and pick a texture from the Artists Surfaces selection – a great way to create natural media effects.

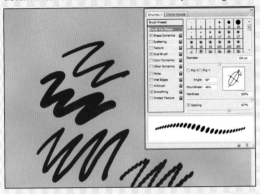

Dynamics: Here you can make Opacity and Size respond to pressure you apply with a pressure-sensitive tablet or stylus. Set Control to Pen Pressure.

Scattering: Modify this slider to scatter brush dabs either side of the central line of the brush stroke – a great way to create brushes with lots of texture.

A brush with history

The History brush does exactly what it says on the tin: it paints with history, at least in terms of what you've already done to an image in Photoshop. To use the tool, you need to have access to your History palette. Display this via Window>History.
In the example on the left, we opened the colour image and then desaturated it (Image>Adjustments>Desaturate). By clicking in the History Brush Source box by the side of the words 'Open state' in the palette, we could then paint with the brush in the image to reveal the original colour from the Open state wherever we wanted it. By using this method, you can paint any kind of History state back into your image. Talk about turning back time!

Selection edges

With all the Selection tools in Photoshop CS3, you have the option of using the Refine Edge command once the selection is active. Choose this facility by hitting the Refine Edge button in the Options bar.

Refine Edge: On White

Within the Refine Edge dialog itself, choose the On White thumbnail to display a white mask over the unselected areas. This makes refining the selection much easier.

Refine Edge: Feather

Rather than set a Feather Radius to use with the Selection tool, use the Feather slider in the Refine Edge box. This is a far more accurate and controllable way of feathering an active selection.

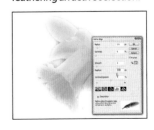

Pencil tool: the straight and narrow Having trouble drawing straight lines with the Pencil tool? Just hold down the Shift key as you draw.

Gradient tool

Using a Black/White gradient on a layer mask is an excellent way of creating a super smooth transition from one image to another on a layer below. To do this, add a layer mask to your top layer (Layer>Layer Mask>Show All) and choose the Gradient tool; select Linear Gradient from the Options bar. Choose Black/White gradient from the Gradient Picker. Click directly on the layer mask thumbnail in the Layers palette and drag your gradient across the image. Black areas of the gradient will hide anything on that layer, and white areas will make it visible. In the Layers palette you can see the layer mask itself containing the gradient. This is the layer that is selected.

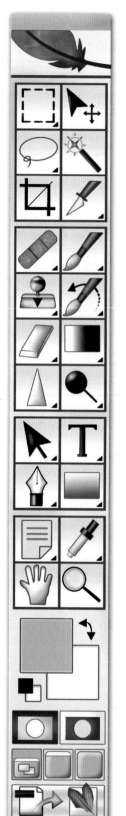

Gradient patterns

You have five patterns of gradient to choose from, all showing as buttons in the Options bar

Linear

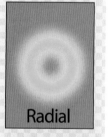
Angle

Radial

Reflected

Diamond

Point to point

To draw from point to point with the Pencil tool, click a start point and then simply Shift-click an end point to draw a line in between. A great way of drawing straight-sided geometric shapes!

The Patch tool

The Patch tool is great for subtle cosmetic retouching, especially if you use it on a duplicate

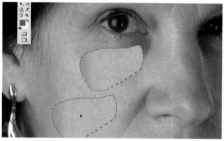

01 Select around the imperfection Open your image and duplicate the background layer. Choose the Patch tool and select Source in the Options bar. Now draw a selection around the area of wrinkles. Click and drag the selected area over a clear section of skin and release the mouse button.

02 Adjust the opacity If the area that has been cloned is a little too smooth, go to Select>Deselect. Reduce the opacity of the duplicate layer until just a little of the original skin texture shows through and the repair looks natural.

03 Alternative method You can also use the Patch tool the opposite way by choosing the Destination option from the Options bar. Now draw a selection around a clear area of skin and then drag and drop it over

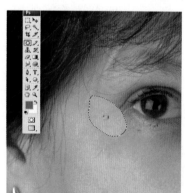

Paintbucket

This is a quick way to fill areas of an image with the current foreground colour. The Tolerance setting determines how similar two colours must be before they are included in the filled area. Contiguous fills continuous areas of the same colours; uncheck this option for those colours to be filled wherever they are in the image.

Cloning tools When you're using one of the Cloning tools, make sure to use a soft brush for seamless repairs.

Attack of the clones

Small and soft: As its name indicates, you can use the Spot Healing brush to clone out small imperfections. Add a new layer to clone onto and choose Sample All Layers in the Options bar, so you can simply delete the layer if things go wrong. Make sure to choose a soft brush to make your healing perfect. Then see it disappear.

Healing brush: If you're cloning out a dark imperfection on a light surface, set the blend mode for the tool to Lighten in the Options bar. Now when you clone, only the dark imperfection will be hidden.

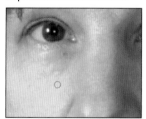

No repeats: With the Spot Healing brush and the Clone Stamp tool, make sure to check Aligned in the Options bar to avoid creating repeating patterns within your cloned area. These can be distracting.

Perfect pupils: When you're using the Red Eye tool, remember that you can adjust both Pupil Size and Darken Amount in the Options bar. It's worth experimenting here to make the correction as seamless as possible – black eyes are scary!

Blur and Smudge tool tricks

Fringe benefits: Use the Smudge tool with a very small brush, with Size set to Pressure in the Brushes palette to 'flick out' around the edge of a cut-out head to break up the outline and simulate stray hairs. Use the tool at a high Strength setting for this.

Instant paintings: Use the Smudge tool with brushes from the Dry Media or Natural Brushes libraries to smudge a digital photo and transform it into a realistic painting. Set the brushes to various strengths.

Blurring masks: When you're using layer masks, if the edges around masked objects are too hard, use the Blur tool to soften them. Make sure to click the layer mask thumbnail in the Layers palette first!

Not so sharp: If you're tempted to use the Sharpen tool to sharpen small areas of an image, it's much better to use it at a very low Strength setting and slowly build up the sharpness by working over the same area repeatedly.

The Clone Stamp tool

It can be quite difficult when you're cloning over an object to know exactly what you're putting in its place. The Show Overlay option in the Clone Source palette makes life much easier!

01 Clone Source palette Once you've chosen the Clone Stamp tool, go to Window>Clone Source. In the Clone Source palette check the box for Show Overlay. Now Alt-click on the clear area of the image you want to clone from.

02 Position and clone You'll now see an overlay image that moves around with your tool pointer. You can use the overlay to match up the pattern of the existing background. As soon as you start clicking to clone, the overlay will fix its position.

03 Repositioning Whenever you Alt-click in another area of the image, the overlay will become mobile again, allowing you to once again find the ideal image section to clone out the next part of the unwanted object.

The mists of time You can even paint with a History state using partial opacity in the brush. Just modify the brush opacity in the Options bar.

Dodgy character

The Dodge tool is a very accurate way to lighten specific areas and ranges of tones in an image, and gives you the ability to almost literally 'paint with light'. First you need to decide which range of tones you wish to lighten – Shadows, Midtones or Highlights. You can choose this range of tones from the Range option in the Options bar. The Exposure setting determines the strength of the effect, and you generally want to use a very low setting here. Now simply choose a soft brush and bush over your chosen area of tone to lighten it. Here' we've chosen Highlights for Range and brushed over the catchlights in the eyes to brighten them.

Words and pictures

When is type not type? When it's a mask! Use this variety of Type tool to fill letters with an image

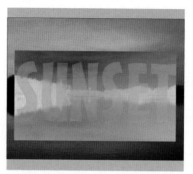

01 **Size and format type** Choose the Horizontal Type Mask tool and enter your type. Highlight the type and change the size and font in the usual way. You can position the type by dragging outside the type area. When you're happy, hit the Commit tick in the Options bar.

02 **Active selection** Now you'll have an active selection generated from the type itself. Go to Edit>Copy, followed by Edit>Paste. This will paste a copy of the selected area on another layer. You can always add a Drop Shadow layer style to this layer, or perhaps even an Outer Glow.

03 **Background fill** You can now fill the original background layer with another colour, or edit it in any way you like. Here we've simply desaturated it and adjusted the levels.

Sponge tool
The Sponge tool can be used to either saturate (make colour more vivid) or desaturate (make colours less intense) the colours in an image. Simply choose Saturate or Desaturate from the Mode option in the Options bar and brush away! The Flow value governs the strength of the tool.

Burning desire

The Burn tool does the exact opposite of its Dodging counterpart, in that it darkens the tones within your chosen range. Again, you can choose Shadows, Midtones or Highlights. Just like the Dodge tool, it's best to use very low Exposure settings. The real advantage of both these tools is that you can choose exactly where in the image you want to darken or lighten the tones, by brushing into that specific area.

Point or Paragraph?
You can use both the Horizontal and Vertical Type tools in a couple of different ways. To create Point Type, simply click wherever you want the type to appear in you canvas. To use Paragraph Type, which is limited by the outer edges of the box around it, click and drag with the Type tool to create the text box. Control the justification of the type (Left Align, Centred or Right Aligned) via the button in the central region of the Options bar.

Let's do the warp
Is your type looking boring? Just click the Warp Text option in the Options bar and choose a Warp style from within the dialog.

Correcting saturation The Burn tool can often oversaturate colours, so use the Sponge tool set to Desaturate after you've burned in an area to correct this.

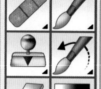

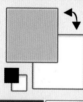

The Shape tools

You might think Shape tools are one-trick ponies, but some gems lie in the little group of overlooked presets!

Shape, Path or Pixels? The Options bar shows three icons. Choose whether you want to make a vector shape, an empty path or a pixel-based shape. Vectors are great, as you can increase them to any size without losing quality and can edit them easily at any stage. Choose Filled Pixels if you won't want to edit the shape too much later.

Shape shifters Once you've drawn a shape as either a shape layer or a path, you can edit the shape easily. Choose the Direct Selection tool to the left of the Shape tool, click on the outline of the shape and manipulate the various nodes around the outside. Curved nodes have direction handles, which you can drag and rotate to adjust.

Putting on the style Once you've created a shape layer, you can easily jazz it up with one of Photoshop's styles. To do this, with the shape layer still active, click in the Style swatch in the Options bar. Simply click one of the preset style thumbnails to apply it to your shape.

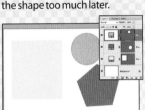

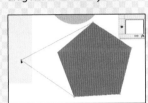

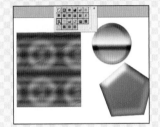

Screen mode

Via the Screen Mode button you can choose from four different workspace views. You can scroll through these views by repeatedly clicking the button, or simply click and hold to activate the fly-out menu and make your choice from there.

Here are your options:
Standard Screen mode
Maximised Screen mode
Full Screen mode with Menu Bar
Full Screen mode

The Full Screen types are useful if you're transforming a layer and need some working space below the image, because in this mode you can hit the spacebar and use the Hand tool to move the entire image within the workspace. Standard mode is ideal when you have more than one image open and want to see each in a separate window.

Pen tool perfection

The Pen tool is one of the most feared but versatile devices. Here are just a few ways it can help you…

Paths as selections Creating a selection from a path is one of the most accurate ways to isolate an object from its background. First draw your path. Now right-click directly on the path with the Pen tool and choose Make Selection from the sub-menu.

Straight or curved? To draw a straight path section from the previous point you plotted, simply click with the tool. For a curved section, just click and drag.

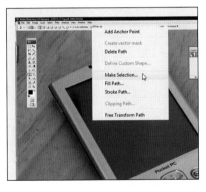

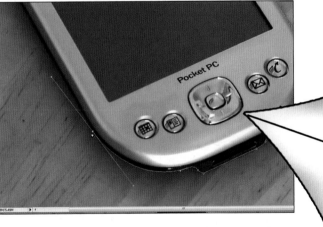

Stroking paths To create really sharp, flowing brush strokes, first draw an open path, right-click it and choose Stroke Path. Check Simulate Pressure and choose Brush for Tool. Your path will be stroked using the current brush and foreground colour.

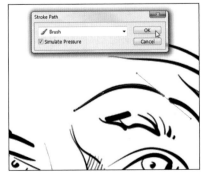

Stay on the right path The current path, known as the 'work path', is shown in the Paths palette. To save this path for future use, simply give it a new name by double-clicking it in the Path palette.

Combine shapes

Use Add to Shape, Subtract from Shape, and the Intersect button in the Options bar to change how two shapes combine as you create them, in the same way as you can when creating selections with the Marquee tools.

Colour be gone! To restrict colour to one area, set the Sponge tool to Desaturate and the Flow to 100%. Now paint over any areas you want to be monochrome.

Eyedropper tool

To choose a colour from your image and set it as the foreground swatch, simply choose the Eyedropper and click on a colour in your image.

To choose a colour from your image and set it as the background, hold the Alt key and click with the Eyedropper. You can set Colour Sample Points with the eyedropper, which makes the RGB measurements for that colour remain in the Info palette. To set a sample point, Shift-click in the image. Shift-Ctrl and drag to move an existing point, and Shift-Alt-click to remove one.

To choose a colour from any window, first restore down Photoshop so you can see the window with the colour you wish to sample in the background. Click and hold in the Photoshop workspace, hold down Shift and move to the area of the screen to sample. When you release the mouse button, the colour below the Eyedropper will be set as the foreground.

Change the area size the Eyedropper samples a colour from, via the Sample Size option in the Options bar.

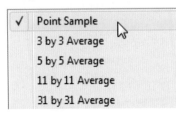

Ruler tool

Got a wonky horizon line in your image? You can easily fix this with the Ruler tool. Choose the tool and click and hold on the horizon line at one side of the image. Still holding the mouse button down, drag over to the horizon line at the other side of the image to create a ruler line. Now go to Image>Rotate Canvas>Arbitrary. Photoshop will automatically enter the required rotation direction and amount, so just click OK. You may need to crop off any areas of blank canvas with the Crop tool.

Using Quick Mask

One of the most accurate ways of making very complex selections is to use Quick Mask mode. Don't draw your selections – paint them!

01 Quick Mask Either hit the Quick Mask button at the base of the toolbar or press 'Q' on the keyboard to activate Quick Mask mode. Next, choose the Brush tool and ensure your foreground colour is black. Set the brush Opacity to 100%. Now simply start to paint over the object you wish to select.

02 Making corrections If you make a mistake and paint over the edge of the object, simply paint again with white to remove the red overlay from that area. You can even paint with the brush at a lower opacity to select an area at partial transparency.

03 Brush variations For selections that will have a soft edge around them, just paint with a soft brush instead of a hard one. To select tiny details, use a very small brush and zoom well into the image. When done, hit 'Q' to exit Quick Mask and generate the selection.

Quick Mask trick

By default, when you exit Quick Mask mode, Photoshop selects the areas outside the area you painted over with black. To change this, double-click the Quick Mask button and choose Selected Areas instead of Masked Areas.

Colour Once you've created a shape on a shape layer, change the colour of the shape by double-clicking the colour thumbnail for the layer in the Layers palette.

Foreground/background colour swatches

These swatches indicate the two colours you currently have to work with – one in the foreground, which your painting tools will use, and another in the background. This background colour, among other things, is the colour that your Eraser will reveal when you use it. To the bottom right of these swatches is a small black and white symbol that you can click to revert to Photoshop's default foreground and background colours.

To swap the current foreground and background colours, click on the arrow to the top right of the swatches or simply press X on your keyboard. You can choose a new colour for either of the swatches, either by clicking on them and choosing from the Picker or by selecting a new colour from the Colors palette.

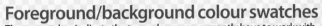

"These swatches indicate the two colours you currently have to work with"

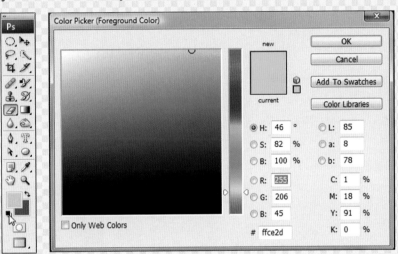

Quick Mask colour
By default, the mask colour in Quick Mask mode is red, but you can change this to any colour. Just click the Quick Mask button, click in the colour swatch and choose a new one from the Color Picker.

Handy Hand tool

Rather than choose this tool from the toolbar, you can access it at any time, whatever tool you're currently using, by holding down the spacebar on the keyboard. Easily pan around your image with just one shortcut!

Hand tool

Double-click the Hand tool button in the toolbar to fit the image within the workspace at the maximum size possible.

Are you ready for ImageReady?

If you need to reduce the file size of your images to send via email or post on the web, ImageReady, sitting at the base of the toolbar, is just for you!

01 Viewing different quality settings Open your image and click the button to launch ImageReady. Within the ImageReady dialog you can choose to view many versions of your images, each at a different quality setting. It's generally best to click on the '4-Up' tab so that you can make a good visual comparison between them.

02 Choose a preset After selecting one of the thumbnails, you can choose your desired file type and quality settings from the Presets list on the right of the dialog. Here we've chosen JPEG Medium. You can always click on another thumbnail and choose another preset for comparison.

03 Size and save Below each thumbnail you'll see the resultant file size. Click on the Image Size tab in the bottom right and enter new dimensions for the final image in pixels. Make sure to hit Apply after doing this. When you're happy, choose the thumbnail with the quality you like and hit Save. Choose Image Only for Save as Type.

Blur to soften When you've painted your Quick Mask, you can use the Blur tool around the edges of the painted selection to soften it.

Chapter I

Photo editing

Fail-safe ways of editing your photos to perfection

Tip

Use layers!

:::: If you don't feel comfortable with using layer masks or adjustment layers, simply duplicate the photo you want to edit onto a new layer. That way if anything goes wrong, you still have the original.

Quick start photo-editing tutorial on the CD

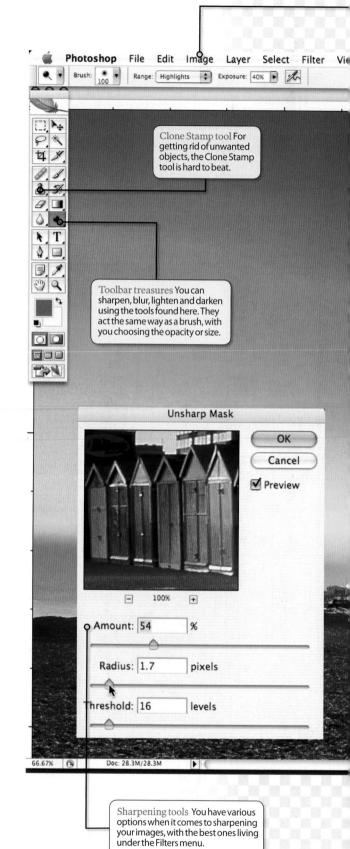

Clone Stamp tool For getting rid of unwanted objects, the Clone Stamp tool is hard to beat.

Toolbar treasures You can sharpen, blur, lighten and darken using the tools found here. They act the same way as a brush, with you choosing the opacity or size.

Unsharp Mask

Amount: 54 %
Radius: 1.7 pixels
Threshold: 16 levels

Sharpening tools You have various options when it comes to sharpening your images, with the best ones living under the Filters menu.

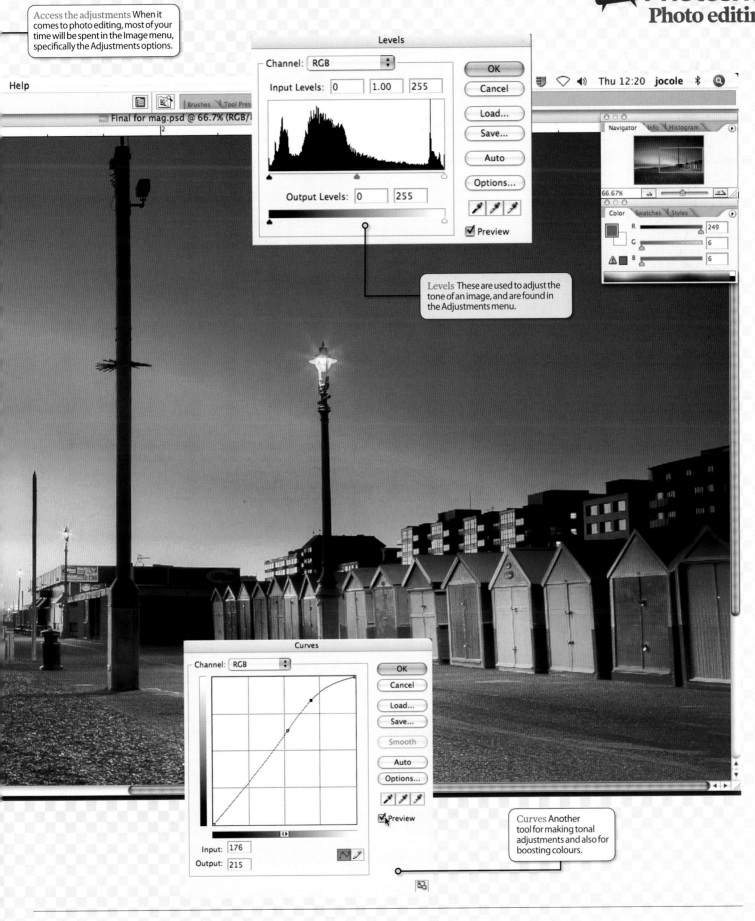

Access the adjustments When it comes to photo editing, most of your time will be spent in the Image menu, specifically the Adjustments options.

Levels These are used to adjust the tone of an image, and are found in the Adjustments menu.

Levels

Channel: RGB

Input Levels: 0   1.00   255

Output Levels: 0   255

OK
Cancel
Load...
Save...
Auto
Options...

☑ Preview

Help

Final for mag.psd @ 66.7% (RGB/

Thu 12:20   jocole

Navigator   Info   Histogram

66.67%

Color   Swatches   Styles

R   249
G   6
B   6

Curves

Channel: RGB

OK
Cancel
Load...
Save...
Smooth
Auto
Options...

☑ Preview

Input: 176
Output: 215

Curves Another tool for making tonal adjustments and also for boosting colours.

Photo editing

Discover the tools to breathe new life into your photos

Essentials

YOUR EXPERT
Jo Cole

ON THE DISC
Quick start
photo-editing
tutorial on the CD

Photo editing is at the heart of Photoshop so it is no surprise to find a merry gaggle of tools and commands that allow you to tame otherwise unwieldy images.

If ever there was a subject to show the full extent of Photoshop's capabilities, it would be photo editing. Users can begin with tweaks that involve a mere mouse-click and progress all the way up to complex edits that call upon a host of different tools, techniques and skills.

Photo editing is a good place for Photoshop beginners to embark on their quest for Photoshop knowledge. To correct common photo problems, you call upon a lot of the essential Photoshop tools. Fair enough, you may be using them in quite a simple way but you are still familiarising yourself with the program and how it works. And that's always the best way to learn – making lots of small edits will soon add up to an invaluable bank of knowledge about what the tools do and how different options will affect the final result. One day you won't even think about what you are doing. You will just see a problem that needs fixing and instinctively go to the best tool for the job.

Over the course of this chapter, you will discover how to use the tools needed to fix common photo problems. You know the sorts of things we mean – unwanted objects creeping into a shot, dull and lifeless colours, slight blur from a wobbly camera… all the usual suspects! While the list of problems you need to fix might seem infinite, the good news is that you only have to worry about a core set of tools. And you can find out about them from here.

 Sharpen tool If you just have a small area to sharpen, try the Sharpen tool. This allows you to paint over an area to sharpen it up.

LEVELS AND CURVES
Making tonal adjustments

Tonal value is very important in photography and images that display a high tonal range are usually more appealing than those that are tonally flat. The aim is to have good shadow, good highlights and plenty of tone in between. The Levels command (found under Image>Adjustments) is the prima ballerina of tonal adjustment tools, as it allows you to target the shadows, highlights and midtones of an image.

All you have to do is decide what it is that needs to be helped and then adjust the appropriate slider. You can also use the Curves command (also found in the Adjustments area) and move the curve to tweak tonality.

THE CLONE STAMP TOOL
Remove unwanted objects

How many times have you got so caught up in what it is you are photographing that you've failed to notice that an unwanted object has also crept into the frame? Photoshop offers various tools that let you make objects vanish, but the king of the castle has to be the Clone Stamp tool as it's just so easy to use. With this, you can select one area of an image and copy the information into another area, hiding your unwanted object. So if someone on a jetski has ruined your shot of the ocean, sample some clean waves and paint the offender out of the image! We will look at the tool and its options throughout the different chapters.

The options You can find the main sharpen tools under the Filter menu.

 Thu 03:44

Tool Presets | Layer Comps

Unsharp mask This is the most popular of the sharpening tools and is very easy to apply. Rather than detect the edges of an image, it emphasises the qualities of areas with similar characteristics. For example, if you had a green apple on a blue background, it would emphasise the green and blue and result in a sharper finish.

Quick start photo-editing tutorial on the CD

Tip

Auto delight

To some, the Auto options are a guilty pleasure. When it comes to photo editing, they might be all you need to fix an image so don't dismiss them! Even if you use them to get part of the way, a quick blast of Auto Levels or Auto Color can work wonders.

CROP TOOL
Zone in on the best bits

Sometimes the simple edits are the most effective and cropping is as easy as it comes! Cropping allows you to chop away 'dead' space in a photo, leaving you with a better composed or more interesting image. The process is simple. Pick the Crop tool from the toolbar, draw around an area on your image and then double-click or hit Enter. Anything outside of the area you have drawn around will be deleted. You can adjust the size of your chosen area once it's drawn and can even restrict the size to a standard format. In our example here, we have decided to zone in on the Empire State Building and get rid of the rest.

COLOUR CORRECTION
Make those colours sing

Often a quick boost of a photo's colours will bring it out of the shadows and turn it into something special. Photoshop has a wide range of different tools to help you achieve colour perfection – here are our favourites, all found in the Image>Adjustments menu

Hue/Saturation
Boost or completely alter
The Hue/Saturation command (Image>Adjustments) lets you edit the colours (hues) in an image, whether it's what the colours are or how bright they appear. You can apply a change to the entire image or use the Edit drop-down menu to focus on a certain colour. Here we have turned the greens into vibrant reds.

Color Balance
Choose your way The Color Balance command is useful when you want to alter the overall colours in an image. For example, Color Balance can be used to boost weak colours in an image. Decide on what colour you want to improve and then use the relevant slider to adjust. In our example here, we have boosted the blues in the photo to get a more life-like finish.

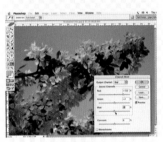

Channel Mixer
Don't be frightened! Now, we aren't going to lie to you – the Channel Mixer is a powerful tool that can be used for complex tasks. For nice and easy edits, though, it can also be employed to good effect. The dialog offers different colours to edit using the familiar slider system. Pick the colour that you want to improve or remove and wiggle the slider!

Photo filters
Life through rose-tinted glasses
Photographers among you might be used to coloured photo filters – small discs of coloured glass placed in front of a camera lens. Well, now Photoshop does all of this for you, thanks to the Photo Filters. You have lots of different filters at your disposal. Have a weak sunset shot? Apply a red photo filter for instant drama.

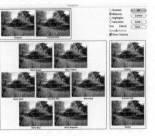

Variations
Pick and choose The Variations command is very easy to use and very addictive too. It basically lays out a choice of colour edits on a platter for you to then decide which one works for your chosen image. It is perfect if you aren't very confident with making edits, as it shows you what the final result will be like before you commit.

Exposure workshop

Exposure is one of the trickiest techniques to master in photography, but with the onset of digital cameras, results are realised instantly.

Comparing exposures and making adjustments is now much easier and cheaper than using film. Once the basics have been mastered, you can utilise exposure for creating special effects. For example, you can use a slower shutter speed to convey motion or a very fast shutter speed to freeze movement. Varying the aperture will change the depth of field and therefore the level of focus in your images. A smaller F stop

number (larger aperture) can be used for softening the background of a subject such as a portrait. A higher F stop number (smaller aperture) can be used to bring more elements into focus.

Aperture is directly linked with exposure, and to achieve full control you're going to need an understanding of how exposure works in conjunction with shutter speed and aperture.

In this feature we'll introduce exposure and show you some examples of how the different metering modes work with certain subjects. We'll also discuss what can be

done to fix over- or underexposed images in Photoshop. We'll then explain how to work with multiple exposures for dramatic effect and increase the tonal range of an exposure. And along the way, you'll find a wealth of general exposure tips for camera and post-camera settings and adjustments. So, if you have your camera at the ready, it's time to start testing those metering modes.

Cameras have varying abilities when it comes to metering light, but most will allow you some degree of manual adjustment. Even the prefixed settings for the right subject will help give you more accurate exposures.

☑ Auto Select Layer ☑ Auto Select Groups ☐ Show Transform Controls

Metering your shot

Camera skills

A photographic exposure combines the amount of light and length of time that light is allowed to fall on a photo-sensitive material within the camera (film or image sensor). The quantity of light is controlled by the aperture ring inside the lens of the camera

The amount of time is adjusted by the shutter speed, which controls the rate that the shutter opens and closes. Exposure is measured in lux seconds; film and sensor sensitivity is measured by an ISO rating. The higher the ISO the more sensitive the

> "It's the independent adjustment of aperture and shutter speed that gives you the most control"

medium is to light.

A larger aperture will allow more light through the lens and therefore increase exposure. A slower shutter speed does the same; the shutter is open longer, so the medium is exposed to more light. It's the independent adjustment of aperture and shutter speed that gives you the most control over exposure.

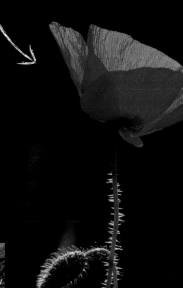

What shutter speed?
You will need to decide on shutter speed – this is dictated by your subject. A moving subject will need a faster shutter speed than a static one.

Search for average tones
Examine the tones in your subject. What you're looking for is average/neutral tones to take a meter reading from. Here the green leaf would be a good average tone.

Choose a metering mode
The metering mode depends on the subject. In this case, Spot metering has been chosen for metering off red petals in the poppy.

Take a reading
With the metering on Spot, camera on Manual, take a meter reading such as green grass (neutral tone). Adjust the shutter speed and aperture until the light meter indicator falls in the o or middle position.

Metering modes

Centre-weighted
Centre-weighted is effective when the subject has a large area of light or dark tone on the edges of the frame

WB A   L N ISO 100

● ⊡ AE-L   125 F5.6 P   [1]

Spot view **Spot metering can be used to take a single reading in the (neutral) shadow area of the snow image to prevent the sunlight areas from being overexposed**

● ⊡ AE-L 125 F5.6 P [1]

WB A   L N ISO 100

● ⊞ AE-L 125 F5.6 P [1]

Matrix view **In this zebra image, the even spread of black and white across the skin works well for multiple point reading in matrix metering**

Underexposure

A quick glance at the digital display on the back will give you a good indication of whether an image is at the desired exposure. Adjustments to the aperture/shutter speed can be made and the image reshot.

But sometimes there isn't time to shoot another frame, because you're in a hurry or the subject has moved out of shot. Or you might have deliberately underexposed the image so you can shoot at a faster shutter speed. Whatever the reason, Photoshop gives you flexibility in adjusting your exposures. Here's a common example, where the sky is at the correct exposure but the land is too dark. Let's see what we can do to fix this.

There are a host of ways to fix an entirely underexposed image. Using Curves and Levels adjustments are very effective if you're shooting in JPEG or TIF and have an early version of Photoshop. The key is to make sure you use adjustment layers. These will let you make further adjustments at a later stage. If you have an advanced digital camera such as an SLR, it's likely to offer Raw mode. This unprocessed format will give you greater flexibility when making exposure adjustments.

The Camera Raw Converter shipped with later versions of Photoshop allows effective exposure control in an easy-to-use dialog. (If you have a recent camera, the Camera Raw plug-in may need updating to support your Raw files – download from the Adobe site.)

The Camera Raw Converter has a host of adjustment options for brightening images. The Exposure control is the key adjustment. This, in combination with Fill Light, Recovery and Blacks lets you significantly lighten images. Opening images from Raw format as 16-bit colour will also allow a higher degree of tolerance and quality preservation when pushing up brightness. As a 16-bit file has more tonal info to start with, drastic corrections to colour or tones will show less degradation.

"The Camera Raw Converter shipped with later versions of Photoshop allows effective exposure control"

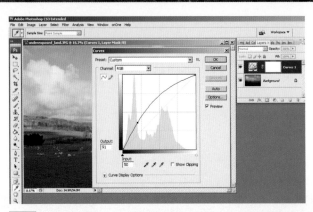

01 Assess the image Open 'underexposed_land.jpg'. Here is a good example, showing a somewhat underexposed foreground that is in shadow and a reasonably well exposed sky, so the land needs selective brightening.

02 Add an adjustment layer The trick is to adjust the exposure of the land while keeping the sky as it is. Click on the Add Adjustment Layer icon at the bottom of the Layers palette and choose Curves.

03 Curves adjustment With the Curves dialog open, add a point near the bottom of the graph. This affects shadow areas of the image. Drag the point upwards until you see lightening of the shadows.

Underexposure quick fixes

Brighten midtones in Levels

Create a Levels adjustment layer by clicking the icon at the bottom of the Layers palette. Move the Midtone slider to the left and the Highlights to the left. This will brighten the whole image.

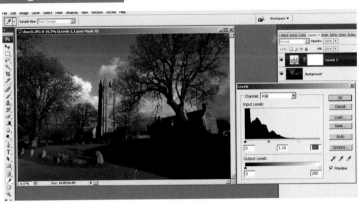

Brighten shadows in Curves

Add a Curves adjustment layer. In the Curves box, place a point near the bottom left. This area affects shadows. Pull upwards to create a curve. The dark areas will lighten.

Raw adjustments

Open 'hillside.dng' in Camera Raw. The Camera Raw box should load. Toggle the preview tick at the top on/off to see a 'before and after' version of your image.

Muddy snow

A camera meter is calibrated for an average tone with average reflectance. An average tone reflects about 18 per cent of the light, whereas snow will reflect about 76 per cent. The camera compensates for this, making the snow look grey. To combat this, you can open up two stops by using the exposure compensation dial [EV =/-] + 2. Alternatively, take a spot reading in the shadow area of the snow.

04 **Select the Gradient tool** Now click on the mask, the white square next to the image in the Layers palette, then select the Gradient tool (G). Set black as the foreground colour and white as the background colour.

05 **Add a Gradient mask** Draw a vertical line from the top of the image downwards. The original exposure of the sky should show through in combination with the brightened foreground.

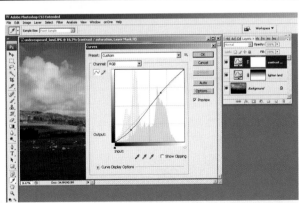

06 **Final adjustment** Finally, add another Curves adjustment layer and create an S-curve, shown in the image. This helps boost the contrast and saturation for the adjusted exposure.

Overexposure

Overexposure quick fixes

Levels
When clouds are overexposed to the point where there is no colour information left, then the white point can be shifted to add off-white back in. Go to New Adjustment Layer>Levels. Move the Highlight Output Levels slider in to 240.

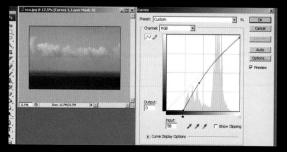

Curves
Some overexposed images can end up looking rather flat and dull. Curves are useful here, because they not only affect contrast but saturation. Go to New Adjustment Layer>Curves. Bring the point in at the bottom. Bring a point at the top down.

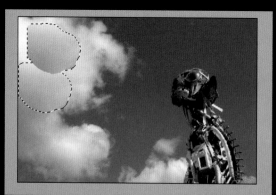

Cloning
Overexposed areas such as clouds can easily be cloned and blended with others that are correctly exposed. Here the Patch tool was used to sample from one area and clone to another. You will notice it's very effective at blending in the edges.

01 **Open the image in Camera Raw** Open Photoshop and go to File>Browse. This should open up Adobe Bridge (CS1 or higher). Find 'overexposed_01.jpg' on the CD and choose File>Open in Camera Raw.

04 **Open it in Photoshop** Now the overexposed area is darkened, we need to selectively adjust the foreground to improve the contrast and brightness. Click Open at the bottom to open in Photoshop.

02 **Highlight the clipping warning** For this demonstration we're using Camera Raw for Photoshop CS3. The interface will vary in older versions. Once the image is open, click on the Highlight Clipping Warning button (O) at the top right.

05 **Curves adjustment** Go to Layer>New Adjustment Layer and choose Curves. Draw an 'S' curve. Now select the Curves layer mask in Layers, and with a black brush paint back the highlight area on the image.

After

After

Adjust the image Overexposed areas show up in red. Now move the Exposure slider on the right to -0.25, the Recovery slider to 60 and the Brightness to -10.

06 **Finishing off** Create a Hue/ Saturation adjustment layer to reduce red and yellow saturation. Select the background layer and the Clone tool (S). Set the blend mode to Darken and Opacity to 8%. Now clone darker patches over the highlights.

Overexposure part 2

Overexposure is common in scenes of dense shadow combined with an area that's in bright sun. If there is detail in the highlights (when the RGB values are not 255,255,255 this is pure white), then the Shadow and Highlights tool can bring back some of the washed-out whites.

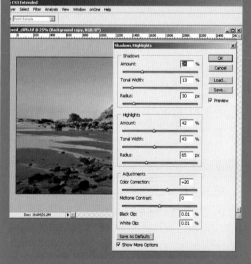

01 **Set up Shadows and Highlights** Open the image 'overexposed_cliffs.jpg'. For CS3 go to Filters>Convert to Smart Filters, and then go to Image>Adjust>Shadows and Highlights. Otherwise, duplicate the layer and then open the Filter menu.

02 **Load up a setting** Inside Shadows and Highlights, click Load and browse the CD for 'reduce_highlights.ssh'. This will add detail to the washed-out highlights. Alternatively, move the Shadows and Highlight sliders to get the desired result.

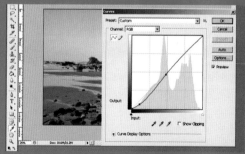

03 **Add contrast** Lastly, add some contrast back into the shadow areas. Go to Layer>New Adjustment Layer>Curves and draw a slight 'S' shape as shown in the image.

Multiple exposures

Before

01 Open the files
Open exposures1', '2' and '3' jpegs. Using the Move tool (V), drag Exposures 3 and 2 onto the Exposure 1 file. Hold down Shift when dragging to snap in the middle.

02 Blending Exposure 3
Hide the top layer. Select Exposure 3 and add a layer mask by clicking the icon at the bottom of the Layers palette. Select the mask, then paint in black the foreground detail from Exposure 1.

03 Blending Exposure 2
Turn on the Exposure 2 layer and add a layer mask. Select the mask and press Ctrl/ Cmd+I to invert to black. Paint selectively in white to reveal the reeds of Exposure 2.

04 Contrast and saturation
Go to Layer> New Adjustment Layer>Curves. Create a gentle 'S' curve to increase contrast and saturation. Use the mask to paint back some of the softer areas at the horizon point.

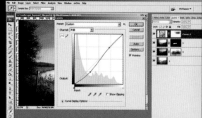

05 Merge and zoom
Press Ctrl/ Cmd+Shift+Alt/Opt+E to merge via Copy onto a new layer. Zoom into the bushes on the right.

06 Lens correction
Go to Filter>Distort>Lens Correction. You'll see a red/cyan fringe. Set Blue/Cyan Fringe to +1. Set Blue/Yellow to -2.

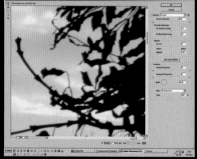

Lighting settings

Sometimes when the lighting in a scene is too extreme for the camera to record all the tonal information in one single exposure, multiple exposures can be taken and then combined in Photoshop.

The six-step walkthrough above shows how to combine three exposures. This covers an exposure for the sky, a midtone exposure and a shadows exposure. The different exposure values can then be revealed or hidden selectively, using masks.

The main advantage over automatically merging multiple exposures is that you can selectively control what areas you want to emphasise or push back.

Like any multiple exposures, the key is to keep the camera in the same place. So for this to work, you'll need a good tripod to prevent camera shake. Ideally you'll then want to put the camera on a Manual or Aperture priority mode so the depth of field does not change between exposures.

> "The key is to keep the camera in the same place. So for this to work, you'll need a good tripod to prevent camera shake"

HDRI images

After

High Dynamic Range Imaging (HDRI) uses methods to increase the dynamic range of an exposure. This often involves merging multiple exposures to produce an image with a wider tonal range, from sunlight to shadows. Everyday computer monitors, such as LCD or CRT screens, have trouble displaying all the tonal information, therefore the resultant image is 'tone mapped' down to a viewable bit depth. Just like the manual method, the images must be taken using a tripod and a fixed aperture. In the example on the right, nine exposures were photographed using the Auto Bracketing feature. Photoshop CS3 Extended was then used to merge all the images together into an HDR file. This file was then tone mapped to a viewable exposure.

01 **Merge files** Go to File>Automate> Merge to HDR and now browse for the images. In this case we've used nine exposures. This will take a long time to process on older computers.

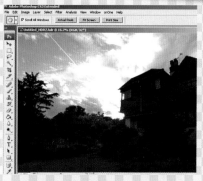

02 **Open HDR file** Once the images have been processed, you can save the file out as an .hdr file.

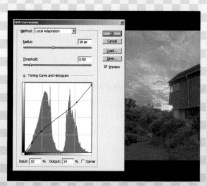

03 **Tone mapping** The HDR file doesn't look much at the moment. Go to Image mode 16bits/channel. Set the HDR conversion to Local Adaptation and adjust the Curve, Radius and Threshold to show the best tonal range.

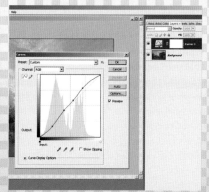

04 **Contrast** Add some curve points to improve the shadows, and add a little more contrast and saturation in the midtones. Convert down to 8-bit for displaying on the web.

Exposure tips

Long exposure – show movement
A long exposure emphasises movement. This was shot at 1/2 second. The water has become a long curtain of soft streaks.

Fast exposure – freeze the action
The waterfall here was shot at 1/500th of a second, fast enough to freeze the water in mid air.

Think in tones, not colours
Look for average tones to take a meter reading. Green grass is a good average tone for metering. A grey card is also handy, if metered next to the subject.

Underexpose if you have to
There may be insufficient light to get the shutter speed you want. A slight underexposure can be fixed in Photoshop, so always take the picture.

BEFORE

AFTER

Essentials

TIME TAKEN
30 minutes

YOUR EXPERT
Matthew Henry

ON THE DISC
High key
before.jpg
High key
after.jpg

High-key portrait

The high-key effect has been popular with portraiture since the early days of the darkroom. Here's how to do it Photoshop-style

Key Photoshop Skills Covered
What you'll learn

INCREASING
CONTRAST
WITH
SHARPENING

PRECISION
CONTRAST
CHANGES
WITH CURVES

DODGING
AND BURNING
WITH CURVES
AND LAYER
MASKS

SMOOTHING
SKIN WITH
GAUSSIAN
BLUR

ADDING NOISE
TO SMOOTHED
AREAS

High-key portraiture is typically characterised by a mass of bright, light tones that produce either a soft, dreamy, ethereal feel or a more dazzling, punchy and gleaming look.

Either way, white is normally the unifying colour of choice, and photographers often dress models in white, place them against white backgrounds and, where possible, choose models with blonde hair for that true high-key effect. The subtle shadow areas of the image ensure that the subject outline and features don't disappear into the background – as do the slight nuances of colour, which typically make colour the format of choice over black and white for the high-key portrait. Photoshop is used to push tones as light as possible, before detail (or too much detail) becomes

clipped. For a dreamy look you'll want to ensure that any darker tones are further lightened, so contrast is really at a minimum. It's a delicate balance, because if you don't leave enough difference in tonality, you'll end up with an image that appears washed out. For a punchier look, these tones may be darkened instead, with the lighter tones pushed even brighter for a greater sense of contrast.

Remember too, that if you're starting out with an image that isn't comprised purely of bright tones, all is not lost. The beauty of Photoshop is that you've also got the opportunity for dodging and burning with precision, enabling you to focus on dodging any less-than-suitable areas, such as the red and blue polo shirt in the demonstration image. Just a quick brush with the Dodge tool and all is good!

WORKS WITH | ALL VERSIONS

LAYING OUR HIGH-KEY FOUNDATIONS
Improving edge contrast lets us dodge hard later on

01 Convert for Smart Filters We want a punchy looking image with defined shadows, which will also allow us to really push our light tones hard, so we're going to start by adding local contrast with Unsharp Mask. Go to Filter>Convert for Smart Filters, or duplicate the background layer with Ctrl/Cmd+J.

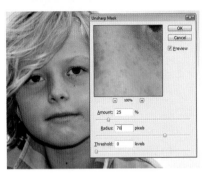

02 Sharpen for contrast Now go to Filter>Sharpen>Unsharp Mask. Start by trying Amount at 25%, Radius at 70 pixels and leave Threshold at 0. Notice how the edges are enhanced and the highlights lightened slightly. This works in a more intelligent way than simply boosting the contrast with Curves.

THE TRANSFORMATION
Three vital stages

The three images shown on the right illustrate the crucial stages of transformation for a high-key finish.

The first image shows high Radius and low Amount settings in Unsharp Mask in order to add edge contrast, which will eventually enable us to over-brighten the image without it appearing washed out.

The second one demonstrates how we set a good general base contrast that will act as a starting point for our dodging work.

The third image illustrates how we dodge hard in certain areas without destroying detail in others. This helps you get the high-key look and still keep definition.

03 Tweak the sharpness If your shadows aren't defined enough, increase Amount by 10%, Radius by 30px each time. Beware of going too hard, as it is a high-key effect after all. You may need to alter the settings later – until the lighter tones are bleached out, it's hard to tell if you've got it right.

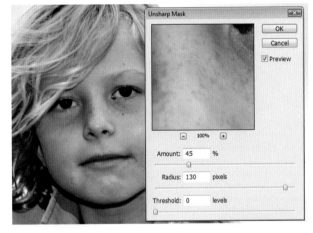

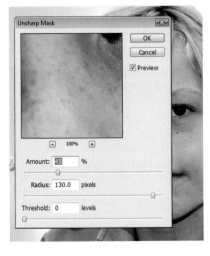

04 Edit the settings If you have CS2 or CS3, you can double-click the Smart Filter dialog and change the settings at any time in the future. If you don't, you'll just have to delete the layer duplicate, duplicate the background layer again and apply Unsharp Mask with different settings.

05 Add a Curves adjustment layer Now we want to alter contrast globally as opposed to along edge detail, as is done with Sharpness. Click the half-white, half-black circle at the bottom of the Layers palette and select Curves. A Curves adjustment layer is now initiated to protect the original.

06 Plot Curves points Click a point in the shadow quarter tone (top corner of the bottom left box) and one in the highlight quarter tone (bottom corner of the top right box). Click another point further up in the highlights, about two thirds in, fairly close to the end point. Refer to the screenshot for guidance.

NOW FOR THE HEAVY LIFTING
Dodge with Curves to give that real high-key look

07 Alter the curve Push the lower highlight point upwards fairly hard, then push the higher highlight point up very hard, so it's near the top of the square. This lightens the brightest highlights, in this case the white background. Push the shadow point up slightly. This ensures the curve is natural without lightening the shadows too much.

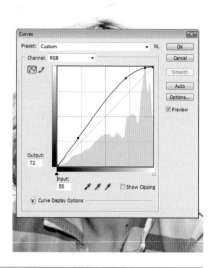

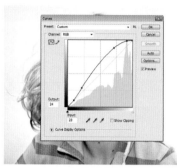

08 Tweak if necessary If your shadows look too heavy, you can push the shadow point up a little more. If they look weak, you can go back and add a little more sharpening or add another lower point two thirds in and drop this instead. This way, the curve stays gradual and the midtones in the skin still get lightened a little.

09 Change the blending mode Now change the Curves layer blending mode from Normal to Luminosity so that there's no increase in saturation that can make skin tones look too yellow or red. Click the Add Adjustment Layer button and add another Curves layer.

DODGY BUSINESS
Use a Curves layer for dodging

Ready to go Once we've increased contrast with USM and Curves, we can start our dodging work with a Curves layer and its mask.

Start work Start by working over the skin, background and shirt with a white brush at 100%, making sure you don't touch the hair.

Work the hair Change the Brush Opacity to 50% and work over the hair, so that detail isn't lost in the bright hair areas.

Switch over Press X to switch from white to black, and brush over the fine hair edges with a 50% brush to rescue detail.

Another layer Complete the dodging with another Curves lightening layer and focus on the base of the hair near the shoulders.

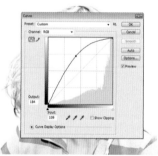

10 Lighten with Curves Our first Curves layer set the contrast, establishing where our highlights and shadows would be in relation to each other. We can now dodge certain areas of our image using another Curves layer. Lighten the image by pushing the curve up hard with a single point. Don't worry about clipping at this stage.

12 Dodging with Curves With the brush at 100% Opacity, work carefully over the face and shirt and any areas of the background that aren't yet completely white, being careful not to touch the hair edges. We want to keep a bit more detail in the hair, so switch to 50% Opacity before working over the hair.

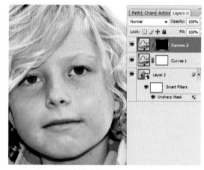

11 Set up layer mask Now invert the layer mask on the Curves adjustment layer with Ctrl/Cmd+I. It will go black and the effect will be removed. Press D to reset the colour palette and make sure white is the foreground colour, using X to swap if needs be. Select the Brush tool and set to 0% Hardness.

13 Rescue hair edges We can pull back a bit of lost detail from the fine hair edges simply by switching to black at 50% and brushing over. Make sure the brush is large and at 0% Hardness, because if the white background is affected, we want to make sure that the blend is nice and gradual.

TIME TO ADD A LITTLE POLISH
Remove blemishes and smooth the skin to finish

14 Lighten the hair base The hair at the bottom near the shoulders is now a bit dark, so we can lighten it separately without having to fiddle with previous layer masks. Simply add another lightening Curves adjustment layer, invert it as before, then paint into the hair with a brush at 100%. Lower the layer opacity if it looks too light.

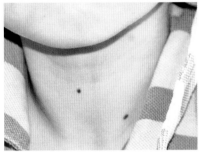

15 Create a new layer Select the background layer, and add a new layer above with the button at the bottom of the Layers palette. Hit J for the Spot Healing brush. Any changes we make from this layer position in the palette won't be affected if we then alter the Curves above. Make sure Sample All Layers is selected in the Tool Options bar.

16 Blemishes Click to remove blemishes. For areas near edges of detail, eg just below the eye, switch to the Clone Stamp and use Alt/Option to sample from similar proximate detail. Make sure Current and Below is selected in the Tool Options bar for Clone Stamp.

LAYER STRUCTURE
Achieving the high-key look

17 Create merged layer Now click the layer at the top of the stack and then add a new layer using the button at the bottom of the Layers palette. Use Alt/Option+ Ctrl/Cmd+Shift+E to Merge Visible to this layer. Go to Filter>Blur>Gaussian Blur and select a 20-pixel Radius.

18 Selective skin blur Add a layer mask to this layer with the circle in the square button in the Layers palette, and use Ctrl/Cmd+I to invert the layer mask. Use a soft white brush at 100% to paint the blur into the skin areas only, excluding areas of detail like lips, eyes, eyebrows, mouth and strands of hair.

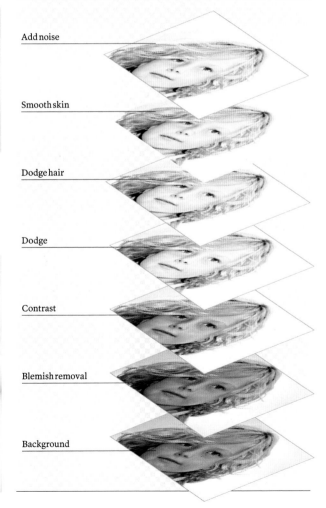

Add noise

Smooth skin

Dodge hair

Dodge

Contrast

Blemish removal

Background

19 Skin noise Avoid face edges like the chin, using a 50% brush as you get close. Hold Alt/Option; create a new layer, change the mode to Overlay and tick the box below. Go to Filter>Noise> Add Noise, and add 6% Gaussian Monochromatic. Hold Alt/Option; drag the Blur layer mask up to the new layer.

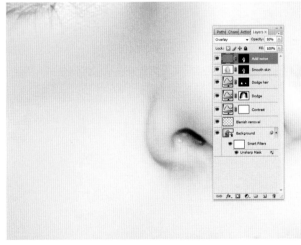

AFTER

BEFORE

Essentials

TIME TAKEN
1 hour

YOUR EXPERT
Matthew Henry

ON THE DISC
Portrait
before.psd

Key Photoshop Skills Covered
What you'll learn

BASIC BLEMISH REMOVAL

LOCAL CONTRAST WITH UNSHARP MASK

GLOBAL CONTRAST WITH CURVES

TEETH AND EYE WHITENING

PAINTING WITH MASKS

PROTECTING TONES WITH CURVES

SMOOTHING SKIN

WORKS WITH | ALL VERSIONS

Give photos contrast

Create a high contrast look popular with painters for hundreds of years with a few fail-safe Photoshop steps

Chiaroscuro is Italian for 'light-dark' and is a term commonly used in art to describe a scene that displays bold and dramatic contrast between light and dark areas. The term has become most popularly associated with 16th Century paintings that depict dark subjects lit by a shaft of light by painters like Baglione and Caravaggio.

The chiaroscuro effect is also very popular in photography and is a great look for portraits, never ceasing to please a sitter or wow an audience. What the effect does need is a decent amount of contrast to start with, and plenty of shadow. It's an enormous and near-impossible task to create detailed shadow on a face where there is none, so Photoshop is there to really make the most of what you've got rather than to create the effect from scratch.

You only have to look at the before and after images to see how Photoshop can make a fairly ordinary photo into a chiaroscuro masterpiece, but it's important to remember that it's the lighting that

> "What the effect does need is a decent amount of contrast to start with, and plenty of shadow"

makes the retouching possible. However, fear not, you don't need a barrage of professional studio lights to create this effect – ordinary window light will suffice!

RAW CONVERSION AND CLEAN-UP
Process for maximum detail and then clean up the skin

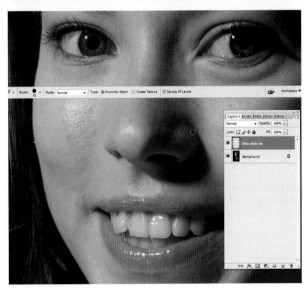

01 Maximise shadow and highlight detail If you can, shoot in Raw mode so you have access to the full range of information. Open your file in whichever Raw converter you use, and set Blacks or Shadows to 0 and choose Linear for the tone curve. With Adobe Camera Raw, you can find the Linear option in the Tone Curve 'Point' sub-menu.

02 Adjust colour temperature Your image will look flat, but you'll have access to the full range of shadow and highlight detail so you can choose where to clip to pure black or pure white in Photoshop. Finish by adjusting the Color Temperature slider to remove any colour cast if necessary, then open up your image in Photoshop.

03 Healing preparations It's good to start with a general skin clean-up. Add a new layer and press J to select the Spot Healing brush (add Shift to cycle to it if necessary). Make sure Sample All Layers is selected in the Tool Options bar above. Use Ctrl/Cmd+Alt/Option+0 to zoom to Actual Pixels.

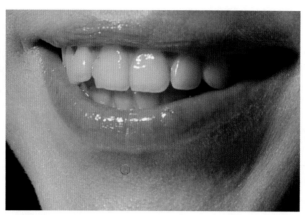

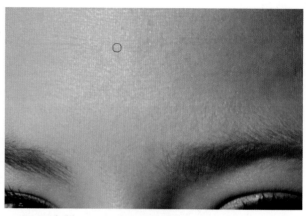

Camera capture tips

You'll probably need a high ISO setting indoors and a wide aperture such as f/4.0, because light will be fairly low. Make sure the shutter speed is no slower than 1/100sec, or mount your camera on a tripod to go as low as 1/25sec if necessary, but keep your model very still! If you're not sure about settings, use Portrait mode and ensure that the flash is off. You'll need a dark background behind your model and remember to dress your model in dark clothes.

04 **Skin clean-up** Now adjust the size of the brush with the '[' and ']' keys until it's slightly bigger than each blemish, and single-click on each to remove, avoiding areas near edge detail. Switch to the Clone Stamp tool (S) and use Alt/Option to source from nearby detail, then click to remove spots on or near edges such as lips or hair.

05 **Wrinkle removal** We can then use the same tools in order to remove lines and wrinkles on the neck and forehead. Click away at each line bit by bit, rather than covering the whole line in one big swoop. Be careful when working on the neck area, where you get near to shadow transitions.

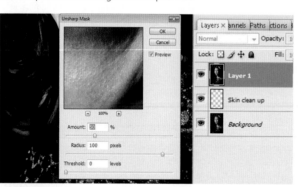

06 **Increase edge contrast** Now we're going to increase the edge contrast a touch. Create a new layer and hold down Alt/Option+Shift+Ctrl/Cmd+E to Merge Visible to this layer, preserving everything below it. Now go to Filter>Sharpen>Unsharp Mask and select Amount 50% and Radius 100.

07 **Brush detail back in** Add a layer mask to this layer using the button at the bottom of the Layers palette. Take a soft black brush set to 20% and brush in any shadow or highlight detail that you want to retain, bit by bit. No doubt you'll find the eyes need working over fully because they've gone very dark.

LIGHTING FOR CHIAROSCURO
It's a delicate balance

It's easy enough to shoot your own chiaroscuro photo at home. Obviously a studio setting will give better results, but don't write off your living room just yet!

To begin with, you'll need a decent sized interior window on a bright day. Place your model fairly close to the window, without the window itself being in shot, and sit them so that their face is three quarters to the window, with the quarter side falling into shadow. Now take a test shot. You should be able to see both eyes, but one side of the face should begin to fall into shadow. You can increase contrast by blacking out half or more of the window with black card, and hanging black material on the other side if necessary. White material can be hung if you need to reduce contrast.

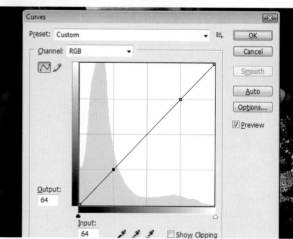

08 **Contrast increase** Now we want to increase contrast globally. We add a Curves adjustment layer via the Add Adjustment Layer button at the bottom of the Layers palette, selecting Curves in the menu. We plot two points on the curve – one on the shadow point and one on the highlight point.

LOCAL AND GLOBAL CONTRAST INCREASE
Use Curves and Unsharp Mask to make that image pop

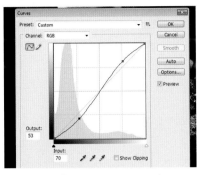

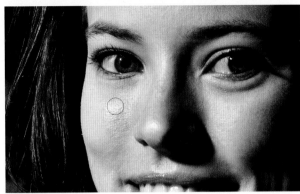

09 **Gentle S curve** We now push the highlight point upwards and the shadow point downwards to produce a fairly gentle S curve. We don't want to turn the highlight areas of the skin too white, so we go a touch harder on the shadows than on the highlights.

10 **Brush back detail** We can use the layer mask which is selected by default on an adjustment layer to brush detail back into areas of shadows and highlights that we don't want affected by the curves. We use a black brush at around 30% and slowly brush out the brightest skin highlights, which can look a bit nasty.

11 **Eye detail** We use the same brush, this time at 100% to brush all the detail back into the iris, pupil and white corners of the eye nearest the nose, which have all fallen very dark. We can leave the large white areas. We use the brush at 30% to slowly brush a bit of detail back into the neck shadow and hair behind the ear.

CREATING ATMOSPHERE
A few subtle techniques can make all the difference

Whiter whites A Curves adjustment layer with a mask has been used to lighten the whites of the teeth and eyes without affecting darker edge detail surrounding the eyes and between the teeth.

Crowning glory Another Curves adjustment layer has been used here along with a mask, with lightening brushed into the highlight areas of the hair to really make them shine.

Keeping it real Blemishes have been removed from the skin with the Healing brush, then the skin smoothed, with Gaussian Blur and noise added to prevent it looking too plastic.

Increase the contrast Global contrast was increased with an Unsharp Mask and a Curves adjustment layer to make highlights pop and shadows fall much darker, while retaining some detail in important areas.

Paint it black The background wasn't uniformly black, showing lots of lighter areas, so a Curves adjustment layer was used along with a layer mask to darken this area to complete blackness.

BACKGROUND DARKENING AND BEAUTY TWEAKS
Once we've darkened the background, we add our final touches

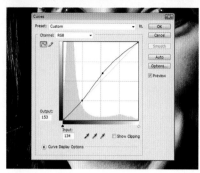

12 Lighten eyes and teeth Now we add a further Curves adjustment layer to lighten the whites of the teeth and eyes. Fix a point in the shadows so that edge detail isn't lightened, and use a further single point to lift the curve. Use Ctrl/Cmd+I to invert the mask. Paint the eye whites and teeth with a white brush.

14 Fine-tune edge detail Now switch to 50% Opacity and work close in to the hair edges. You will find it necessary to destroy some of the hair in order to get the background completely black, but it will blend into the background anyway, so it won't be noticeable.

16 Smooth skin Create a new layer at the top of the stack and use Alt/Option+Ctrl/Cmd+Shift+E to Merge Visible to this layer. Now go to Filter>Blur>Gaussian Blur and select 10 pixels. Next, go to Filter>Noise>Add Noise and add 4% Gaussian Monochromatic noise.

13 Black out the background Now add another Curves adjustment layer and darken hard with a single point until the background detail disappears. Invert the layer mask with Ctrl/Cmd+I. Now take a very large soft white brush at 100% and move around the background, just catching the edges of the hair. Try not to kill too much of the edge hair detail at this point in time.

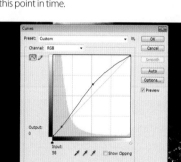

15 Lighten hair highlights Add another Curves adjustment layer, and this time fix a point low down in the shadows and lighten with another point further up. Use Ctrl/Cmd+I to invert the layer mask, then start brushing into the hair highlights with a 30% brush, building up as necessary.

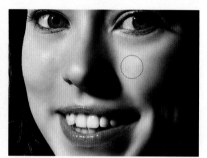

17 Brush in smoothness Add a layer mask to this new layer then invert it with Ctrl/Cmd+I. Now take a soft-edged white brush and carefully brush the smoothness back into the skin areas, avoiding the hair, eyes, lips and any edges such as the edges of the nose, cheek and jawline. Finally, drop the layer opacity to suit.

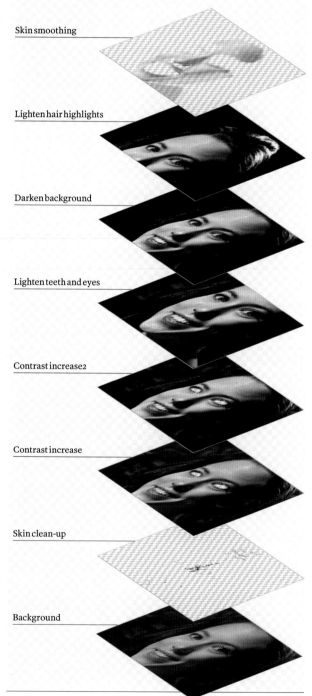

Skin smoothing

Lighten hair highlights

Darken background

Lighten teeth and eyes

Contrast increase 2

Contrast increase

Skin clean-up

Background

Dell recommends Windows Vista® Home Premium.

adamo
BY **DELL**

Genuine Windows Vista® Home Premium
Profile 0.65"
Casing Aluminium
Colour Onyx/Pearl
Keyboard Scalloped, Back-lit
Screen 13.4", 16:9 HD, Edge-to-Edge Glass
www.adamobydell.com

⊞ Windows

Windows® and Adamo. Visually stunning.

The simple guide to HDR

Discover the secret Photoshop tool capable of producing perfectly toned images at the touch of a button

No matter how adept you are at photography, shooting at night or in low-light conditions can be a tricky task. In an ideal world we'd love to capture the scene in all its glory, from the depths of the shadows through to the twinkle of the street lights.

Unfortunately, capturing all this wonderful detail in a single image usually comes at a price – namely 'noise'. Noise is the nasty grainy effect you often see in low-light images, plus a huge lack of detail. Thankfully, there is a way to maintain the details at either end of the light spectrum, while eradicating noise at the same time. The answer? High Dynamic Range (HDR).

This technique is a culmination of photography and image-editing skills brought together to produce stunning results. We know that the term 'HDR' may sound scary, but trust us, it's easy to achieve.

"We know that the term 'HDR' may sound scary, but trust us, it's easy to achieve"

To introduce the subject of High Dynamic Range, we must first think about how we humans see things. Think of a well-lit place at night. We're able to distinguish various tones in shadow areas, and interpret bright areas as having various intensities. Now compare this to a regular photo of the same scene. You'll see it registers most shadow areas as black and the brightest lights as pure white. The huge contrast between the dark shadows and bright lights makes it near impossible for a camera to capture this scene realistically. It's this difference that we refer to wit the term 'dynamic range'.

In order to produce an image capable of representing a high level of dynamic range, you need to take a series of images throughout the brightness scale – from the depths of the shadows through to the brightest lights.

Create this HDR image! page 45

100 8839 100

HDR: The basics

Great images are all about maintaining as much detail in both the shadows and highlights as possible. In traditional photography, filters are often used to help control the amount of light and dark in a scene, but the results are restricted to the types of filters available. So how can Photoshop help? High Dynamic Range (HDR) imaging enables you to combine a number of images together in order to achieve optimum detail at both ends of the brightness range. Each image is taken at a different exposure in order to collate as much detail information as possible. When combined, the result is a detail-rich image.

Dedicated HDR software

Obviously we're going to tell you to create your HDR images the Photoshop way, but there are other programs designed to help you achieve the effects too. The most well known program is Photomatix from HDRsoft. This standalone software automatically merges your images and provides you with a range of controls to adjust the contrast, saturation and tones. Many HDR images that have heavily saturated colours are created with this program. You can download the basic version for free from www.hdrsoft.com or take a look at the premium versions, which start from $99.

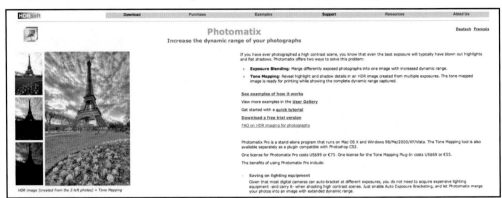

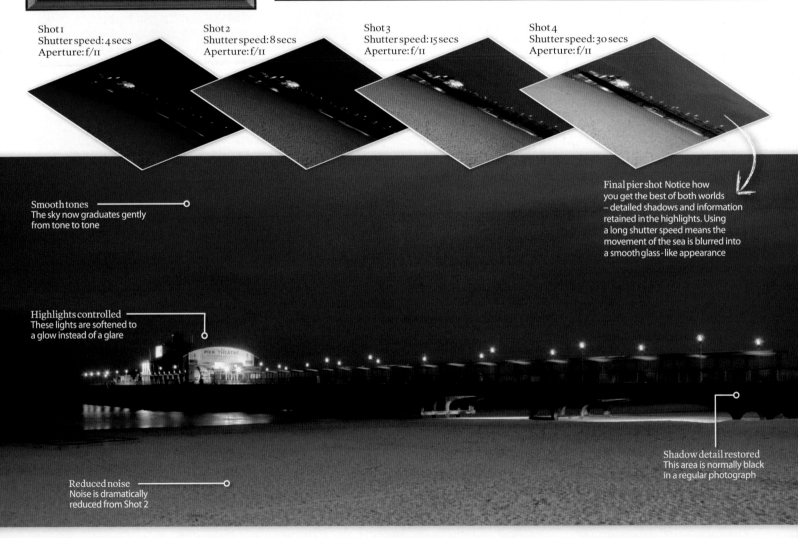

Shot 1
Shutter speed: 4 secs
Aperture: f/11

Shot 2
Shutter speed: 8 secs
Aperture: f/11

Shot 3
Shutter speed: 15 secs
Aperture: f/11

Shot 4
Shutter speed: 30 secs
Aperture: f/11

Smooth tones
The sky now graduates gently from tone to tone

Final pier shot Notice how you get the best of both worlds – detailed shadows and information retained in the highlights. Using a long shutter speed means the movement of the sea is blurred into a smooth glass-like appearance

Highlights controlled
These lights are softened to a glow instead of a glare

Shadow detail restored
This area is normally black in a regular photograph

Reduced noise
Noise is dramatically reduced from Shot 2

Case study:
Ryan McGinnis

Ryan McGinnis is a real pro it comes to HDR photography. As a keen stock photographer, he has had plenty of practice at perfecting the art.

"I got into photography back in '99," says Ryan. "I love storm photography – the weather we get out here in rural Nebraska, complete with massive hail, blow-you-down winds and two-mile-wide tornadoes can't be found anywhere else on Earth. HDR gives me nearly infinite latitude in post-processing an image. It captures all detail in all areas of an image, even under extremely challenging lighting, and is a technique that can produce extraordinary images. I have a blog up at http://backingwinds.blogspot.com, a Flickr gallery at http://flickr.com/photos/digicana/ (complete with an HDR section), and sell stock photos through The Photoshelter Collection and Alamy."

Tell us how you first got into HDR photography

I'm a bit of a weather nut, and every spring I gear up my car with mobile internet, radar and GPS, and spend a week or so driving around the great plains of America looking for good storms. When taking photos of storms, there's often a massive difference between the brightness of the sky and the ground. My storm-chasing partner and good friend, Darren Addy, pointed HDR out to me as a possible solution. It turns out that HDR doesn't work terribly well for storms, because with current camera technologies you have to take several photos, and storm clouds tend to move too quickly between photos. However, through experimentation I discovered that for any photo in which a subject stays put, it can produce exceptional images that would be highly difficult or even impossible to create using any other method.

What do you find so appealing about this medium?

With photography, you're always trying to capture the essence of a scene or a moment, and so much of the craft in photography is working around the inherent shortcomings of the technology. I mean, say you take a picture of a man napping in the shadow under a tree on a clear blue day. If you take the picture so that the sky will be blue, the

Top tip
Want to see more? backingwinds.blogspot.com is a page showcasing Ryan's photography. See also Flickr – http://flickr.com/photos/digicana/ – and http://psc.photoshelter.com/user/digicana (Photoshelter), http://tinyurl.com/2zt37b (Alamy).

Kearney Home: A house in Kearney, Nebraska, October, 2006. ©Ryan McGinnis

Shot 1
Shot 2
Shot 3
Shot 4
Shot 5
Shot 6

NYC Sculpture: A sculpture by Marc Di Suvero in New York City, New York, September, 2006. ©Ryan McGinnis

man and the tree will be almost entirely black in the final image. If you take the picture so that the man and the tree aren't completely black, the sky will end up washed-out and white. For years photographers have bought things like flashes and filters and reflectors to try to get around the fact that cameras just aren't anywhere near as good as the human eye at capturing all the detail in a scene. HDR evens this out. With HDR you capture all the detail in the scene, and you can show as much or as little of it as you want in the final product.

Why do you prefer using Photoshop compared to other HDR programs?
I've tried a couple of the other programs on the market, but found that for the most part, they have only very limited controls for the final render of the image. Photoshop allows you to tinker with the curves as you make the transition from an HDR file to a TIFF file, which gives much finer control than I've seen with the competition.

Photoshop also seems to do a better job of rendering an image realistically. If you look around for HDR photos, you'll find a great deal of them done with a program called Photomatix. Photomatix has a habit of creating incredibly garish and unrealistic images, in my opinion, and while they seem to go over well with the public, they remind me a bit of when Photoshop introduced the Lens Flare filter, and everyone and their dog started adding lens flares to their images. It's not subtle, and everyone is doing it the same way. The photograph becomes more about the filter you ran it through than the photograph itself. Photoshop has a much steeper learning curve, but then anyone who works with Photoshop knows that summiting that curve is worth it in the long run.

People get scared when they hear about 'bits per channel'. What's it all about?
Computers all run on good old ones and zeros. When your computer thinks about a colour, it assigns it a number, or rather a set of numbers. Everything you see on your monitor is made up of a mixture of the colours red, green and blue. To a computer, each of these is called a channel. So, if you want a nice shade of yellow, the computer will say to itself: "Self, mix red #37 with green #44 and blue #6".

The number of bits per channel dictate how many shades of colours the computer has to pick from when it's saving an image. The more colours you have to pick from, the

better, especially if you plan on doing any extensive editing to the image. Think of it as a kind of 'colour resolution'. Just like a higher resolution file can be blown up larger without getting more blurry than a lower resolution file because it has more pixels, an image with more bits per channel of colour information can have the colours manipulated more without artefacts showing up because it has more colours. And, just like upsampling will never make that tiny thumbnail of an image you found on the web suitable for a poster enlargement, converting an 8-bit image to a 16-bit image will not increase the number of actual colours in the image.

One of the great things about HDR is that HDR files not only save colour information but brightness information as well. There's practically no limit to how much colour and brightness information can be saved in a single HDR file.

How would you explain tone mapping to the common man?
'Tone mapping' is a way to get HDR images to look correct on current monitor technology and prints. Let's go back to the example of the man napping in the shadow of a tree on a bright blue day. Our eyes and brains are much

higher performance machines than the most expensive camera and computer, and so we see the man in the shadow perfectly well, and we also see a blue sky and a bright circle of sun. Yet back on our computer, we either end up with a blue sky and a man completely hidden in shadow, or a visible man with a completely white, far too bright sky. The camera, unlike our eye, just can't get it all in one shot.

Now, with multiple shots, HDR files will capture all the details in the scene – the man sleeping, the clouds in the sky, the shape of the sun... But our monitors still aren't good enough to recreate the scene. After all, in real life the sun is bright enough to burn your retina, and yet you can stare at the sun for as long as you like on your screen without fear of going blind. If we had a magical monitor that could make things as bright or as dark as we wanted, we could actually recreate the scene exactly as we saw it.

However, consumer monitors just can't get that bright or that dark right now (they likely will within the next 15 years...), so on existing technology we're stuck with having to 'tone map' the image to get it to look anything close to what we saw. Tone mapping will try to 'compress' the dynamic range of the image.

The view of Derwent Water (with Keswick and Skiddaw in the distance) from Surprise View near Ashness Bridge in Cumbria, UK, December, 2007

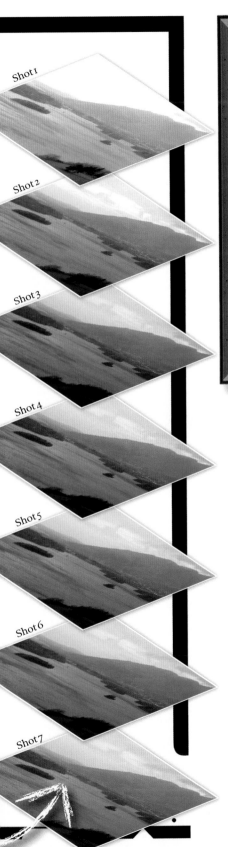

Shot 1

Shot 2

Shot 3

Shot 4

Shot 5

Shot 6

Shot 7

Create your own HDR image

Top tip
Exposure and Gamma This shows how your HDR data appears on a low dynamic range source. If you've brought an HDR image into line at the 32-bit stage with manual dodging and burning, you need to convert the 32-bit image to 16-bit without applying more compression.

Essentials

TIME TAKEN
40 minutes

YOUR EXPERT
Matt Henry

ON THE DISC
Image1
Image2
Image3
Image4
Image5
Final image

Photoshop's Merge to HDR facility means no more burnt-out skies and blocked-up shadows

There are two main options for working with HDR images.

The first is to leave the image in 32-bit mode and manually dodge and burn the blocked-up shadows and/or burnt-out highlights to reveal detail in the 16-bit space your screen is able to display. Where normally that detail would be gone for good, it will magically reappear if

you've captured the full HDR range.

The second option is to convert the image using one of the semi-automated methods offered by Photoshop in the HDR dialog drop-down menu. Of these, only Local Adaptation is really worth its salt.

We've covered both methods below in this simple tutorial.

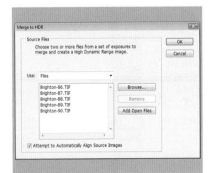

01 Browsing for files Once you've shot a range of exposures to capture a scene (typically at least five), you need to go to File>Automate>Merge to HDR. In the dialog box click Browse, then navigate to your files (Raw files are best) and select each one by Ctrl/Cmd clicking.

02 Auto align layers You've then got a choice of whether or not to tick the checkbox Attempt to Automatically Align Source Images. Unless you've sandbagged your tripod down and operated your camera remotely, it's a good idea to check this as it will prevent ghosting from minor camera movements.

100   8839   100

Ryan's top 5 tips

1. Get a sturdy tripod
If the camera moves between shots, you're at the mercy of the Auto Align feature. It doesn't always work, and it takes forever. But you won't need it if the camera is steady. It also helps to use a 'cable release', which keeps you from bumping the camera every time you take a picture.

2. Set your camera to Manual This shuts off much of the camera's brain – important for HDR. Your camera is constantly adjusting settings based on what you see through the viewfinder, but when taking HDR photos you need to keep all the settings the same for each photo, except for the shutter speed, which you use to vary the exposure.

3. Shoot RAW Actually, this is a good tip for any photography. For HDR, RAW files are better because they store a great deal more info about the lighting in the photo, and so your final product will have fewer artefacts.

4. Take at least three photos One exposed correctly, one darker, one brighter. Make the photo darker by increasing the shutter speed, and brighter by decreasing. If you have a lot of time and know a bit about photography, take even more.

5. Check the settings Before you load photos into the HDR Merge feature, ensure that the Adobe Camera RAW settings are at 16-bit and each image has the same colour temp. You can do this by setting the colour temp of one of them, selecting the rest and clicking Sync.

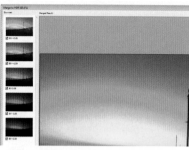

03 Choose images Once you click the Open button, the Merge to HDR preview window appears with all of the images arranged in terms of exposure on the left-hand side. Look carefully at the combined result. If you've mistakenly included irrelevant images, you can deselect them in the film strip on the left.

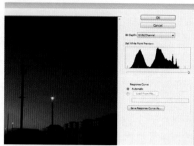

04 Examine preview Moving the White Point preview slider right the way across the histogram left and right gives you the chance to check that you've captured all the detail necessary in the shadows and highlights. If it's not there, you may have missed an image when browsing, or you might need to shoot the scene again.

05 Set White Point preview The point at which you set the White Point preview is the basis for your work when dodging and burning manually, so it's a good idea to tweak the slider so the midtones appear spot-on. Ignore shadows and highlights, as we'll be recovering those next.

06 Add Dodge and Burn layers Leave the Bit Depth at 32-bit and click OK. Click the Create New Adjustment Layer button at the bottom of the Layers palette, select Exposure and pull the slider hard left. Rename the layer 'Burn'. Add another and move it hard rightwards. Rename this layer 'Dodge'.

07 Invert layer masks We can't invert the layer masks of our Dodge and Burn layers with Ctrl/Cmd+I in 32-bit mode, so we zoom out to make our image small with Ctrl/Cmd and -, and paint across the whole image with a large black brush at 100% Opacity on each layer.

08 Burn layer This brings us back to our starting point and gives us a good base to dodge and burn selected shadows and highlights without touching midtone areas that are already looking good. Select the Burn layer first and take a brush at 0% Hardness.

09 Burn street lamps We want to burn in the street lamps first, bringing back some much needed detail. We zoom in with Cmd/Ctrl and +, set our brush to 50% Opacity and click carefully to build up the detail in each lamp without touching the surrounding areas.

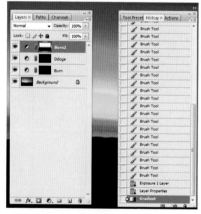

10 Burn Sky layer There's very little detail in our sky at all, so we need plenty of burning in. Doing it manually with a brush is going to leave obvious signs of burning, so we need to make use of the Gradient tool. We need another Burn layer separate from the street lamps, so we add this and invert as before.

11 Gradient for sky We press 'D' to ensure our Color palette is reset to black and white, and drag from the base of the sky to about half way up. Reduce the layer opacity so the blend looks realistic, or alternatively run some strong Gaussian blur with Filter>Blur>Gaussian Blur if you don't want the strength reduced.

12 **Dodge layer** Next, we want to dodge any shadow areas that look like they might be blocked up or just in need of a little lightening. The beach and promenade need lightening as a whole, so we attack them using a gradient on the Dodge layer drawn upwards from the shoreline to the height of the flats behind the beach huts.

13 **Dodge foreground** We drop the layer opacity a little and brush some detail back into the sea area affected, with a large soft brush at 30%, and a little into the beach at 15% to blend. We finish by choosing Image>Mode>16-bit, Merge, and leaving the slider settings as they are, and then make a few Contrast adjustments in 16-bit mode.

14 **Start again** We're going to start from scratch again for this second method, so go to File>Automate>Merge to HDR and select the same files via the Browse dialog. Check the Align box and hit Open again. Leave the White Point preview and change 32-bit to 16-bit.

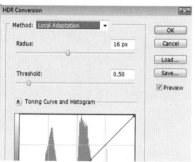

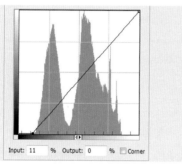

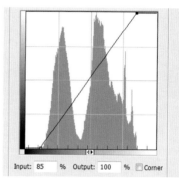

15 **Choose conversion method** The conversion now goes ahead, and this time a dialog box opens up with options for conversion from 32-bit to 16-bit. Select Local Adaptation from the drop-down menu and click the button underneath the sliders to reveal the Curves dialog.

16 **Set black point** First drag the endpoints in the Curves dialog to meet the information. Now click the point on the bottom left of the curve and drag it inwards until it meets the edge of the shadow info on the histogram. Don't go too far or you'll clip shadow detail.

17 **Set white point** Now do the same for the highlights. Drag the point on the top left of the curve leftwards until it meets the edge of the highlight info. Again, don't go too far. The default settings on the sliders can be left as they are for now.

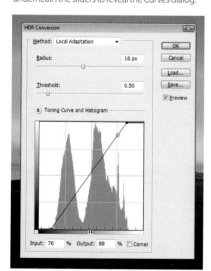

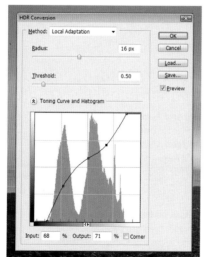

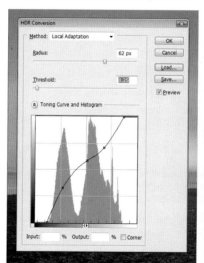

18 **Check tonal points** The image should now have a good overall contrast, with detail in both the highlights and the shadows. If you need to adjust areas of tone, you can now do so in the usual way using the Curves dialog. Hold down Ctrl/Cmd and click a tone in your image to check where it falls on the curve.

19 **Manipulate curve** In this case we decided to plot a point in the darks to lighten the pebbles, one in the midtones to continue the lightening curve, and a further point in the highlights to keep the sky area dark. You can add as many points as you like and produce more extreme changes than is possible in 16-bit mode.

20 **Check sliders** When you're done with the curve, it's worth checking the sliders to see the effect on the image. Depending on the type of image, you may want to reduce or increase the Threshold slider to counteract a soft blurry look, or to remove the presence of halos. The Radius slider is worth experimenting with as well.

HDR quick tips

1. Scene Almost any scene is suited to HDR photography. For the most dramatic results, choose a scene which has a large contrast between lights and darks.

2. Setup Take a few sample shots until you manage to get shadows in the middle of the camera histogram. Now decrease the exposure by 1 or 2EVs and take a second shot.

3. Settings Keep decreasing by 1 or 2EVs and taking images until you manage to get all the highlight detail inside the histogram edge. You should end up with at least three exposures.

4. Other settings Compression is designed to ensure that all highlight detail is preserved, but rarely offers decent overall results because images typically appear overly dark. You can do the same job better in Photoshop's Local Adaptation function. Equalize Histogram finds the peaks in the histogram and spreads these out locally, ensuring that the majority of pixels receive a contrast boost. The effect is striking but tends to crunch the range at both ends together, producing heavy-looking shadows and highlights that often appear a little weak.

BEFORE IMAGES

Auto-Align and Auto-Blend

There's more to Auto-Align and Auto-Blend Layers than stitching panoramas. They're great tools for montage as well...

The Auto-Align and Auto-Blend features were introduced in Photoshop CS3 and caused quite a fuss. Indeed, there are photographers out there who'd happily shell out hundreds of pounds simply for these features alone.

These features are most famously known for their ability to work as part of Photoshop's existing Photomerge feature, perfectly stitching together a sequence of images to form a panorama and compensating for differences in exposure, and blending edges seamlessly.

But there's more to Auto-Align and Auto-Blend Layers than Photomerge. They're actually fab as tools for single frame montages too. There are many situations where you might want to combine parts of several similar images into one frame, and don't

have a tripod handy to ensure that everything stays perfectly lined up.

The example we've used here is a good one – a busy thoroughfare at the height of summer made it almost impossible to capture the seafront without someone walking past. The Auto-Align feature correctly lines up our backgrounds, leaving us free to mask out each person with a quick brush stroke without the need for any complex cutouts or transformations. And the Auto-Blend feature sorts out differences in exposure that may have occurred due to metering issues or changes in the lighting. The same techniques can be applied to similar frames where you want to keep some parts and not others – a family portrait with people smiling in only some shots is another great example.

WORKS WITH | PHOTOSHOP CS3 AND ABOVE

AUTO-ALIGN ALL FOUR IMAGES
Watch Auto-Align Layers work its magic on these four shots

Key Photoshop Skills Covered
What you'll learn

AUTO-ALIGN LAYERS
AUTO-BLEND LAYERS
ADDING LAYER MASKS
PAINTING WITH MASKS

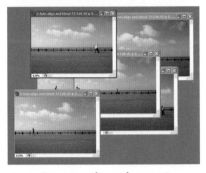

01 Open constituent images Open up all the images you want to work with. Press F to move through screen modes until you can see all images on the screen at once to make sure they're all there. Pick any image as a base that you'll lay all other images on top of.

02 Copy and paste Press F for Full Screen mode and use Ctrl/Cmd+Tab to move through to the next image. Use Ctrl/Cmd+A to select all, then Ctrl/Cmd+C to copy. Move back to your original image with Ctrl/Cmd+Shift+Tab, and use Ctrl/Cmd+V to paste. The second image will appear on top.

03 Repeat for all images Now use Ctrl/Cmd+Tab twice to move through to the next image and do the same. Repeat until all of the images are pasted as layers onto your base image. Now Ctrl/Cmd-click each of the layers (or Shift-click the bottom and top) to highlight them all.

Essentials

TIME TAKEN 30 minutes

YOUR EXPERT Matthew Henry

ON THE DISC Constituent images and the final montage image

04 Auto-Align With all layers highlighted, go to Edit>Auto-Align Layers. A dialog box will appear with a range of options for alignment. Choose Auto, which is nearly always the best option. Now sit tight while Auto-Align does its thing.

05 Inspect results You can inspect the results by playing with the visibility icons for each layer to examine how they sit together. For our series, Photoshop has thankfully decided to ignore the moving cloud and happily aligned the images based on the rail in the foreground.

06 Add layer mask If things haven't worked out as they should, you can always use Ctrl/Cmd+Z to undo them, and try one of the manual Auto-Align options instead. When you're done, add a layer mask to each layer by highlighting each one in turn and clicking the button at the bottom of the palette.

Tip

Number of images

You'll notice we used four images when theoretically we only needed two. But when shooting without a tripod, the hand movement may mean you lose important areas. Four images can maximise the amount of background and foreground info available prior to cropping. With only two you might end up with a clear scene but poor composition.

SMOOTH AND SEAMLESS
How we made four become one

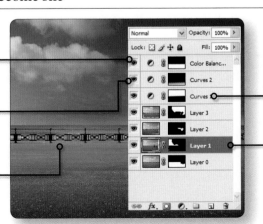

Color Balance A Color Balance layer with red and yellow added to the midtones gives a warmer tone to the path so it fits with the deep blues of the sky.

Curves 2 Our second Curves layer in conjunction with a gradient on its mask burns in the path base to add drama and direct the eye upwards.

Going straight Notice how the fence is completely straight despite being made up of four images shot at varying angles.

Curves 1 Our first Curves adjustment layer darkens the sky. A gradient from the top of the sea to the bottom ensures there's no obvious sharp line.

Masks Auto-Blend flattens any original masks and adds new ones of its own, masking and revealing certain areas of each layer to ensure a seamless blend.

MASK, AUTO-BLEND AND POLISH!
We paint out the people before using Auto-Blend Layers

07 **Top layer masking** Now we're ready to brush our people out. Start by ensuring the top layer is active, and its layer mask selected. Take a largish, soft black brush at 100% Opacity and paint over the cyclist and the jogger in the foreground. Don't forget to paint out any shadows as well.

08 **More layer masking** Now click the eye icon for the top layer to turn off layer visibility temporarily, and select the next layer down. Again make sure the layer mask is selected, then paint over the runner with a soft black brush. Don't forget the shadow.

09 **Last but one** Now turn off visibility for this layer too, and select the next layer down, ensuring its layer mask is active. Repeat again, brushing out the woman and her child and any associated shadows. We've now just got the background layer left.

10 **Background masking** We can't normally add a layer mask to the background layer, but the process of Auto-Align automatically turns the background layer into Layer 0, allowing us to use a mask. Ensure visibility is on for this layer only, and paint out the man with the mask. You'll see blank canvas below, but don't worry.

11 **Auto-Blend Layers** Now turn on visibility for all layers and select them all by Shift-clicking the bottom and top layers. Go to Edit>Auto-Blend Layers and watch while all the sharp transition lines and areas of uneven exposure suddenly disappear!

12 **Crop and burn the sky** Select the Crop tool and carefully crop so no blank canvas shows. Add a darkening Curve adjustment layer and draw a line the height of the sea with the Gradient tool (Shift+G to cycle to it) selected; pick white as foreground and black as the background colour.

LAYER STRUCTURE
Analysing the montage

13 **Burn path and warm tone** Add another darkening Curves layer, and drag with the Gradient tool from the bottom of the path to about half way up to burn its base in. Add a Color Balance adjustment layer, ramp up red and yellow, then draw your gradient the height of the sea, from bottom to top, to colour the path.

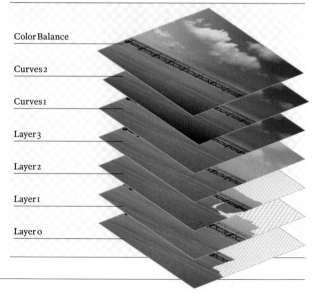

Color Balance

Curves 2

Curves 1

Layer 3

Layer 2

Layer 1

Layer 0

Lowkey images

High Speed Film Grain

Sepia toning

Quick photo process effects

Inject new life into your images by combining some old-school photographic processes and new Photoshop techniques

Y ou are constantly under pressure to do more and do it quickly, and here we give you seven quick Photoshop tutorials that reproduce traditional photo processes. The aim is to breathe new life into your current library of photos in the quickest way possible. You don't have to be a technical genius in order to accomplish stunning work!

Since the advent of photography, people have worked hard to improve the process. Several techniques were invented and many of these processes have resurged in popularity, largely due to the ease with which they can be re-created digitally without getting your hands dirty.

In some cases, the process was a result of the equipment used. In others, the quest for a better image took a more artistic route, and creative licence gave rise to toning techniques such as sepia tones and tritones. Another kind of tonal play is at work in high or low-key images, where specific ranges are widened or reduced.

This feature explores ways in which many of these techniques can be applied to your own images. Since every image is different, the approach was to build each effect with as much versatility as possible. Explore alternate settings as you work through the feature – let creativity be your guide! You will find all the source files on the free disc and you'll also find a nice selection of additional 'goodies' to make things even easier.

High Speed Film Grain

There is a special kind of grain that occurs traditionally in high-speed films (generally ISO ratings of 800 and above). With these films, the emulsion is packed with larger grains of silver halide, which gives them a greater sensitivity to light. The higher the speed, the better the film is for night photography and the more granular the print becomes. This is known as High Speed Film Grain. Favour with this effect comes and goes but it serves as a good starting point, because you can combine this technique with any of the others in the feature to produce a unique combination of effects.

BEFORE

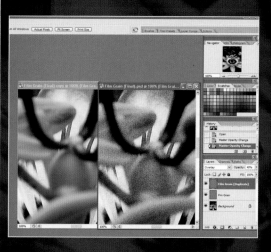

AFTER

01 **Film grain – part 1 (colour)** Start with a colour image and create a layer above it. Fill the layer with 50% grey (Edit>Fill), then add 15% Noise (Filter>Noise>Add Noise). Change the blend mode to Overlay and Opacity to 40%. Finally, duplicate this film grain layer. You should now have two film grain layers which, when applied, provide a colour film grain.

AFTER

02 **Film grain – part 2 (black and white)** Next, to quickly convert the image to a black-and-white film grain, change the top film grain layer's blend mode to Color, and Opacity to 100%. Now you can strengthen the grain by raising the bottom film grain layer's opacity, or reduce the effect by lowering the opacity. Somewhere around 90% is a good middle ground.

Sepia toning

Sepia toning has its roots in the 1880s, where pigments were applied to a positive print to produce a brownish-yellow monochrome image where the tonal range is preserved. These prints were highly durable, and perhaps that was part of their popularity. They also tend to give the image a warm, earthy quality. Today, silver sulphide is used in place of silver during black-and-white photo processing to achieve the same results. With the advent of digital photo processing, sepia toning has become synonymous with colourisation, where any single colour can be applied to the image. This also makes sepia toning a perfect candidate for digital processing in Photoshop, where colour can be separated from the luminosity of an image. Currently, you can find sepia tone settings on almost all commercially available digicams – a testament to the popularity of this process.

01 Color Fill sepia tone
This process is probably one of the easiest. Create a Color Fill adjustment layer (Layer>New Fill Layer>Solid Color) and select a brownish-yellow (Red: 183 / Green: 174 / Blue: 99). Then change the Color Fill's blend mode to Color and keep the Opacity set to 100%. Instant sepia tone!

AFTER

BEFORE

AFTER

02 Colourised sepia tone
Alternatively, you can use the Hue/Saturation adjustment layer (Layer>New Adjustment Layer>Hue/Saturation) and click the Colorize checkbox. Change the Hue to somewhere around 57, and Saturation to anywhere from 0 to 60. Here, a setting of 50 worked well. Leave the Lightness slider where it is, unless you want to change the tonal balance of the image.

The Copperplate process dates back to the 1850s, when a printing plate was created from the image and then used to create the paper print. It shares some similarities with a lithograph. The process is rarely used today due to high costs. Traditionally, most of these prints ranged from dark black to brown to copper and orange. While the process can be easily accomplished using the Duotone dialog, you will explore a different approach through adjustment layers. The advantage is that you can easily switch the colours used to create new unique image recipes.

01 Desaturate and separate the highlights
Start by duplicating the image layer and then desaturate the copied layer (Image>Adjustments>Desaturate). Go to Select>Color Range, and in the Color Range dialog use the Select drop-down to choose the Highlights. Click OK. Now save this selection (Select>Save Selection) and name the selection 'Highlights'. When done, be sure to deselect to remove the marching ants (Ctrl/Cmd+D).

02 Separate the midtones and shadows
Go back into the Color Range dialog and create/save two more selections – one for the midtones and one for the shadows. Be sure to deselect (Ctrl/Cmd+D) after saving each selection, otherwise you may get a warning message indicating no pixels are selected. When you're finished, click on the Channels palette. You should see your three selections as alpha channels.

AFTER

Copperplate print

BEFORE

03 **Blur the channels** Select the Highlights channel and blur the channel (Filter>Blur>Gaussian Blur). Use a setting that matches your image resolution. Since this is a large image, a large blur setting of 15 pixels is used. Apply the same blur to the Midtones and Shadows channels as well. When done, go back to the Layers palette and select the desaturated layer.

04 **Load each selection and map colours** Go to Select>Load Selection and select the Highlights channel. Click OK. Now with the selection active, create a Color Fill adjustment layer (Layer>New Fill Layer>Solid Color). Use the following colour: R:241/G:203/B:141. Repeat this process for the midtones and shadows selections. Use the following colours for each Color Fill adjustment layer: midtones: R:188/G:145/B:90 and shadows: R:102/G:67/B:35.

05 **Blend and add some grain** Change the blend mode for all three Color Fill adjustment layers to Color. To add texture, create a new layer at the top of the layer stack and fill it with 50% grey (Edit>Fill) Then apply some grain (Filter>Texture>Grain). Use the Clumped grain type with Intensity: 22 and Contrast: 73. Desaturate this layer and change the blend mode to Overlay.

BEFORE

AFTER

High-key

High-key images are the opposite of simply overexposed photos. The while the shadows are rich in contrast with this technique are incredibly striking. Here, photo can use this technique. By tweaking the can achieve interesting results.

01 **Create a curve adjustment** Duplicate the original image layer and desaturate it (Image>Adjustments> Desaturate). Create a Curves adjustment layer (Layer>New Adjustment Layer>Curves). Create an evenly sloping curve in the top left quadrant. You can achieve a relatively accurate and evenly sloped curve using three points (as shown above).

02 **Blowing out the highlights** Select the desaturated layer and change the blend mode to Screen. Now duplicate this layer twice to create three screen layers sandwiched between the top Curve adjustment layer and the bottom original image. The image will look almost completely blown out. But don't worry, we'll fix that in the next step.

Here we've used a pic
that would actually be
better suited to high-key
treatment – just to show
it can work on any image!

images

low-key images. They use the entire tonal range, so they are not highlight and midtone areas are lightened with a softer contrast, and detail. Like their low-key counterparts, images produced a low-key image is transformed into a high-key image, but any blend mode and parameters of the top Hue/Saturation layer, you

BEFORE

AFTER

03 **Bringing back detail and colour** With the topmost screen copy layer still selected, create another duplicate of this layer and change the blend mode to Multiply. Now select the original image layer, make a duplicate and move it to the top layer. Change this layer's blend mode to Color. This brings back the photo's original colour.

Low-key images

Low-key photos are often thought of as high contrast underexposed images. This is not quite true. While they are high contrast, they're still correctly exposed. The details are not lost, as with a typical underexposed image, and you can still make out all the nuances of the shadow area. The following technique can be used on an evenly exposed image to give it a low-key quality. For added fun, we'll use an image that would typically be better suited to high-key treatment to show that this technique can be used on all sorts of images.

04 **Finishing touches** Now holding your Alt/Option key down, hover your cursor on the line between the Curve adjustment layer and the layer below, and click to group these layers. Do the same for the next three layers below. Go to the top colour layer and create a Hue/Saturation adjustment layer just above it. Change Saturation to roughly +30. Done!

01 **Set up your layers** Duplicate the image layer. Change the blend mode to Multiply and Opacity to 50%. Create a Hue/Saturation adjustment layer, changing Saturation to -50 and the blend mode to Darken. Create a Curves adjustment layer with an 'S' curve to heighten the contrast. Change the blend mode to Luminosity. You should now have four layers: Background (bottom), Copy, Hue/Saturation1 and Curves1 (top).

02 **Soften the midrange** Select the Background Copy layer and then Select>Color Range. Choose Midtones in the Select drop-down and hit OK. You'll see the marching ants selection. Feather this by about 12 pixels, depending on the size of your image (Select>Feather). This softens the selection. Now apply a Gaussian Blur filter of 1-4 pixels. Deselect (Ctrl/Cmd+D) and you're done.

Tritones

AFTER

BEFORE

Strictly speaking, a tritone is a black-and-white photo that uses three coloured inks to map the tonal range of the image (the mapping is done using Curves in the Image> Mode>Duotone dialog). Tritones began as a printing method not a photographic process. However, the process can be easily reproduced in Photoshop. It should also be noted that the printed output of a Duotone mode image is wonderfully deep and rich. This is due to having total control over tonal ink mapping, and because the printer can produce a wider tonal range with multiple inks than one ink for a greyscale image.

01 **Create the tritone** Here you will create an oxidised green tritone using a black base and two colours. Open the image and convert to Grayscale mode (Image>Mode>Grayscale). Now convert to Duotone mode (Image>Mode>Duotone) and load the tritone (Green-Violet).ado file from the CD. Instant tritone! Note: it's usually a good idea to use black as your first 'base' ink, as in the example above.

02 **Review the curves** Reviewing the ink curves, the black base is lightened. The second ink, green, has its Density increased by 30% at the highlights. The inverse is done with the violet ink, where Density is decreased by 70%. This oxidises our original blue statue image. Experiment to find your own colours and curves to create a unique tritone.

BEFORE

Salted Paper Prints

Salted Paper Prints are one of the earliest forms of photography as we know it. William Henry Fox Talbot is credited with inventing the process in 1840. Traditionally, a Salt Print consisted of paper first coated with a salt solution, and then coated with silver nitrate on one side. After the paper was dried, a negative or object was placed in direct contact or in very close proximity with the paper, and exposed to sunlight for several hours (though UV light is more commonly used today). The advent of Albumen Prints in the 1850s heralded the end of Salt Prints due to their superior quality. However, these two types of prints can look the same, and are often mistaken for each other.

Generally speaking, Salt Prints are deep brown, gold or violet. Alternatively, they can be printed greyscale, without any tinting. Another characteristic of the Salt Print is a textured grain that manifests itself in the entire print. Salt Prints almost always have a gritty matt look as opposed to a glossy finish. Here we'll focus on creating a typical violet Salt Print.

01 **Texture and balance** Duplicate the image layer and find the edges (Filter>Stylize>Find Edges). Apply the Dry Brush filter (Filter>Artistic>Dry Brush) with Size: 1, Detail: 7 and Texture: 3. Change the blend mode to Overlay at 25% Opacity. Add a Curves adjustment layer, applying a high contrast 'S' curve. Add a Levels adjustment layer, moving the Gamma/Middle input slider to 50.

02 **Add a second texture** Add a new layer and fill it with 50% grey (Edit>Fill). Then add a Grain filter (Filter>Texture>Grain) and use a Clumped grain set to Intensity: 33 and Contrast: 50. On the same layer, apply the Glass filter (Filter>Distort>Glass) with Distortion: 18 and Smoothness: 7. Make sure the texture is frosted. Set the layer's blend mode to Pin Light.

03 **Colouring and paper texture** Add a Hue/Saturation adjustment layer at the top. Click Colorize and set Hue to 7 and Saturation to 22. Add a layer above and fill it with 50% grey. In Filter>Texture>Grain use the Vertical grain type with Intensity: 2, Contrast: 50. Change the blend mode to Vivid Light.

04 **Finishing touches** Select the first texture layer (above the levels layer). Go to Select>Color Range and then select the highlights. Feather the selection by 12 pixels (Select>Feather), hold the Alt/Option key and add a layer mask. Highlights will be masked out. Optionally, create a new layer above and fill it with clouds (Filter>Render>Clouds). Set the blend mode to Hard Mix at 3% Opacity. Instant water spots!

AFTER

Sharpening techniques

The final step of creating an image in Photoshop should be to add sharpening, but what is this and how do we do it?

Digital cameras take pics that don't appear fully sharp – the focus looks a bit soft by default. It's not an error or bug with the hardware, it's just a characteristic of the recording technology and properties of light.

You may well be thinking your photos are perfectly sharp, and you're probably right. Camera manufacturers have added software designed to add sharpening to your image while it's still in-camera, so if you only ever shoot in Automatic mode, your images have been pre-sharpened. Even so, many images will benefit from sharpening, and if you shoot in RAW mode on your camera, no sharpening is applied in-camera at all, so you should be applying it in Photoshop.

So it's a good thing, but what exactly is sharpening? It's a process by which edges are accentuated to be more obvious than they would naturally look, helping to create the appearance of fine sharp detail. In its simplest form, sharpening increases the contrast between adjacent pixels to heighten the difference between them. Edge-sharpening filters and techniques look for areas of contrast, and impact the pixels surrounding these. The result is a sharpening of any surface blur.

By applying the principles in this guide, you'll give your images apparently new levels of detail – pin sharp and accentuated.

QUICK AND EASY
A simple way to add impact

Sharpening can be as complicated or as simple as you choose. If you want to add impact quickly and painlessly, use this simple technique. As well as being a rapid process, you have ongoing control, as it's a non-destructive approach – always a bonus!

01 Duplicate your artwork
We'll use a filter to grab the edges, then blend it with the original image to highlight the details. To do this we need a copy of our background layer, so highlight it then go to Layer>Duplicate Layer.

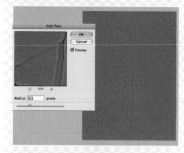

02 High Pass
Go to Filter>Other>High Pass. The Radius slider will alter the amount of detail brought out with contrast; note the highlighting/shading along the edges. Adjust to suit (experiment with it); we chose 5px.

03 Blending In the Layers panel, change the blending to Overlay. You'll see the photo has new levels of detail. Set the layer at various levels of opacity and use a layer mask to remove sharpening where it's not desirable.

AVOID THE PITFALLS
Watch out for the obvious

In most cases sharpening will add to your image, but you do need to be careful as you're applying a wholesale bit of processing to the entire image; there are some major pitfalls to avoid. If you over-sharpen your image you'll create halos around your sharpened edges – areas of unnatural light pixels that follow the sharpened areas. This happens because Photoshop is artificially increasing the contrast around the edges, and can look terrible! Sharpening can also introduce noise to your image. If you continue to work, cloning or toning after sharpening, this noise can become more defined, introducing further artefacts and nasty areas to your image. Try to have a critical eye, and examine your image after each operation to make sure you haven't added unwanted effects.

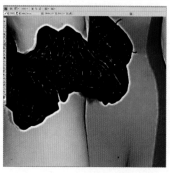

KEEP IT REAL
Everything is best in moderation

As with any Photoshop effect, you'll get best results if you use the techniques in moderation. Sharpening shouldn't be obvious to the viewer; it should pick out the most important detail and leave the blurs in place for a balanced composition. Look at your image and decide which the most important bits are. Target your adjustments at these, and when happy, look at other parts of the image. If necessary, remove sharpening or lessen the effect on the non-focal areas.

BEFORE

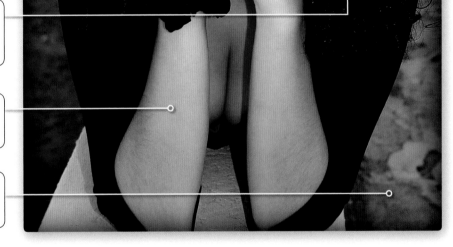

AFTER

Eyes are important If the eyes aren't sharp, it doesn't matter what else in the image is. This is because we connect with people via their eyes. For this reason it's worth creating a separate sharpening layer just for the eyes if necessary.

Sharpening doesn't fix blur It doesn't matter how much sharpening you apply, you can't fix lens blur with these techniques. You can, however, reduce the appearance of soft focus. The best approach is to ensure your start image is well focused, then apply sharpening rather than trying to recover a bad image.

Hair If it's in focus, hair is a good place to look for a nice level of sharp detail. Apply sharpening selectively or generally to get a good level of accentuation, but use care to avoid creating a straw look. Here we've applied a High Pass filter masked to impact only the hair area, highlighting the detail in a controlled fashion.

Be selective Avoid bringing additional attention to undesired areas of the image, imperfections or blemishes. Target your sharpening at the areas of interest, then reduce the impact over arm hair, moles and freckles.

Limit the effects In an image such as this, we only really want to sharpen the primary subject at the heart of the composition: here the main subject is the model. Make use of layer masks to avoid impacting the background.

USE SHARPENING CREATIVELY
Get some unusual results

Don't limit your thinking to regular output. Because sharpening accentuates the edges of an image, you can go to the opposite ends of the spectrum and achieve some wacky, fun and outlandish results. At its extreme, sharpening will give you a highly stylized, posterised look. You can achieve some of the same results with filters, but sharpening will give you very precise control over the edge contrast, so it's well worth bearing this in mind for future projects where you may need to give your image an entirely different treatment.

GET SMART
Use Smart Objects

If you own one of the more recent versions of Photoshop that supports Smart Objects and Smart Filters, get into the habit of using them. In the Layers panel, right-click on your artwork layer and choose Convert to Smart Object. Now you can run filters on your layer, but they'll be smart. You'll be able to apply a mask to the filters to reduce their effect, and you can turn filter effects on and off individually on the layer. This gives you far more control over your image and offers freedom when you make the edits.

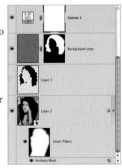

LEARN TO SHARPEN UP
Give this image a makeover

01 **Open the image** Grab the image of the model from the disc. It's worth having a detailed look at the image to get a feeling for what needs to be done. The eyes look a little soft, and the hair could have more detail brought out, but otherwise it's quite a very nice image.

02 **Colour correct and fix blemishes** If you want to make corrections, do so before adding sharpening effects. Check out our Retouching Photos chapter starting on page 168 for techniques to remove blemishes. Here we've brightened the iris of each eye and removed some facial hair and fluff from the clothes. We also desaturated the red item in the background.

03 **Convert to Smart Object** If you're using an older version of Photoshop you may have to skip this step, but if you have the more recent editions it's worth converting your photo to a Smart Object. This will allow you to go back and change the settings of any filters you apply at a later date. Right-click on the layer and choose Convert to Smart Object.

Tip

Sharpen tool

 It's possible to add manual localised sharpening with the Sharpen tool, located in the same part of the toolbox as the Blur tool. Both of these are limited in their usefulness however, so while you might get away with it from time to time, you're nearly always better off with the full control offered by the various techniques discussed in this tutorial. Our advice is to avoid the tool!

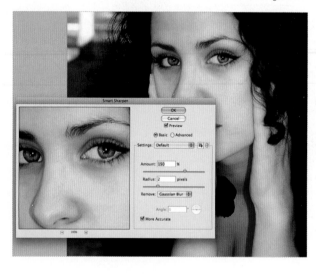

04 **Sharpen for eyes** We're going to apply selective sharpening to our image. First of all we'll sharpen for the eye area. Select Filter>Sharpen> Smart Sharpen. In the dialog box choose 150%, 2px and Gaussian Blur. If you're using a Smart Object, you can paint onto the layer mask to reduce the halo effect outside the eye area.

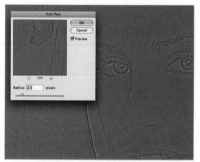

05 **Sharpen for hair** Next, we'll add a copy of the original layer and run a filter to sharpen just for the hair. Duplicate your layer, remove any Smart Filters that came with the copy, then choose Filter> Other>High Pass. Choose a value of 2.5px and click OK. Change the blending mode of the layer to Hard Light.

UNSHARP MASK
The obvious first choice

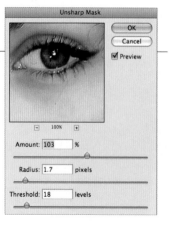

The Unsharp Mask is the automatic default choice of the Sharpening filter to run because it offers a good degree of power and control within a simple set of three options. The Amount option is a straightforward decision over the level of contrast to introduce. Radius specifies the areas over which Photoshop will consider contrast to have been identified (the bigger the radius therefore, the greater potential for sharpening). Threshold describes the amount of tonal range before two pixels are determined to be an edge. This is important because it allows fine control over where the sharpening effect is applied. Use the Preview checkbox to see the difference between the original image and the one with the edits and be sure to glance over the entire image.

SMART SHARPEN
Direct control over shadows/highlights

Smart Sharpen is like Unsharp Mask but better. As well as the same controls you'll find in that filter, you can get Photoshop to attempt removal of various types of blur. If you've got time to play with settings, Smart Sharpen is the tool of choice. Click the Advanced button to get access to individual settings for areas of shadow and highlight. This gives you direct control of the appearance either side of the edge and lets you temper halos from within the Filter dialog.

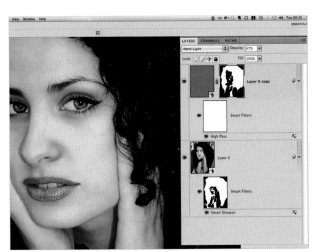

Tip

Add noise after sharpening

Many images also warrant adding noise. It's important to add noise after sharpening rather than before – you want to ensure that you don't accentuate the noise as an edge.

06 Selectively show the effect Add a layer mask to the High Pass layer. Fill the layer mask with black to completely hide the sharpening effect, then paint back in with white over the hair area to limit the impact to the hair area alone.

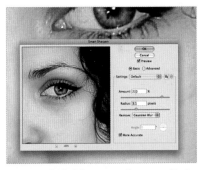

07 Add general sharpening Hold down Ctrl+Alt/Option+Shift while clicking on the Layer Panel menu and choosing Merge Visible. This should create a composite of your artwork onto a new layer. If not, undo and try again. Add a final small amount of sharpening to the composite by choosing Filter>Sharpen> Unsharp Mask. Don't overcook the amount here. We opted for settings of 57%, 1.2px and 2.

08 Add noise Create a new blank layer and choose Edit> Fill. Select 50% grey from the drop-down box and click OK. Select Filter>Noise>Add Noise, then enter 2%, Gaussian and Monochrome in the Filter dialog box. Finally, set the blending mode of the layer to Overlay for a non-destructive noise effect.

09 Add a vignette Finally, create another new empty layer at the top of the stack. Fill it with any colour you choose, then reduce the Fill level to 0 in the Layer panel. Add an Inner Shadow layer style and set the values to suit, making sure Distance is set to 0. The aim is to slightly darken the edges of the image, helping to create a natural frame.

10 Printing it? Over-sharpen a little Printers tend to add a little softness to images, so if you're planning to print your image you should go back and alter your settings to marginally over-sharpen. Only do this for the print version of the image, but you'll find it gives more pleasing results to deliberately go a little beyond what you would otherwise set your values to.

RECOVER FROM HALOS
All is not lost if you add undesirable halos

Sometimes you need to sharpen to such an extent that you can't avoid creating halos around your edges. If this happens, don't despair – there are a couple of different ways to deal with the problem. The easiest is to create a copy of your unsharpened layer over the top of the original. Apply the sharpening to the copy layer, then add a mask by holding down Alt/Option and clicking on the Add Layer Mask button in the Layer panel. Now simply paint on the layer mask in white to reveal sharpened artwork. Wherever you don't paint, the original unsharpened artwork will shine through, without the halos!

SHORTCUTS
Set up quick keyboard shortcuts

Photoshop helpfully allows you to record 'actions', which can be a real time-saver. As you're going to be sharpening

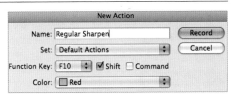

often, it makes sense to record your basic default sharpening settings as an action, and to assign the action to a shortcut key. In that way you can apply sharpening to an image using your favourite default settings with the click of a button. Choose Window>Actions, then select the New Action button and start recording your steps. Once saved, apply to any image you open that might need a bit of definition.

BEFORE

AFTER

Colour replacement

Essentials

TIME TAKEN
30 minutes

YOUR EXPERT
Matthew Henry

ON THE DISC
Before and after images

Change the colour of any subject or object using manual selections, the Color Replacement brush or Replace Color command

It's perfectly possible to change the colour of any subject to a colour of your choice, and there are two main way of going about your changes.

The first is the manual type, which involves making a careful selection around the object you wish to alter, and then using an Image Adjustment such as Color Balance, Hue/Saturation, Levels or Curves.

The second method is the semi-automated type, where Photoshop produces its own on-the-fly selection based around a chosen colour and then allows you to manipulate that colour. The two main examples of this method are found in the Color Replacement brush and the Replace Color command.

Which method you go for will depend largely on the context. Where the colour is very distinct in comparison to surrounding colours, you may get much success with Photoshop automation and save yourself precious time on cutouts, especially for subjects with complex edges. Where the automated methods start to fall down is in cases where there isn't such a clear distinction and edge contrast is low. Here you might start to find colour changes bleeding into areas they shouldn't, and you might spend more time cleaning things up than making a selection from scratch.

We've got one tutorial for the manual approach and two for the other, so by the time you've finished all three you'll have a much better idea of which to use and when.

WORKS WITH | PHOTOSHOP CS ONWARDS

THE MANUAL METHOD
Alter colour the manual way with paths and adjustments

Key Photoshop Skills Covered
What you'll learn

SELECTIONS WITH PATHS

SUBTRACTING FROM A PATH

HUE/ SATURATION ADJUSTMENT

LUMINOSITY WITH CURVES

COLOR REPLACEMENT BRUSH

LAYER MASKS

REPLACE COLOR COMMAND

01 Start your path We're going to start out with the manual method, and an artificial object with curves like the taxi here is perfect for the Pen tool. Select it with 'P' and make sure Paths is selected as opposed to Shape Layers in the Tool Options bar above. Now plot your first point.

02 Continue path Click your second point further along, but hold the mouse button and pull to shape the curve to suit your object. The object outline we have continues along a similar curve, so we do the same again for a few more points. When the shape changes direction abruptly, hold down Alt/Option and click the last point before clicking another.

03 Close path Continue around the car exterior using this method until the path is complete, by joining at the starting point. You can adjust any point by holding down Ctrl/Cmd and dragging. Now go to the Tool Options bar and change the mode to Subtract From Path Area.

04 Subtract from path We can use the same method to remove areas we don't want touched by the colour changes inside the initial path. Take out the windscreen, headlights, front grills, side windows and wing mirror. Go to the Paths palette and hit Load Path as a Selection. Go Select> Modify>Feather and feather by 1 pixel.

TAXI TRANSFORMATION
Ring the colour changes on this fleet of taxis

Background The background is fairly warm, so will be cooled a little with Curves to complement the taxi blue.

Rear taxi The rear taxi will be altered using the same Replace Color command as the mid-ground taxi, and altered to the same shade of blue.

Middle taxi The taxi in the middle will also be turned blue, but this time we'll use Photoshop's Replace Color command.

Taxi on the right The taxi on foreground right will be used to demonstrate the same colour change, but using the Color Replacement brush instead.

First taxi The first taxi in the foreground has been altered via a path selection, a Hue adjustment layer and a further Curves adjustment layer.

05 Alter hue Our selection now needs to be inverted with Ctrl/ Cmd+Shift+I. Now we go back to the Layers palette and add a Hue/ Saturation adjustment layer via the button at the bottom of the palette. Move the Hue slider to get the colour you want. We've gone for a turquoise blue.

Tip

Colour reflections

You have to remember that colour reflects around in its environment as light bounces off it, so as well as altering the colour of your object, you may need to alter the colour cast on a surrounding area. Had we kept the taxi on the right as yellow, a slight yellow cast would have been seen in the door panelling on the taxi left, which we would have added with curves and a layer mask or something similar.

Tip

Replace Color command

Note that with the Replace Color command we isolated our subject roughly first. This prevents other objects with similar colours being affected and saves time brushing them out on the layer mask afterwards. Note in the dialog window that only the taxi appeared in the monochrome area and the rest of the image was ignored. The initial selection need only be a quick one.

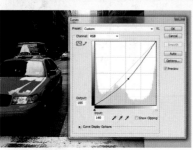

06 Darken colour We want to alter the lightness of the colour, but Lightness in Hue/Saturation doesn't do the best job, so we Ctrl/Cmd-click the Hue/Sat layer mask to reload the selection, and this time add a Curves adjustment layer. Now we bring the curve down with a single point to darken it slightly.

07 Sample blue We're going to attack the second taxi with the Color Replacement brush. Go back to the background layer and duplicate it with Ctrl/Cmd+J. Cycle to the Color Replacement brush with Shift+B. We want to use the same colour, so we Alt/Option sample the taxi blue, but ordinarily we could select via the Color palette.

08 Set up the brush Now we make sure that the brush is set to Color in the Tool Options bar, and that Contiguous is set in the Limits and Sampling is set to Once rather than Continuous. Both these settings give us a little more control in preventing colour spilling into areas where it shouldn't.

09 Start painting Click the Brush Preset picker and make sure that Size is set to Off and not Pen Pressure or Stylus Wheel. Now we need to start painting in an area that has a strong shade of yellow, as all subsequent guess-work by Photoshop will be done where you first click when using Sampling Once mode. We start on the right side of the bonnet.

10 Adjust the Tolerance setting The brush hasn't picked up all the yellow, leaving some untouched areas, so we need to alter the Tolerance to include more of the yellow. We Undo with Ctrl/Cmd+Z and then change the Tolerance level from 30% to 50%. Now we have another go.

11 Increase Tolerance again At 50% parts of the bonnet are still untouched, so we go all the way to 70%. We have to be careful about our precision now at this Tolerance setting. We can also click again at the light areas in the bonnet to make sure these are picked up when we paint.

12 Work over the taxi We continue to keep working slowly around like this, re-clicking on areas that don't get taken and then going over them. Use Undo if you make a mistake. If you find later that you have gone into areas you shouldn't, simply add a layer mask and then paint it out with a black brush.

13 Tweak Saturation The taxis are looking good, but the original has too much saturation on the bonnet and roof in comparison to our new one. We add a Hue/Saturation adjustment layer, drop Saturation, invert its mask with Ctrl/Cmd+I and then paint the adjustment into the areas we want with a white brush. We now go back and tweak Hue and Lightness a little as well.

REPLACE COLOR COMMAND
The third and final method uses Replace Color

14 **Make a rough selection** Now, for the final taxi we're going to try and achieve the same effect with the Replace Color command. Start by selecting the Lasso tool with Shift+L and make sure the duplicate background layer is active. Then go to Image>Adjustment>Replace Color.

15 **Select the yellows** In the dialog, select the + Eyedropper and click in a few different yellow areas of the taxi. Include a dark yellow, a midtone yellow and a light yellow. Now play with the Fuzziness slider until the areas in the taxi that you want to alter appear white in the monochrome dialog image.

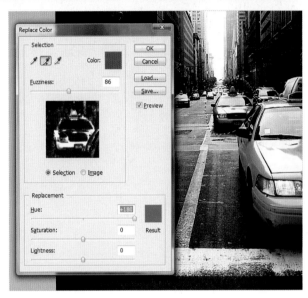

16 **Tweak the dialog** Now alter the Hue to change the colour, which will show you just how good your selection is. If it doesn't look good, simply play with the Fuzziness slider to alter the selection or use the + and - Eyedroppers to take out or add in areas as required.

17 **Repeat for rear taxi** Now we can repeat the process for the taxi in the rear. Do this by making a rough selection first with the Lasso tool, adding different tones of yellow in Replace Color, before altering the Hue and tweaking Fuzziness and using the Eyedroppers to get the desired result.

18 **Colour the headlights** As a little embellishment we can give the headlights a bluish hue on the front two cars. Select the second background layer and choose the Color Replacement brush again. Use the same settings as before and sample the blue from a taxi before brushing over the lights.

LAYER STRUCTURE
How we created our colours

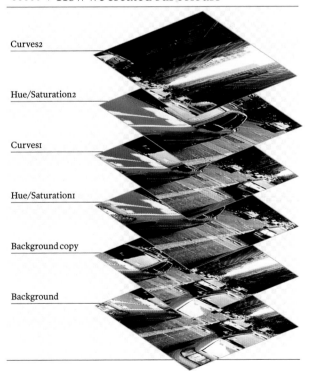

Curves2

Hue/Saturation2

Curves1

Hue/Saturation1

Background copy

Background

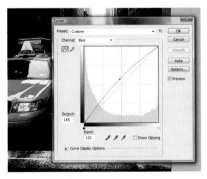

19 **Add a blue wash** Now we want to give the background image a slight bluish hue to match the colouring of the cars. Add a Curves adjustment layer and select Blue from the drop-down menu, then push the curve up slightly. Now select Red and pull the Curve down slightly.

20 **Knock back for taxis** Next, make sure the layer mask is active, take a black brush and brush out the adjustment from the taxis because they already have enough of a blue tone and we don't want to overdo things. Change the layer blending mode to Color so the contrast isn't affected.

BEFORE

AFTER

Key
Photoshop
Skills Covered
What you'll learn

PEN TOOL
CHANNELS
PALETTE
LAYER
MASKING
LEVELS

Spotless backgrounds

Save hours of studio time and use Photoshop to make clean, pure white backgrounds

Cleaning up messy backgrounds is an important technique for any photographer to master. Whether behind the camera or using Photoshop, it's vital to keep a white background entirely white.

It's a lot quicker to clean up backgrounds using Photoshop rather than adjusting multiple studio lights to minimise irritating shadows. In this tutorial, you'll learn exactly how to do it. With the tools and techniques we've used here, tidying things up doesn't need to be a lengthy or painful process.

In the following steps you'll discover how to use the Pen tool to make new selections around a subject to eventually cut them out, plus how to add a new layer mask to make the whole effect work. Tweaking adjustments such as Levels is also covered to make sure the subject will look balanced with the white background that you'll eventually have.

So it doesn't matter if you have a black background or just a very dirty-looking one that needs whitening. It can all be sorted within a handful of steps, and won't take you long. It doesn't have to stop there, because you can also change the colour of the background to anything you want – depending on how you intend to use it.

"It's a lot quicker to clean up backgrounds using Photoshop than adjusting studio lights"

If you don't have your own images to practise on, simply load up the CD and then search for the picture 'SmallDoll. jpg' in order to get started on this tutorial.

Essentials

TIME TAKEN
30 minutes

YOUR EXPERT
Simon Skellon

ON THE DISC
SmallDoll.jpg

WORKS WITH | PHOTOSHOP 6 AND ABOVE

SMARTEN UP USING A LAYER MASK
Make a selection and say goodbye to the grey areas

01 Select the Pen tool Open 'SmallDoll.jpg' from the disc. Make the image editable by double-clicking its layer in the Layers palette. Select the doll's shadow with the Lasso, go to Image>Adjustments>Hue/Saturation and reduce Saturation to -40. Now choose the Pen tool to draw an outline around the doll.

02 Draw the outline With the Pen tool selected and zoomed in closely, begin marking the points around the edges of the doll, adjusting the lines to fit its curves. Try to be as accurate as possible, so the final result will have seamless edges.

03 Make Selection When you've completed the whole doll, Ctrl/right-click inside the selection and hit Make Selection. This will transform the line into a live selection, making it a new Alpha channel in the Channels palette. If at any point the selection disappears, simple hold Ctrl/Cmd and click on the Alpha channel's layer to restore the selection.

04 Create a new layer In the Layers palette select the Create New Layer button at the bottom of the palette. Now drag the new layer, while inside the Layers palette, so that it sits below the layer with the doll. This new layer will form the spotless white background that we are aiming for.

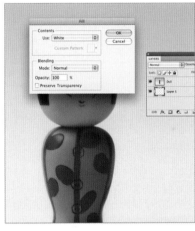

05 Make grey into white With the new layer selected, hit Ctrl/Cmd+D to deselect the live selection around the doll. Go to Edit>Fill, and in the Fill menu set Contents to White, Normal for the blend mode, and use 100% Opacity. Press OK and the new layer will fill with pure white.

06 White before your eyes Go back into the Channels palette and while holding Ctrl/Cmd, click on the Alpha channel. The selection made earlier will now become visible around the doll. Go to the Layers palette, select the Doll layer and hit Add Layer Mask. This will hide the grey and also show the white layer underneath.

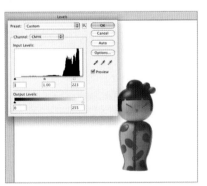

07 Levels adjustment Select the thumbnail of the doll in the Layers palette. It's the perfect time to brighten it up, so head to Image>Adjustments>Levels and boost the highlights and midtones levels of the doll. Hit OK when done.

08 Reveal the shadow The finishing touch is to add the shadow. To do this, select the Layer Mask thumbnail in the Layers palette and use a soft brush to take away the area of the mask covering the shadow. The doll should now be on a perfect white background.

Remove unwanted elements

Don't despair if stray hairs are ruining your stunning portrait. Photoshop has just the tools

There's barely a photo most of us could take that hasn't got a small niggle somewhere in it. It might be a telegraph pole, a stray hair, or you might want to touch up a model's makeup. Whatever the issue, it needn't cause a headache. With the advent of digital imaging, we have the ability to distort reality and create perfect scenes by removing any objects we don't want.

Photoshop ships with some incredibly powerful tools for getting rid of objects, imperfections and even ex-partners – but there are some basic rules to follow to avoid destroying your image. Recognising which tool is most appropriate for the job, blending and correcting in a convincing manner will all take practice. Even as a seasoned Photoshop user you'll find it easy to over-cook your corrections. The end result should look natural and believable, but most importantly it shouldn't be obvious that you've done anything to the image at all.

In this tutorial we're looking at an image of a horse. The horse is partially obscured by a gate, and the desired result is to free the horse from its metal shackles. There are a few other bits of tidying we can do at the same time, and by

> "Most importantly, it shouldn't be obvious that you've done anything to the image at all"

the end of the steps you should have a clear idea of how to tackle removing objects and imperfections from images.

This is a core retouching technique, but it does take patience and lots of practice to master, so stick with it and don't despair if you don't immediately get the results you were hoping for. Persevere and soon you'll be living in your own perfect digital world.

Key Photoshop Skills Covered
What you'll learn

CLONING TOOL
PATCH TOOL
HEALING BRUSH
ESSENTIAL TECHNIQUES

IDENTIFY THE TOOL, THEN GET STUCK IN
Half the technique is knowing which tool to use when…

Essentials

TIME TAKEN
30 minutes

YOUR EXPERT
Sam Hampton-Smith

ON THE DISC
Horse © jkingsbeer www.sxc.hu

01 Identify the issues Our image is of a horse behind a gate. The issues here are obvious: we don't want the gate, and there is a bit of trash attached to the fence. First we'll tackle the gate – we need to decide which tool we're going to use. As the gate extends over different areas (the horse, the background, the skyline), we'll need to call upon a number of different approaches.

02 Take a copy We must ensure we're not damaging our original artwork – we may need to come back to it later – so create a duplicate of the photograph on a new layer by choosing Layer>Duplicate Layer. We'll do all our work on this duplicate layer so that the original is safely stored at the bottom of the stack.

03 The Clone Stamp tool The Clone Stamp tool works by borrowing pixels from elsewhere in the image and copying them where you apply the brush. You select the point to copy from by holding down the Alt/Option key while clicking on the area to sample from. Alt/Option-click in the field to choose this as the source point.

WORKS WITH | PHOTOSHOP 7 AND ABOVE

BEFORE

AFTER

BEFORE

AFTER

PRACTICE (AND PATIENCE) MAKES PERFECT
Take the time to learn how the tools work, and see the benefits

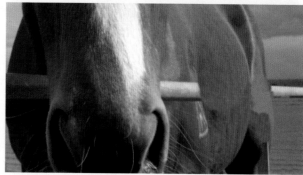

04 Paint in new pixels Now we've chosen our source pixels, we can paint in with these pixels over the top of the offending areas. Try to align your brush with the furrows to match the area you selected as the source point, and then paint over the central rung of the gate.

05 Little and often Hold down Alt/Option and select a new source point on the horse's midriff. Paint over the central top part of the gate as it crosses the horse. Paint with short strokes, a bit at a time. This way, if you make a mistake you can choose Edit>Undo and you won't lose all your corrections in one go.

TOOLS OF THE TRADE
 Find out how they can help you produce a perfect image

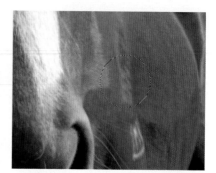

06 Choose many source points To be convincing, you'll need to choose lots of different source points and avoid creating multiple adjacent copies of the exact same pixels. The human eye will immediately spot patterns formed from sampling the same areas repeatedly.

Sharpening As a final step, add sharpening and see the detail come out of your image. Choose Filter>Sharpen>Unsharp Mask from the menu and experiment with the settings to get a sharper image with much more impact.

Combined effort Some areas will require manual reconstruction of the image. Here we're going to have to create an artificial horizon as it's totally obscured. Use combinations of the tools to achieve a good result.

Patch tool The Patch tool allows wholesale replacement of areas of an image. Draw a marquee around the area you want to replace and drag your selection over the area you want to use as a replacement.

Clone Stamp The Clone Stamp tool makes quick work of low-detail areas like the field here. Simply Alt/Option-click on the field nearby, align your brush to match the furrows, and paint over the gate.

Healing brush This is ideal for replacing textured areas while retaining tonal characteristics of the image. Use it as the Clone tool; Photoshop applies processing to the pixels, matching them with their surroundings.

07 Blend for believability You won't always have exactly the right pixels available – they'll either be too dark or too light, or at the wrong orientation. In more recent versions of Photoshop you can rotate, scale and distort your cloned pixels as you paint, but a simple technique to blend the pixels is to vary the opacity of the tool.

OTHER USEFUL TOOLS
Don't limit yourself to the Clone tool

Tip

08 Complete the easier areas It makes sense to complete the easy elements first, and then move on to the more complicated areas. Once you've blocked out the areas without an edge, you can start to focus on the finer detailed areas.

09 Patch tool Photoshop doesn't restrict you to one tool for re-creating areas of an image. Select the Patch tool from the toolbox, and draw a marquee around the fence post with litter. Once you've made a selection, click inside the marching ants and then drag to the right so that you frame up a copy of the post closest to the horse.

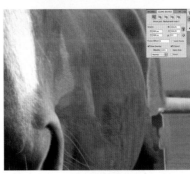

10 Healing Brush tool Choose the Healing Brush from the toolbox. This is used in a similar fashion to the Clone Stamp, but instead of just pasting new pixels over the top of the old, the Healing Brush attempts to retain tone from the area being replaced. Try using it to get rid of the horse's tattoo.

Less is more

It can be tempting to go mad with the Clone Stamp tool. It's so powerful that it's easy to lose track of your changes and end up in a horrible mess. To avoid this pitfall, only make the changes absolutely necessary to remove the elements you don't want. Periodically view your artwork at different zoom levels. If you're lucky enough to be using CS4, this is a perfect excuse to use the new Bird's Eye view. Hold down the 'H' key to select the Hand tool, then click and hold your mouse button to view the full document temporarily.

11 Spot Healing tool If this were a portrait of a person, the Spot Healing tool might be useful. It works by simply painting over the area you want to fix. Photoshop automatically samples the area around the 'spot' and replaces pixels as necessary. Give it a try here, but don't expect great results on this image.

12 Creating artwork from nothing In most images you'll find certain areas have nothing comparable in the rest of the image to sample from, no matter how hard you try. In these circumstances, for example where the gate obscures the horizon on the left-hand side of this image, you're going to have to get creative.

13 Patch, then clone Start off using the Patch tool to replace the whole area, but limited only to the area that you don't want. Drag up to the sky to use these pixels. Fortunately, the far background is softly focused, so we can get away with cloning from the sky and remaining ground to create an artificial horizon.

14 Finish the rest All that remains is to work around the rest of the image, dealing with each of the difficult areas in turn. Take your time and follow the existing contours to ensure a believable result. Remember to watch out for repeating patterns and shifts in tone.

15 Colour correct, sharpen and add noise As with any image, the final step should be to sharpen and add noise, but as we didn't colour correct this image in the first instance, it's worth considering that now as well.

Fix white balance

Essentials

TIME TAKEN
30 minutes

YOUR EXPERT
Katty Houtmeyers

ON THE DISC
Before file

Don't let annoying white balance blight what is an otherwise excellent image. Simply bring the Levels palette into play

One advantage of living in a world where the light is always sunny and bright is that white balance problems would be practically non-existent. But an album full of photos taken in the sun would make for a very boring photo collection indeed, so there's something to be said for risking an odd duff image here and there.

When you have white balance issues, you will see a colour cast occur when one of the RGB colours is stronger than the others and usually happens when

photos are taken under artificial light. With fluorescent lights this is often green and with tungsten lighting it will be yellow. If the flash is involved, you're looking at a blue cast. However, as this example shows, you can also suffer from colour casts even if the photo is taken outside. Natural daylight is far from consistent and changes depending on location and time of day. For example, photos taken early in the morning will appear more 'bluish' than those taken at midday. As the day ends, colour will become redder and warmer. But in addition

to the natural light, you have to think about location. Photos taken under a canopy of trees, for example, can suffer from a green colour cast.

Photoshop provides the perfect tools for removing these colour casts and bringing back your neutral, natural colours. We're going to use the Levels palette here to restore this photo to its rightful glory, by neutralising and defining the black, white and middle grey points. Use this tutorial on colour faded or old pictures; you'll be amazed what it can do.

WORKS WITH | PHOTOSHOP ELEMENTS 3.0, 4.0, PHOTOSHOP 7.0 AND ABOVE

COLOUR CAST BEGONE
Get your gleaming whites back

Tip

01 First things first Copy the start image file from the CD onto your desktop. Open it up Photoshop and take a good look where the problem areas are situated. The most obvious problem is the white in the car that has a yellow, greenish cast. Duplicate the layer by going to Layer>Duplicate Layer. Name the first layer Original and call the duplicate Retouch.

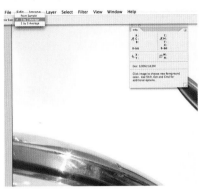

02 Prepare the workspace Pick the Eyedropper tool and set the Sample size to 3 x 3 Average. Bring up the Info palette and go to View>Fit On Screen. Now we're ready for optimising the image.

03 Levels In the Image>Adjustment menu, bring up the Levels palette. In this dialog box, beneath the Auto button are three eyedropper tools; these are used to set the black, grey and white points of the image. Double-click on the Eyedropper at the left to set the black point.

Alternative Another way to remove colour casts is by using the Match Color palette. This can be found in the Image>Adjustments menu. Here you can select the Neutralize checkbox to give standard values to your RGB values. Also take a look inside Photoshop's Help Centre to find more tips for working with colour casts, white balance and overall colour adjustments. You can find it by going to Help>Photoshop

04 Setting the back point After clicking on the left Eyedropper tool, the colour picker box will appear. Click in what seems the darkest, most black part of the image and look at the RGB Values. Here we have: R: 4, G: 9 and B: 2. Set all the values to '4' and click OK to conform. Click with the Eyedropper once more in the darkest area.

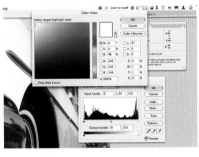

05 Set the white point We will do exact the same thing for the white neutral point. Double-click on the right Eyedropper tool to bring up the colour picker. Set the eyedropper on a white part that has colour cast. Set all of the RGB values to 246. Click OK and click with the white loaded Eyedropper inside the image. You'll notice that the cast disappears.

06 More white The white in an image is one of the most important values; we don't want to make it too white. The minimal white shouldn't be less than 5% colour and the black shouldn't be more than 95%. Check with the Eyedropper tool and see what values crop up in the Info palette.

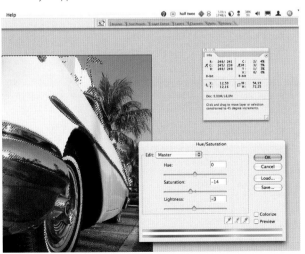

07 Hue/ Saturation Go to the Select menu and choose Color Range. Select the white of the car with the Eyedropper and set the Fuzziness to 95. Bring up the Hue/Saturation box and set the Saturation to -14 and decrease the Lightness to -3. This will remove the last bit of colour cast from your image.

08 Sharpen Click out of the selection from the Color Range and examine your image. An Unsharp Mask on top of this would be useful. Go to the Filter menu and choose Unsharp Mask in the Sharpen menu. Set the Amount to 50 and click OK.

Chapter 2

Restore photos

*Invaluable tricks for restoring
old photos back to life*

Tip

Be realistic

::: This is probably not the best way to start a chapter, but don't expect miracles when restoring really badly damaged pictures. Photoshop can certainly do a lot, but you need to be realistic about how far it can stretch!

Photo restoration tutorial on the CD

Healing brush/Patch tool Old photos will have area of missing information. Use these tools to simply clone parts back in.

Clone Stamp tool For a more precise finish, the Clone Stamp tool is need to sample information from one part of the image into a damaged area.

Curves Old photos often lack tonal interest. To give a boost to the image, use the Curves dialog.

Dust and scratches The Dust and Scratches filter allows you to smooth out small imperfections.

Blending modes If you are adding colour to a black and white image, the Blending Modes will help you achieve a desirable result

Restoring photos

Don't let your treasured photos succumb to the ravages of time

Essentials

 YOUR EXPERT

Jo Cole

 ON THE DISC

Photo restoration tutorial on the CD

It's a sad fact that traditional print photos don't suffer wear and tear well, especially photos from previous generations.

The best-case scenario is that they have just gone a bit musty and faded from being stored in a photo album for decades. Unfortunately, a lot of us have to face up to the worst-case scenario, which is that the photos have been sat in a shoebox in the bottom of various cupboards, picking up rips, folds dust and scratches over the years. Even if you've been careful with the storage, camera technology isn't what it is today and so an image that might be perfect in terms of condition could still need a helping hand in terms of colour or sharpness.

There's a lot that can be done in Photoshop to help rescue neglected or abused photos. The first task is to get the photo in a digital format. Scanners are getting cheaper – just make sure to scan in at a decent resolution (300ppi is good).

There's more good news. You'll find there is a lot of crossover between the tools used in retouching photos and the tools used to restore photos, with emphasis being put on the easier tools such as Spot Healing Brush and Healing Patch. Cloning plays a big part in most restoration projects too. Since a lot of the photos in this Photoshop work are black and white or sepia, you'll find that you'll reach for Levels and Curves more than other colour correction options.

By following our techniques in this chapter, you will be able to restore your favourite photos to their former glory.

Levels If you want to further boost the image, try the Auto Levels command from the Image menu and see what happens!

 ## DODGE AND BURN
Lighten and darken

The Dodge and Burn tools (found in the toolbox) take their characteristics from traditional photographic methods of darkening and lighting images. The Dodge tool will lighten areas that you brush over, while the Burn tool will darken. You can treat each tool in the same way as a brush, and just move over where you want to edit. You can adjust how severe the edit is and pick a soft brush for more subtle effects.

SHADOW/HIGHLIGHT
Bring out details

Old black-and-white photos can sometimes be very dark, which means that a lot of areas are lost in the shadows. The Shadow/Highlight command is excellent for rescuing these details and restoring your image. Simply adjust the relevant slider until you are happy. You can also use the command if you have a photo that is very bleached out and is in need of some dark areas.

Adjustments The Adjustments menu offers a few options for fixing colour casts, from the Channel Mixer to reduce the offending hue, to the Variations command for instantly combating the problem.

Photo restoration tutorial on the CD

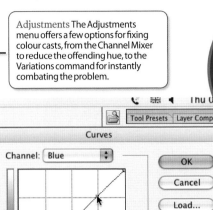

Curves In this case, we chose the Curves dialog to fix the colour cast. By choosing a hue from the drop-down menu, you can remove it from the image.

Before and after Old photos often suffer from colour casts, where a distinct hue can be seen all over an image. Here you can see how it's been fixed.

Tip

Sharpen tools

You will often have to apply a small amount of sharpening to old photos to crisp them up a bit. Unsharp Mask is a good all-rounder for this task, and you can easily see the effects of the edit in the Preview window.

NOISE REMOVAL
Smooth out the surface

Old photos can suffer from a lot of noise, which can make your image look as though tiny bits of dust have settled on it – not so much of a issue with modern cameras. This problem can be even worse if it's a photo taken at night. To fix this annoying effect, pay a visit to the Filters menu and select the Despeckle filter. You could also apply a very weak blur in areas most affected by noise.

FIXING TEARS
No more tears over tears

Old photos always suffer from the odd rip or damaged area and for these occasions, you need a way to rebuild the areas. As you may have guessed, Photoshop has a good selection waiting for you

Clone Stamp tool

Stamp it out The mother of all restoration tools, this allows you to sample part of an image and paint it in another area. Pick the largest brush you can and go for small dabs for the most realistic effects. This can help you to fix everything from rips and tears, to dust and scratches, giving you a perfect image that you can treasure forever.

Healing Brush tool

Heal over the cracks This also allows you to replace unsightly areas with information from other parts of an image, but the Healing Brush also matches the texture, transparency, lighting and shading of the sampled pixels to that of the original, making it perfect for complicated areas, such as some of the more obvious rips on our example image.

Spot Healing Brush

On-the-spot fixing power Good for smaller areas that need fixing. Again, you pick an area that is the desired finish and just click over the area that needs fixing. Pick a large brush and try to make the edit in one click, otherwise you might find that you can see the joins and have to do even more work to the image – there's no point making it hard on yourself!

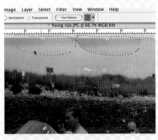

Patch tool

Patch it up This is a fun tool and very easy to use. The Patch tool does the same as the Healing Brush and Spot Healing Brush tools, except that you haven't got to brush the edit on. Instead, you draw around the area you want to fix with any of the selection tools, and then drag to get to the part you want to replace it with. It can heal large areas in seconds.

Dust & Scratches

Clean up your photos If you have small areas of an image that have suffered damage, go to the Filter menu and pick Noise>Dust & Scratches. The surface area will smooth out. You can adjust how smooth it becomes using the Radius slider. Use it at the smallest setting possible to get a balance between smooth surface and keeping the details.

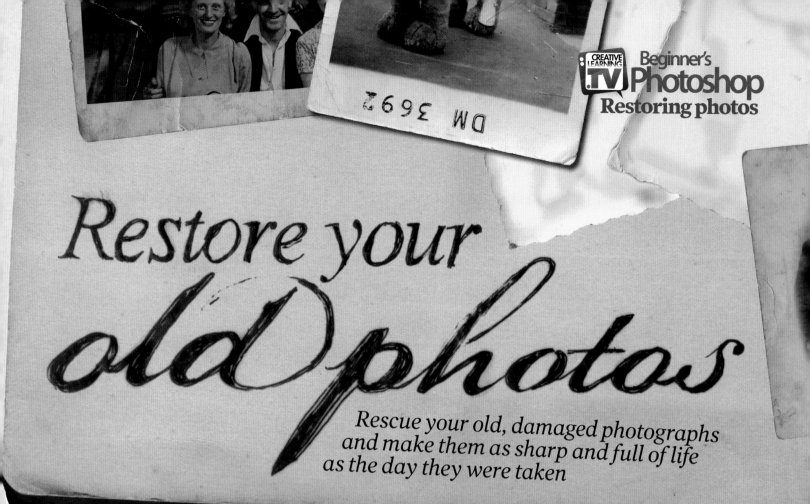

Restore your old photos

Rescue your old, damaged photographs and make them as sharp and full of life as the day they were taken

Most of us have collections of old family photos hoarded away. And even though we try to protect them from damage, over time they can become discoloured, worn and torn.

Now there's no excuse for keeping them hidden in a box at the back of your cupboard, because they can be returned to their full glory using Photoshop's powerful restoration capabilities. But before you can begin clicking away in Photoshop, cleaning up your photos, they need to be in a digital format which is done through the magic of scanning.

When scanning old photos there are many handy techniques to get the best quality from your images. These will be revealed in our step-by-step tutorials on how to tackle the most common problems that occur with old photos. Most scanners come with software, but getting your photos on-screen and ready to repair is just as easily done using Photoshop's Import function in the File menu. Photoshop can take you all the way from scanning right to the final restored image.

Software that comes with scanners normally features adjustments such as dust removal and colour restoration which generally do a good job. However, Photoshop is not only excellent when it comes to producing artistic projects, it also excels in its restoration capabilities, giving you greater control over its adjustment settings. Therefore our main focus will be on restoring your photographs using Photoshop rather than the software that comes with your scanner.

Remember that both stages of the process are equally important. There's no point in selecting the correct

> ## "Our main focus will be on restoring photos using Photoshop rather than your scanner's software"

settings to achieve optimum scan quality and then doing a poor retouching job in Photoshop.

Selecting your scanner

The first thing to consider when buying a scanner is the type of documents you will scan most often. If you have lots of old, damaged photographs stashed away in need of restoration, it's best to choose a high quality scanner offering a better resolution. If it's old negatives and slides you want to scan, select a model with a transparent media adaptor.

Modern scanners are easy to connect to your computer. They're also becoming more slimline all the time and feature software that's straightforward to install. If you've looked at scanner specs you may have seen they feature two numbers describing their resolution, for example 1200dpi x 2400dpi. The first, smaller number refers to optical resolution, or how many colour samples are taken per inch. The second number is the enhanced resolution that can be achieved by manipulating the scanner's software. You only need focus on the first one, as it specifies the true resolution in dots per inch.

The main scanner types available are flatbed, photo, drum and slide. Drum scanners are the most expensive and best quality but are mostly used in the publishing industry. Some models are in the region of £30,000 and obviously not ideal for home users! Flatbed scanners are made up of glass through which a bright light is shone and a moving sensor which reads the image according to the amount of reflected light.

Photo scanners did have a reputation for producing scans of unimpressive resolution, but recent models are much improved. The old photos we've used in this feature were scanned using a photo scanner and the results

OLD

NEW

02 Retain the detail There are many small and large scratches on the image. You can reduce the small ones with the Dust and Scratches filter, but it can reduce the detail, making areas look slightly blurred. Therefore pick the Lasso tool, enter a Feather value of 10 and select Add to Selection in the top Options bar.

03 Select dusty background areas Now you can go around the areas that have the most detail in them. This is usually not the background, but areas such as faces. We chose to select these areas here. The feather will also soften the edge. Choose Select>Inverse in order to select the part of the photograph that you will apply the filter to.

04 Adjust your filter settings In Filter> Noise>Dust and Scratches, set Amount to 100%, Radius to 2 pixels and Threshold to 1 pixel. Turn the Preview on and off to see the effect of the filter on certain areas of the image. If it's too severe increase Threshold or reduce Radius to 1. Hit OK to see your specks and scratches fade.

06 Tools to turn back time Alt/Option-click to select the source area you want to copy. Now click on the scratch or dust to paint over it with the sample you just selected. For seamless cloning try to sample regularly and from either side of a scratch or speck. Prevent it from looking too smudgy or fake by avoiding large strokes and building up using single clicks.

07 Reduce brush size for detailed areas The Dust and Scratches filter reduces smaller defects, but larger cracks will still need removing with the Clone tool. For areas with more detail, zoom in and reduce your brush size in the Options bar, but for less detailed background areas use a larger brush. Use this method to erase all trace of scratches and specks.

08 Convert the image Choose Image>Mode>Grayscale. You will be asked if you want to discard the colour information – click OK. This will transform your cleaned up and despeckled image into black and white. When you save your photograph, if saving as a JPEG also make sure that you choose the highest quality.

at 100dpi, it will be made up of 800 dots. So when you set the output size and resolution, think whether you'll need to enlarge it when you print. If you're scanning damaged photos, resolution should be set no lower than 300dpi and they should be saved using the highest quality setting. When scanning old photos at such high resolution, they will be large files so make sure you have enough space to store them. If you plan to scan a large quantity of images, perhaps it's worth investing in an external hard drive to keep them all on.

It's also useful to hit Preview first to see a quick, low-res overview of your image on-screen before you commit it to scan, in case of problems – eg being placed at an angle on the scan bed. Most scanning software lets you crop the region scanned at the Preview stage using the mouse to mark out the selection area. When you hit Scan, only

> ## "A highly useful filter which many people avoid because they don't understand it, is the Custom filter"

this segment of the screen is scanned, which saves having to crop it later in Photoshop. If you're carrying out other adjustments in the scanning software such as dust removal, the results usually don't show in the Preview window – you only see it when the final image appears.

Filter away the flaws

Now you've created a digital copy of your old photo you can get to work on it in Photoshop. Once you take your scan into the program you can clean up the imperfections using the app's tools and filters. If the image is covered in dust specks and scratches, Photoshop has a filter perfectly suited to getting rid of them – the Dust and Scratches filter.

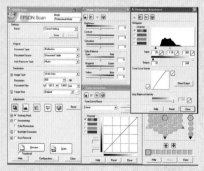

Your scanner should come with software for getting images into a digital format, but these options are also in Photoshop

Although it does a great job of reducing them, it also has a blurring effect that reduces detail. You should therefore use it carefully or only apply it to areas with detail that can afford to be lost.

Filters such as Unsharp Mask bring detail back and enhance images. Again, this should be applied with care to avoid over-sharpening, which can look just as bad as blurring. Another highly useful filter which many people avoid because they don't understand it is the Custom filter which also helps bring back detail and is good at fixing underexposed images. See page 87 where we use this filter after fixing a

Whether photos have dust and scratches, colour casts or tears, Photoshop can rescue them with its filters and tools

photo's colour cast to create a high-pass version of the image to overlay, adding more contrast.

Bring back colour and contrast

Not all Photoshop's restoration powers lie in its filter selection. Colour casts are a common curse of old photos. Colour tinges are easily removed from photos with some crafty tweaking using Curves. By selecting the image's problem colour channel in the Curves dialog window, adding a few points to the line on the graph and moving them slightly, the original vibrant colours are brought back as if by magic.

Photoshop's tools allow a higher level of control than those in scanning software. One useful tool to enhance old photos' faded colours is Levels. A histogram is displayed in the centre of the Levels dialog. The left slider is for shadows and the right one is for

01 **Time-saving scanning techniques** Open 'ripped.jpg' from the disc and right/Ctrl-click the background layer thumbnail in the Layers palette. Choose Layer From Background. Select one half with the Marquee tool. Choose Layer>New>Layer via Cut, placing them on independent layers. If they are too large, scan them separately and copy and paste them both into a new larger document.

Piecing together a ripped photograph

Use our digital method of reattaching ripped photos; it's far better than using sticky tape

fixed

Some severely damaged photographs are beyond repair. For example, if your photograph has a large chunk missing it can be difficult to make up what was there before, unless it is a fairly plain area of landscape or flat colour that you are cloning. A photograph such as the one on the left, however, is easily pieced together in Photoshop. The tear is quite a clean one and there are no sections missing, making it even more straightforward to fix. Although using the Clone tool is very simple, there are a few handy techniques to make sure you produce a seamless area where the two halves meet. For example, by checking Aligned in the Options bar the clone source moves in accordance with where your cursor is placed, creating the perfect cover-up.

02 Delete unwanted areas Click on one of the layer thumbnails and pick the Magic Wand tool. Click on the white background area around the edge of the photograph and hit Delete. Repeat this for the other layer so you have two halves of the photograph on separate layers with no white around them.

03 All in the layer order When piecing together parts of a photo check that it displays according to the way it was ripped. Experiment with the layer order by dragging one above the other in the Layers palette to see which fits best. In this case the layer with the lower half of the photo should be higher in the Layers palette.

04 Precise alignment If the halves don't align, select one of the layers, choose Edit>Free Transform and rotate it. Use the Move tool and arrow keys to align the photographs precisely and then select both layers in the Layers palette by Shift-clicking. Choose Layer>Merge Layers. Create a new layer for your cloning. Move it to the top of the Layers palette.

05 Clone on a separate layer Zoom in and pick the Clone tool. Set Size to 45 pixels, Opacity to 50%, check Sample All Layers and Aligned. Hold Alt/Option while clicking one side of the tear. This is your sample area. Now click the tear, painting over it with the sample. Click rather than stroke to avoid smudging.

06 Keep on cloning Keep repeating this method of cloning for both sides of the tear and build it up until you've concealed the rip. For fairly flat areas such as the animal's fur you can use a larger brush, whereas a smaller brush is needed to clone in areas such as the edges.

07 Scrub out the scratches We used the same method as in the previous tutorial, using the Dust and Scratches filter and Clone tool to remove scratches and creases. Although it was tricky, the Clone tool was also used to paint over the red mark. After cropping it is up to you whether you choose Image>Mode> Grayscale or keep the original colouring.

highlights. Dragging them towards the middle to meet the point where the histogram raises, enhances an image's shadow and highlight areas. The contrast can then be improved by experimenting with the middle slider.

Attack of the clones

A familiar problem in old photos is creases or tears where photo collections have been moved from place to place. Don't dismiss these as irreparable, even if they're ripped in half. Photoshop's Clone tool enables you to repaint over a damaged area with a nearby sample from the image, making it miraculously

> ## "Don't dismiss old photographs as irreparable, even if they are ripped in half"

disappear. By doing this you're sampling the detail and colour of an area that's intact and using it to cover a damaged section. This is also handy for removing unwanted objects and even attaching pieces of a ripped photo. To use the tool, hold down Alt/Option while clicking the source point you want to sample from, then click in the problem area to paint over it with your sample.

You can customise how the Clone tool works in the Options bar. If working on a multi-layered image, checking Sample All Layers means your source is taken from all the document's layers. For your sample points to update according to where your cursor is, check Aligned.

You want the areas of the image you've repaired to be as unnoticeable as possible, so a softer, more realistic effect

Previewing a scan gives a speedy, low-res example of your image, then use the Marquee to crop/select the area to scan

Scanning slides and negatives

Apply the scanning and restoration techniques you've used for your old photographs to the original negative film and slides

Developments in scanning technology mean the quality of scanned slides and negatives is impressive. However, a severely scratched transparency can be challenging due to its small size. Scanners can be transformed in seconds, as attaching transparent media adaptors is very simple, but this type of model can be more expensive. Most include a holder that transparencies are inserted into and placed on the scanner bed. Some of the latest even feature automatic film loaders where film is inserted into the top of the scanner then fed into the scanner bed.

When selecting a model to scan negatives, check it has a resolution high enough to capture the right number of pixels if you want to enlarge the scanned negatives to print. A high dynamic range is also vital when scanning transparencies to capture shadows

and highlights accurately. After scanning, save your scanned negatives as TIFFs. You can then apply the same restoration techniques as to photos. Adjust the resolution to give an appropriate file size in pixels, and for scans for print, multiply the print size in inches by 300 to give the size in pixels, eg for a 6 x 4-inch print you need 1800 x 1200 pixels.

Many scanners can now handle slides and negatives

is essential. This is easy by making sure your brush size is suitable and the brush's hardness is on a minimum setting. A delicate effect can also be created by reducing the opacity in the Options bar. Once you've finished your cloning and adjustments, it's also important to save the document on a high quality setting or all your hard work will be wasted.

Make use of the History feature

When retouching old photos you'll carry out many enhancement techniques and experiment with a selection of tools and settings. It's therefore a good idea to back up your image and work on adjustment layers when applying adjustments such as Curves or Levels. This means your changes are made on a separate layer, keeping your original scan intact.

When cloning to cover up marks and tears, it's also worth doing this on a separate layer. One of the most essential tools when carrying out operations like this is the History function and multiple undo capabilities. The History palette has a record of all your actions. By clicking one of them you revert to an earlier stage in the restoration process. When using the Clone tool to cover up marks on detailed areas, you may have

to try many times, and this is therefore an indispensable tool offering a high level of control.

This shows a crease and marks being cloned away using the Clone tool

Do it yourself

Many companies offer 'professional' photo repair services, but the methods they use are no more expert than the techniques we've shown here. Some of them may not even accept severely damaged images which we know can be repaired if you're familiar with Photoshop's tool and filters. All you need is a scanner, Photoshop and some time to invest in restoring your worse-for-wear photos to make them sharp, shiny and new. The beauty of fixing old photos using Photoshop is you now have a digital copy of a pristine-looking image that you can print out as many times as you like on high-quality photo paper for your friends and family to enjoy.

Before.

After

Remove colour casts from old photographs

Even photos that are severely tinted by time can have their original colours revived

Photos can age in bizarre ways, not only by collecting dust and scratches but in their colour. For example, they can acquire an odd overpowering tint, making it look like special photographic films have been used. If you'd like to restore the original colours, Photoshop has some incredible features that let you remove this colour cast in a few easy steps. There are some alternative methods to the one we've chosen, such the Variations filter or Levels. This old landscape shot has become tinged with red and it's doubtful that anyone would be proud to display it in their album. However, this can be removed to leave no trace of overpowering red with some nifty Adjustment Layer Curves action…

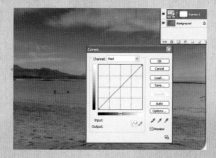

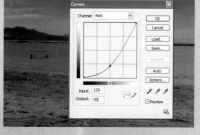

01 **Channel surfing** Open up 'colour cast.jpg' from the CD. Boost the contrast slightly using Levels. The first step is to identify the problem colour in the image, which is red. Choose Layer>New Adjustment Layer>Curves and click OK. Once the Curves window comes up select Red from the Channel drop-down menu.

02 **Remove the red** Colour casts can normally be removed by simply clicking in the middle of the line to create a point. Drag this point down to reduce the amount of red and miraculously see the original colour come back to the photograph. We found it was correct when the Input value was 129 and the Output value read 55.

03 **More detailed Curves adjustment** We then created another point towards the top end of the line and moved it to the right slightly until the Input value was 226 and Output value was 192. Hit OK for your Curves adjustments to be made. Choose Layer>Merge Visible.

04 **Rectify underexposure** Right-click on the layer and choose Duplicate Layer. Our photograph is a little dark, so select this new layer and choose Filter>Other>Custom. Enter the same numbers into the boxes as we have, enter 1 into the Scale box and leave the Offset box blank. Click OK. Don't panic at the result – it will be faded!

05 **Soften the effect** Set the blending mode to Overlay and reduce opacity to 20%. Turn the visibility on/off to see the difference applying the filter to a low opacity layer has had on the underexposed image. We used the same method as before to remove dust and scratches.

Tip

Finding your way around

When you are zoomed in close and cloning away your scratches and specks, you may want to move around your image. Hold down the spacebar and the cursor will turn into a hand. Click and drag to move around the document.

Colour cast removal

Remove colour casts and see old photos as they were intended with Color Balance, Curves and Levels

Photographs age with time, and very often certain colours will fade more quickly than others, leaving the impression of a colour cast.

Thankfully, colour casts are relatively easy to remove, enabling you to bring time-worn photos truly back to life. You'll need to work by sight, so it's important that your monitor is calibrated and profiled if you're planning on having a print made of the image in its correct colour state (try the Pantone Huey calibrator for around £60). And, if you're printing the image yourself, you'll need a profile made for your paper/printer combination as well (£15 from **www.pureprofiles.com**).

Colour casts may be extremely obvious or more subtle. They're most noticeable in midtone and highlight areas, but are very difficult to spot in the shadows. They are generally easiest to pick up in areas of neutral tone – such as the whites of clouds or the greys of a pavement, for example.

Colour has a lightness element as well as hue, so integral to the correction of colour is the correction of contrast. Hence we need a combination of Levels, Color Balance and Curves adjustments to bring our original colours back to life.

EVALUATING THE HISTOGRAM

SETTING END POINTS WITH LEVELS

REMOVING COLOUR CASTS WITH COLOR BALANCE

MEASURING COLOUR WITH THE COLOR SAMPLER TOOL

TWEAKING CONTRAST WITH CURVES

Essentials

TIME TAKEN
20 minutes

YOUR EXPERT
Matthew Henry

ON THE DISC
Before and after images

BEFORE

AFTER

WE NEED TO CROP THAT PHOTOGRAPH
We rotate our image before applying a crop

01 **Rough crop** We've scanned a couple of photos in at the same time, so the first thing we need to do is crop the image we're working on. Hit C for the Crop tool. We make a rough crop around the image, but it's clearly wonky so needs a bit of rotation before we crop the edges. Let's make things neat and tidy.

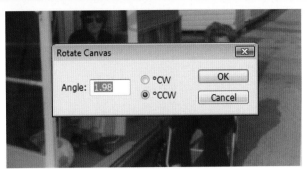

02 **Precision rotate** A shortcut to precise rotation is to take the Ruler tool (Shift+I to cycle to it) and draw a line somewhere along the top or bottom of the photograph. Now go to Image>Rotate Canvas>Arbitrary, and the exact figure you need to rotate by will appear. Press OK in that dialog box.

03 **Crop tight** Now the image is straight, we can select the Crop tool again (C) and go in tight. It looks best with a little bit of the original border left around the image. Once the crop is lined up on all sides, hit the Enter key to complete it.

CONTRAST CORRECTIONS
We bring the contrast into line with Levels

IN GREATER DETAIL
A closer look at the histogram

04 **Add Levels layer** Now we can begin our colour cast removal. First, we want to make sure the blacks and whites are set up correctly to ensure the contrast is good, so we add a Levels adjustment layer via the button at the bottom of the Layers palette.

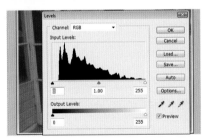

05 **Histogram** We need to examine the histogram to see if we've got the full range of contrast. On the right, the lightest tones appear to go right up the histogram end, but our darkest tones are quite far from the left edge, so these tones need redistributing.

Incomplete picture You can clearly see here that image information stops well short of the darkest shades found at the very left of the histogram.

Full range The lightest shades in the image seem to go right up to the right side of the histogram, suggesting there's a full range of the lightest tones.

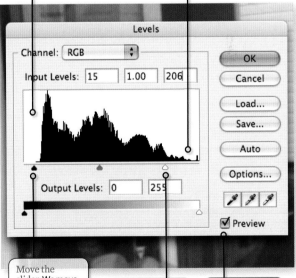

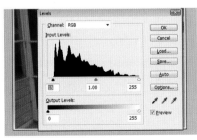

06 **Set black point** The way we do this is to drag the black slider inwards to meet the information on the left edge. The most accurate way is to hold down Alt/Option and drag until some specks of information appear in the image window. then go back a touch until they disappear again.

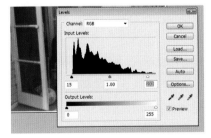

07 **Check white point** The white point looks good, but use the same method holding down Alt/Option as you drag the white slider inwards to double-check. The clipping display shows us that the information at the end of the histogram is actually the border, not the info we want in the photo.

Move the slider We move the black slider inwards to the information edge, which turns the darkest shade in the image into the darkest shade available.

Get the lightest tones The clipping display showed we need to move our slider quite far inwards to get the lightest tones in the photo itself.

Preview button We can toggle the Preview button on and off to see the effects our corrections have had on the image.

Tip

Color Balance adjustments

The Midtones slider actually works on the highlights and shadows too, to some degree, so is usually enough to correct any visible colour cast. However, you may find that no amount of correction here gets rid of a cast entirely, so it may be necessary to make some tweaks in the highlights and/or shadows. Be very subtle here, because unlike the Midtones control, the changes made with small increases and decreases will actually have a very strong effect.

NOW FOR COLOUR CORRECTION
A Color Balance layer is the easiest route to cast removal

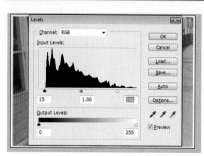

08 Set white point Keep dragging the slider across until information appears in the actual photograph. Once you reach this point, move back a touch until it disappears. You can see now on the histogram how far we've had to move in to extend our tones to the lightest shades.

09 Add Color Balance layer We now have a full range of tones from darkest to lightest, which has improved our contrast. We don't want to make final contrast tweaks until we've removed our colour cast, so we start by adding a Color Balance adjustment layer using the button at the bottom of the Layers palette.

10 Evaluate the image Initial inspection suggests the colour cast has a very orange feel. As red and yellow are the constituent elements of orange, we will want to try reducing both of these colours. Keep the Midtones button checked and start by dragging the top slider towards Cyan.

11 Removing the orange cast The best neutral starting point appears to be -65. Next, we switch to the bottom slider and find a point at +40 that appears to bring the image to a fairly neutral state in terms of blues and yellows.

12 Check green/magenta Although this type of colour cast rarely has a green/magenta element to it, it's worth experimenting with the slider anyway. A setting of -3 appears to be the most neutral to the eye, showing there may be a slight tinge of green in the colour cast.

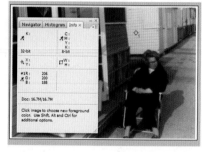

13 Plot Color Sampler point Lucky for us, there are some neutral whites in the shot that give us a chance to check the neutrality of our settings. The hut in the rear looks like it should be the most neutral white, so take the Color Sampler tool (cycle to it with Shift+I) and plot a point there.

14 Tweak the colour Making sure the Info palette is visible, check the Red, Green and Blue readings, which should be equal. They show too much red and not enough blue, so open the Color Balance layer and tweak the settings until the right-hand set of numbers are all equal.

15 Revert to previous state The image now looks too blue and cold, which shows us that either the white wasn't neutral or it was a very overcast day. The shadows suggest not, and a warmer look is more pleasing anyway, so use Ctrl/Cmd+Alt/Option a few times for multiple Undo to take us back to our previous state.

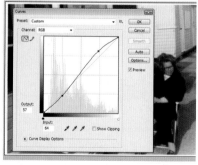

16 Curves to finish Change the Color Balance layer blending mode from Normal to Color to ensure contrast and luminosity aren't affected by the changes, and finish by adding a Curves adjustment layer and increasing the contrast slightly by lightening highlights and darkening shadows a touch.

adamo
BY DELL

Intel® Centrino® 2 Processor Technology

Profile 0.64"
Casing Aluminium
Colour Onyx/Pearl
Keyboard Scalloped, Back-lit
Screen 13.4", 16.9 HD, Edge-to-Edge Glass
www.adamobydell.com

AFTER

BEFORE

Tackle dust spots and fading

You'll be amazed at what can be salvaged from faded old family photographs with just basic Photoshop techniques

Precious aged photos are prone to suffering from any number of different problems, depending on age, the type of print, whether black and white or monochrome and, crucially, how well they've been stored and treated.

A badly stored, poorly treated and cheaply printed vintage photograph might, for example, suffer from corner, spot or general fading; light or dark fungal patches; cracks, tears and fold marks; colour casts (yellowing for black and white photos); pen scribbles and scratches, or staining from liquids such as tea or coffee. Not good news for the memories of older relatives that you'd like to pass on to later generations. But if you know your way around Photoshop, you'll be relieved to hear that every one of these blemishes can be treated and, as long as the damage isn't catastrophic, you'll

be amazed at the level of restoration success that can actually be achieved.

The starting point for an aged photo of any kind is always a Levels correction to make sure you're getting the best possible brightness and contrast – of particular importance to faded photos that can be given a new lease of life in an instant. The same adjustment can be used with a layer mask to correct faded areas of a photo. Curves or Color Balance should then be used to correct for colour casts in colour images, and a Black and White or Hue/Saturation adjustment can be used to remove the yellowing in monochrome images. The standard clean-up tools of Clone Stamp, Healing and Spot Healing, as well as Patch, can then be employed to treat the vast majority of blemishes – as long as you use the correct tool for job.

BRIGHTNESS AND CONTRAST CORRECTION
Most improvements will come from a single Levels adjustment

01 Review image We've got an image here suffering from general fade, some corner fade top left, and there are also a few scratches and bit of fungus to throw into the mix. At the bottom right we've also got a piece missing from edge – possibly done at the printing stage.

02 Contrast and brightness correction The first thing we need to do is to sort out the contrast and brightness with a Levels adjustment layer. We bring the black and white sliders inwards to meet the edges of the information if they don't already. We can then use the middle slider for overall lightening or darkening of the image.

03 Another Levels adjustment Once the general brightness and contrast is sorted, we can take a look and see if there are any more localised fade issues. You can see that there's fade from the top left of this corner to the centre, so we need to fire up another Levels adjustment layer.

CS2, CS3. PHOTOSHOP 7 (SUBSTITUTE SPOT HEALING BRUSH FOR HEALING BRUSH) | WORKS WITH

DEALING WITH LOCALISED CORNER FADE

The Gradient tool and layer masks are called for here

Drawing a gradient

The line drawn by the Gradient tool represents the transition from foreground to background colour. So if you drag a small area across the centre of a blank canvas, everything preceding the starting point will be foreground colour and everything after the point of release background, with an area the width of the line moving from white right through to black. Drawing edge to edge gives only a small amount of white and black at the start and finish, with everything else as grey tones.

04 Rough correction We start by making a very rough correction, dragging the middle slider rightwards to darken the image a little more. It darkens everything as a whole, which we don't want. So we select the Gradient tool (G or Shift+G) and click the drop-down menu in the Tool Options bar to select the Gradient Editor.

05 Set up the gradient We then make sure that Foreground to Background is selected in the Gradient Editor before closing it and ensuring Linear Gradient is selected in the Tool Options bar (the first of five icons). We finish by pressing D to reset the foreground and background colours to black and white.

06 Draw the gradient Now we need to experiment to get the gradient right – fade of this kind is nearly always gradual. We start by dragging from the top left to the centre of the frame to see if this matches the fade. Make sure white is foreground and black background. Use X to swap if necessary.

07 Test the gradient Before we can measure the success of our gradient we need to double-click the Layers adjustment layer to open the dialog and move the centre slider back and forth to give a better sense of the area we've affected and whether it will need more alteration or not.

08 Tweak the gradient By making it very dark we can see the fade correction needs to move a little further into the picture, so we select the tool again, make sure the layer mask is selected on the Levels adjustment layer and have another go.

09 Tweak the adjustment This time we get a better match, so we open up the Levels dialog again and get the brightness spot on with the centre slider. We bring the black slider in to meet the info on the left edge again to ensure the contrast is matched too.

SCANNING HINTS
Get it right from the start

Before you start the scanning process you need to stick on some white cotton gloves to avoid fingerprints (you can buy them from most photo stores), or handle the edges only. Next, rid your film and prints of dust with a blower brush before you attempt scanning, and clean film too if necessary. Clean the desk space area around your scanner so it's dust-free, and use manufacturer recommended cleaner and a lint-free cloth to clean the glass platen of a flatbed scanner. Load your film into the film holder, or place your prints square onto the platen surface – use its centre where possible, as this is where you can achieve optimum quality. Most scanner software can be loaded up from inside Photoshop, so once you've installed your scanner, restart Photoshop and go to File>Import and select the plug-in. Be sure to scan in RGB rather than Grayscale, even for black and white photos.

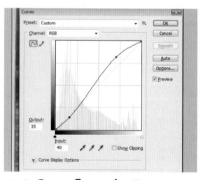

10 Curves fine-tuning The woman's face is now a bit dark, so tweak the contrast with a Curves adjustment layer. Hold Ctrl/Cmd+Alt/Option and click the face to plot a point, then do the same with a shadow area. Push one up, the other down to boost contrast.

REMOVE COLOUR CAST AND CLEAN UP
The final push to clean up scratches, dust and fungus

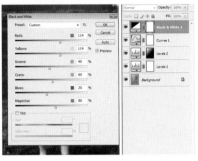

11 Remove yellowing Now we want to remove the yellowing, so we fire up a black and white adjustment layer. As we have some red and yellow colour information in the Channels, we can tweak these sliders to affect contrast a little and we end up with a more punchy result.

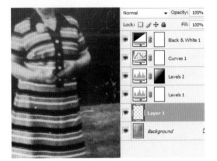

12 Add clean-up layer Next is the clean-up process. We select our background layer and create a new layer here, which ensures we can change the above layers later without affecting our clean-up. We start with the Spot Healing Brush tool set to Sample All Layers and zoom in at 100%.

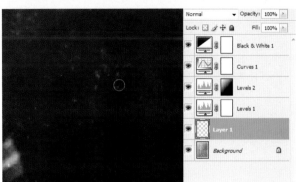

13 Do the healing work We carefully click away at all the isolated dust spots, small scratches and fungus marks. For any blemishes clustered in groups, switch to the Healing Brush and source from a clean area to avoid repeating blemishes. We don't touch blemishes near the edges at this point.

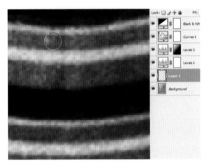

14 Switch to Clone Stamp For those spots situated close to edge areas, such as the lines on the dress, we need to use the Clone Stamp tool, otherwise we end up with a muddy blur. Source from an appropriate area nearby with Alt/Option as with the Healing Brush tool, and correct with a single click.

15 Select the missing piece Now we need to repair the missing edge piece bottom right, so start by roping off the surrounding area with the Polygonal Lasso tool (L or Shift+L to cycle to it). Make sure you're exactly flush to the edge with the selection. Ensure the clean-up layer is still selected.

LAYER STRUCTURE
Good as new

16 Clone to replace Select the Clone Stamp tool using S, make sure it's set to 0% Hardness and use Alt/Option to source from an area next to the missing piece. Now work over the offending area to cover it up. Use the same technique on the small white area at the bottom frame edge.

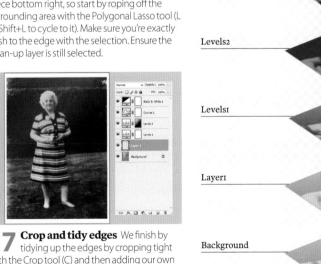

Black and white1

Curves1

Levels2

Levels1

Layer1

Background

17 Crop and tidy edges We finish by tidying up the edges by cropping tight with the Crop tool (C) and then adding our own neat canvas edges back by increasing the canvas size with Image>Canvas Size. We change the units to Per Cent and set Width to 104 and Height to 106%.

Restore colour to your photos

BEFORE

Save your memories using this tutorial to recover and re-establish your old family snapshots

Over time, many items of value gradually deteriorate, and photographs are no different when it comes to the ageing process. It's a terrible shame when you come to reminisce about your past and your photo album is full of grimy old pictures with faded colours, scratches and other blemishes all over them.

You may be tempted to get a professional to fix your images, but this can be very costly, and rather than paying out a huge amount or throwing out the faded photos, try giving this tutorial a go.

It might seem like a daunting task to restore these damaged photographs to their former glory, but with this guide to help you through, the job can be achieved quite easily. Using a combination of Photoshop's expansive toolbox and a little bit of patience, you'll

be able to go some considerable way towards recovering those precious memories.

For the best results, we scanned the image in full colour at 600dpi resolution. Despite this, you'll notice the colours have been badly drained to an almost greyscale state. In this tutorial we'll guide you through step by step, looking at how we can improve our image, boosting the colours using various methods. We'll be using adjustment layers – the central button represented by a black and white circle at the bottom of the Layers palette. By using these layers we'll be able to combine many effects, blending them to accomplish our goal.

There's no greater sense of joy than reliving your childhood memories, so make yourself comfortable and savour the opportunity to ensure your memories are preserved forever.

Key Photoshop Skills Covered
What you'll learn

USING PATHS AND MASKS

CREATING ADJUSTMENT LAYERS

BLEND MODES

APPLY IMAGE

Essentials

TIME TAKEN
45 minutes

YOUR EXPERT
Simon Lincoln

ON THE DISC
FadedPhoto.jpg

TIME TO BEGIN
Create a base image to modify

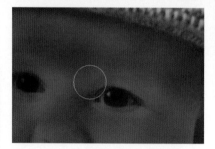

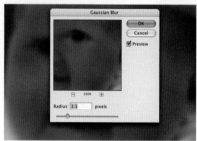

01 Colour removal First we'll make some changes that will let us create a base which we can adjust to our preferences. Open 'FadedPhoto.jpg' on the disc, copy the background layer then desaturate this new top layer (Image>Adjustments>Desaturate). This removes the colour from the pic, but keeps the colour channels for use later on the other layers.

02 Colouring the skin Now we have our desaturated layer, we can boost the colour of the skin. Pick a soft round brush from the Brush-preset menu and a deep red colour to paint with; we used Pantone 175C – a reddish brown. Select a brush size you're comfortable with and use the brush with a low 10% Opacity, painting onto the desaturated layer, around the skin on our subject's face.

03 Fleshy tones Skin tones always have some areas that are slightly lighter, and some darker, so vary the opacity to add extra detail. If you know the colour of your subject's eyes, select it and roughly paint this onto the layer. Ensure all skin is carefully covered to avoid white patches, and apply 10 pixels of Gaussian Blur (Filter>Blur>Gaussian Blur) in order to reduce sharpness.

WORKS WITH | PHOTOSHOP CS ONWARDS

04 **Layer blending** To blend the two layers, go to Apply Image and set Layer: Background, Channel: RGB, Blending: Overlay. Name the layer 'Base'. Preview the image to check the skin tones. If the face looks orangey, you can rectify it via an Overlay blend mode to the base layer, but leave it for now – we'll apply it later. If you're not happy, try again.

05 **Paths to work with** Each segment needs a different adjustment to help restore colour detail. The best way is to use the Pen and create some paths. Open the Paths palette and at the bottom select Create New Path. Select the Pen tool and create a path for the back of the armchair. A path is needed for each image element, so repeat for the hat, body and background, naming each one.

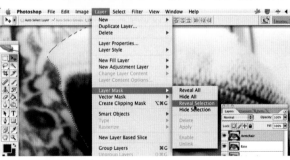

06 **Masking the selection** Let's start with the armchair. First duplicate the base layer and rename it 'Armchair'. Hold down Cmd/Ctrl and select the Armchair path to load the selection. Choose the Armchair layer and then Layer>Layer Mask>Reveal Selection to create a mask. Desaturate the layer and repeat steps 2 to 4, this time painting the armchair brown. Cmd/Ctrl-click the Armchair path to make the selection again and apply a Photo filter (Layer>New Adjustment Layer). Use the Warming filter (85) with a Density of 60%.

Tip

Clone Stamp

::::: Using the tool much like a regular paintbrush, you can adjust opacity, flow, hardness and size. To select an area to clone, hold the Alt key and click to define an area, then simply paint short strokes over the damaged area. When working with files that have numerous layers, it's often easier to flatten the image to restore an area – remembering to save a layered PSD file in case you want to make further adjustments at a later date.

Tip

Adjustment layers

::::: You might be aware that all changes made via adjustment layers are also in Image> Adjustments, so why use layers? Well, applying these effects in this way lets us return later and modify them if we need to. By applying the effects through the Adjustments menu we're restricted with what we can modify. A new layer isn't created for us to individually change, and editing complex images in this way can get messy.

BACKGROUND WORK
Making things easier

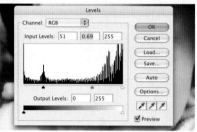

07 Colour correction Now we'll make some changes to the hat. Duplicate the base layer, rename it 'Hat', Cmd/Ctrl-click on the Hat path to make the selection and apply a mask as before. Load the selection again and select Color Balance from the Adjustment Layer menu. Assuming the hat was initially a tweed green or brown, adjust the sliders for each of the three tones until you get a colour you like.

08 Adjust levels You'll notice that the underneath of the hat has taken on a tint of the colour we just applied. To remove this and restore this area to a deep black, make the selection again and open Levels in the Adjustment Layer menu. Slide the black arrow towards the centre of the histogram to darken the area and adjust the grey arrow slightly to darken and enhance the midtones.

09 Whiten clothes To adjust the clothes, repeat the duplicate/mask process, naming the layer 'Clothes'. Make the selection again and add a Brightness/Contrast layer. Increase Contrast to +17 to improve whiteness. To bring out creases in the clothing, use a Levels adjustment layer. Select the area and move the middle, grey arrow slightly to the right, just enough to darken the creases.

THE OVERALL PICTURE
How we made the most of our baby pic

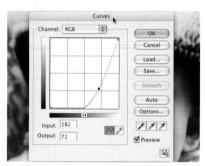

10 Lighting curves Take the final path for the background and repeat the process. Make the selection and apply a Curves layer – focus on the background area further away, not the coloured bit near the foreground. Make the area more defined by pulling the curve to the bottom right corner of the grid.

> **Hat** We'll use a combination of levels and colour balance layers to restore the flat cap.

> **Background** By splitting the background in two we are able to concentrate on getting the best out of both areas.

> **Face** Painting the skin, blurring it and then blending the layers together is the easiest way to restore skin colour.

> **Armchair** The colour of the furniture can be enhanced with a Photo filter and blend mode.

> **Clothes** Recovering the whiteness of the clothes is a simple process; ensure that you lighten the material further using the Dodge and Burn cheat.

11 Divide the background We can now make further adjustments to layers by double-clicking. This is the big advantage in applying effects as adjustment layers, as we can tweak colours, levels and contrasts. Copy the Curve adjustment layer we just created. On the original layer, edit the mask to hide the top half of the background, and on the new layer, mask the bottom half. View the mask by Alt-clicking it.

FINISHING OFF
Our cute baby just gets cuter

LAYER STRUCTURE
It's child's play... really!

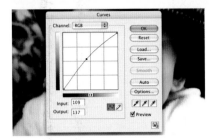

12 Minor adjustments To adjust the bottom half of the background, first select the original layer, double-click the Curve adjustment. Reset the curve by holding Alt and clicking where the Cancel button was. Drag the curve slightly up to lighten the area. Select the Photo filter applied to the armchair; apply an Overlay blend mode to make the colours more vivid, with Opacity at 40% so they're less harsh.

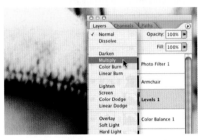

13 Changing the blend In step 4 we mentioned applying an Overlay blend mode to the base layer – apply this now. Apply the Multiply blend mode to the Levels adjustment layer we gave to the hat; this will further darken areas and help define detail. There are still more adjustments we can make to the image to iron out any rough edges and help bring out some of the details even further.

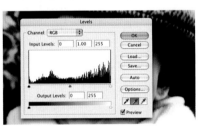

14 Alter levels First, with no selection made, we'll apply a Levels adjustment layer that'll affect the entire image. There are three Eyedropper tools in the bottom corner – black, grey and white. Use these to adjust the levels easily. Select the black one first and pick the area under the hat to define the black level. Now choose the white, and select an area of white clothing. Lastly, use the grey to pick a neutral colour – lower background on the right.

15 Layer placement Ensure that this new Levels adjustment layer is placed at the top of the Layers palette. This should help to equalise the colours throughout the image, ensuring they are consistent. At this stage you may also choose to apply a Photo filter to warm or cool the image.

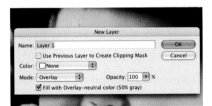

16 Dodge and Burn cheat We can now create a similar effect to the Dodge and Burn tools to bring out further detail in the image, such as the hat or face. Press the Alt key and create a new layer from the Layers palette. A New Layer window will appear. Change the mode to Overlay and check the box below to fill the layer with grey, again ensuring this layer is at the top of the Layers palette. With a low opacity, use a black brush to paint on the layer to darken areas, or a white brush to lighten areas.

17 Final touches Once happy, check for damaged areas that have appeared as a result of the improved quality, eg bottom edge of the baby's clothes. Use the Clone Stamp and Healing Brush to repair the area. Apply the Dust & Scratches filter (Filter>Noise) to old pics, to help remove damage/dust. You can also apply the Unsharp Mask to sharpen the image.

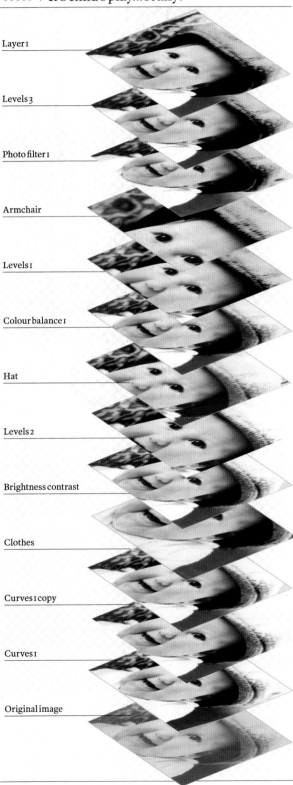

Layer 1

Levels 3

Photo filter 1

Armchair

Levels 1

Colour balance 1

Hat

Levels 2

Brightness contrast

Clothes

Curves 1 copy

Curves 1

Original image

Crease removal

Fear not, a fat crease down the length of a prized family photograph can be removed with some healing TLC! Read on to find out how it's done...

There's nothing like a big fat crease running down the length of a photograph to ruin its precious content.

And preserving our photographic history is now much more pertinent in the wake of the digital era, where few images seem inclined to leave our hard drives to be seen beyond the monitor screen. But if you have an old creased family photograph or even a new one that's been treated in a similarly unkind manner, don't even think about tossing it away. Removing even the most stubborn creases is not too difficult a task, provided they don't run through important and complex detail, like someone's face.

In our example, the crease can quite easily be removed beyond all trace, because a large part of it runs through relatively unimportant areas such as grass and sky, and all the important facial detail of the two children isn't touched at all. And, as is sometimes the case, we have a colour shift along the crease line to work out, and this needn't cause us any real trouble either. A simple layer set to Color blending mode takes care of the colour shift with some careful sampling and painting, and the crease itself can be worked out with a combination of Patch, Healing Brush and Clone Stamp tools. Job done.

Once the crease has been removed, you can set about doing the normal colour and contrast tweaks with Curves, Levels and Color Balance adjustment layers to bring the photo up to scratch – often necessary in an old one. The Auto options in the Image>Adjustments menu are good here and they can work instant wonders.

Key Photoshop Skills Covered
What you'll learn

COLOURING USING LAYER BLENDING MODES

BLENDING COLOURS USING OPACITY CONTROL

REMOVING BLEMISHED AREAS WITH PATCH TOOL

CLEANING UP WITH HEALING BRUSH TOOL

USING CLONE STAMP TOOL FOR DETAILED AREAS

Essentials

TIME TAKEN
30 minutes

YOUR EXPERT
Matthew Henry

ON THE DISC
creaseremoval before.jpg

PREPARE FOR SOME CLEVER COLOUR WORK
A layer with Color blending sets us up to start

01 Examine the damage We start by zooming in to 100% with Ctrl/Cmd+Alt/Option+0 and then use the spacebar to drag around the crease areas to see how bad the problem is. In the example we're using here, the crease damage is worsened with some surrounding discolouration.

02 Create a Colour layer We'll need to Clone or Heal to remove the crease itself – but it's best to salvage as much as we can from the discoloured area, so the amount we need to clone is as small as possible. To start the process we add a new layer and name it 'Colour Change'.

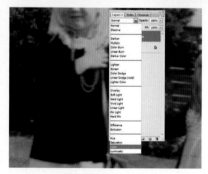

03 Set the blending mode In the Layers palette, the blending mode of our new layer is set to Normal by default. We want to change just the colour of the discoloured area and not the underlying detail, so we need to change this blending mode to Color, which you'll find near the bottom of the drop-down menu.

WORKS WITH | PHOTOSHOP CS ONWARDS

AFTER

BEFORE

04 **Set up the Eyedropper tool** Now we select the Eyedropper tool (I) so we can change the area we sample our colour from. You can find the Sample Size drop-down menu in the Tool Options bar. The 5 by 5 Average setting ensures that the colour we choose isn't determined by stray pixels of a different colour.

05 **Set up the Brush tool** Switch to the Brush tool (B) and use the [and] keys to get a brush slightly bigger than the height of the discoloured area. Make sure Brush Hardness is set to 0% as we want to blend the colouring as best as possible with surrounding areas.

06 **Sample nearby grass** Starting at the far left side of the crease, hold down Shift to turn the Brush tool temporarily into the Eyedropper tool. Now sample a colour from nearby grass not affected by the discolouration, then carefully brush over proximate red discolouration.

KEEPING IT REAL
Some careful colouring needed here

07 **Sample and resample** We don't want to brush over the entire red area with the same selected colour, as the effect won't look real, so we need to continually sample and brush bit by bit as we move along the crease. If you get an unrealistic colour at any point, use Ctrl/Cmd+Z to Undo and have another go.

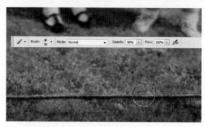

08 **Blending colours** If things look a different shade either side of the crease line and you're having trouble sampling the correct shade, you can set the brush to 50% Opacity, paint with one colour, sample another and paint again. This technique effectively allows you to mix two colours and is a good blending solution.

09 **Other grass area** You'll also notice that on the right side of the photograph there's a large area of grass which differs in colour outside of the crease and discoloured area. It's worth painting over this as well, so the whole grass area has a consistent colour tone.

IN GREATER DETAIL
Analysing the crease mark

Sail through the sky The sky is easy as long as we start off using the Clone Stamp, because we don't want the Patch tool to pick up tones from the conifer.

Colour cast The colour cast runs through the flower bed, but the crease itself isn't too visible so not too much work is needed here.

Vertical crease The vertical crease mark running up the shot goes through the flower bed. However it is quite faint so it should not be hard to remedy.

Grass of a different colour Notice the area to the left of the vertical crease – the grass is a different colour to other areas and needs to be brought in line.

Get rid of that red tinge The horizontal crease mark down here is made worse by a nasty red tinge that needs to be removed first of all.

Tip

Cloning vs healing

You'll notice in the tutorial that we move between the Healing tools such as Patch and Healing Brush to the Clone Stamp for particular areas. This is because while the Healing tools are our preferred choice where possible, they're no good where there's surrounding detail that deviates from the source. In the case of the sky for instance, using the Patch tool too near to the conifer will drag the darker shades of the conifer into the sky, producing ugly dark patches.

HEALING, PATCH AND CLONE STAMP TOOLS
Once the red colour's gone, we can go to work on the crease

Tip

10 **A sprinkling of dried grass** There are several dried areas of grass in this shot, so for ultimate realism we don't want to colour these green, but sample dried grass colour and use a small brush to paint these lighter parts. Even if you just do a few here and there, it should give a more realistic feel than painting everything green.

11 **Finish colour cast removal** We can now apply the same technique to continue our corrections past the grass into the flower bed and upwards into the sky, by brushing and resampling to get appropriate colours – completing the removal of the red discolouration.

12 **Select the crease** Now we can attack the crease itself. Create a new layer and hold down Alt/Option, then select Merge Visible from the Layer menu. Rename it 'Clean up', then select the Rectangular Marquee tool (M or Shift+M to cycle to it) and draw a box around the horizontal crease, leaving a little space around it.

Colour shift
You may find that once you've applied the Patch and Healing Brush tools to the grassy area, some of the grass colour goes a bit awry as it attempts to blend things together. The solution is simply to add another blank layer on top, changing the blending mode to Color once again and sampling, painting and resampling as before until the areas of grass are brought back to their original or your preferred shade.

13 **Patch removal** Next, select the Patch tool (Shift+J to cycle to it) and drag from inside the box upwards to the selection of grass above that's crease-free. Release the mouse and watch the crease disappear.

14 **Clean up with the Healing brush** Now do the same with the vertical crease, stopping short of the flower bed. Once this crease is removed, we can use the Healing Brush tool (cycle with Shift+J) to clean up any signs of the Patch tool at the box edges, sampling from nearby grass first with Alt/Option.

15 **Putting detail back in** We can also use the Healing Brush tool to put back some sharp detail into areas that may have gone soft with Patch work, or may have been soft originally, by sampling sharp areas and clicking where needed. Do this bit by bit rather than using large brush strokes.

16 **Switch to the Clone Stamp tool** Luckily, little of the crease appears visible in the flower bed, but the small line seen in the tall greenery is best removed by sourcing adjacent pixels with the Clone Stamp tool (S), as there's too much detail for the Healing tools to handle. Repeat for the trees and in the sky just past the top of the conifer.

17 **Back to Patch to finish** Finally, section off the crease area in the sky (not too close to the conifer to avoid contamination) with the Marquee tool (M); select the Patch tool (J) and from inside the box, drag rightwards and downwards so the electricity cable lines up correctly before releasing. All creases gone!

Chapter 3
Photomanipulation

The tools and techniques needed to alter photos into new creations

Tip

Selections

▓ If ever a Photoshop task needed some selection savvy, it's photomanipulation If you have shoddy cutouts, you will find that any composites or edits will stick out like a sore thumb. The aim is to practise, practise, practise!

Photo manipulation tutorial on the CD

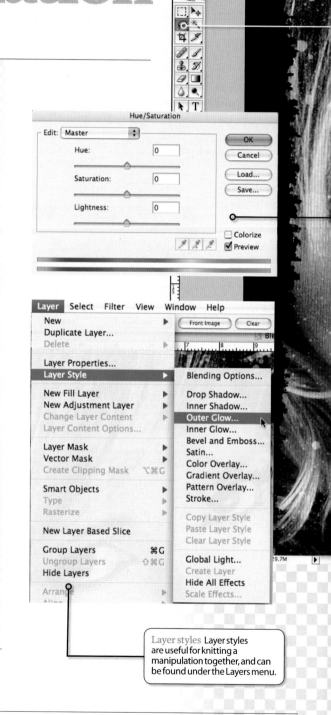

Layer styles Layer styles are useful for knitting a manipulation together, and can be found under the Layers menu.

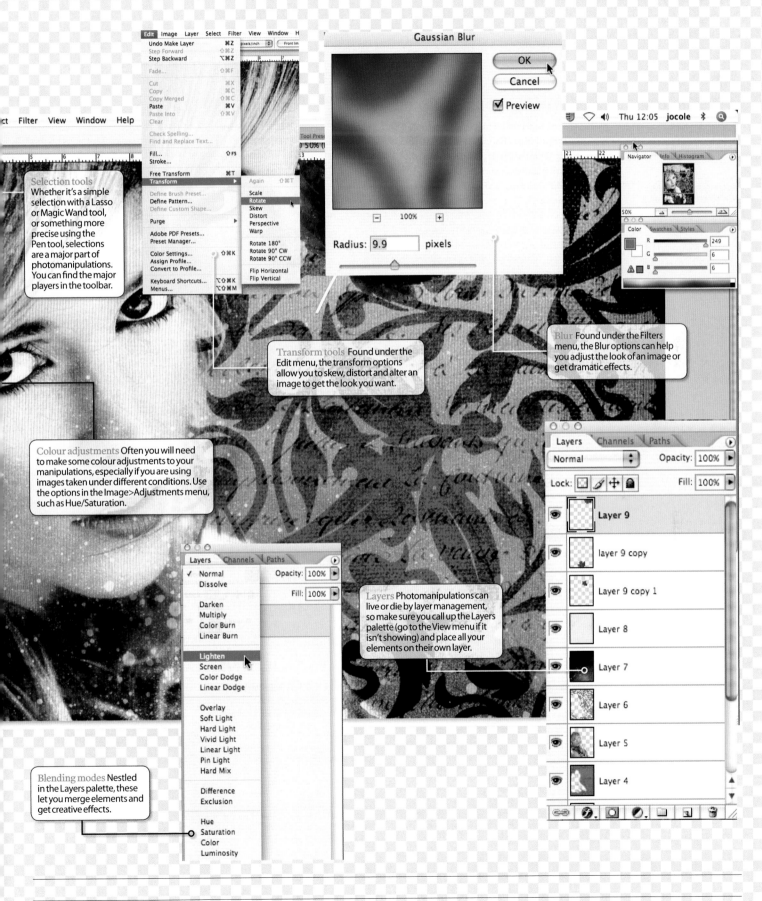

Selection tools Whether it's a simple selection with a Lasso or Magic Wand tool, or something more precise using the Pen tool, selections are a major part of photomanipulations. You can find the major players in the toolbar.

Gaussian Blur

OK
Cancel
☑ Preview

Radius: 9.9 pixels

Transform tools Found under the Edit menu, the transform options allow you to skew, distort and alter an image to get the look you want.

Blur Found under the Filters menu, the Blur options can help you adjust the look of an image or get dramatic effects.

Colour adjustments Often you will need to make some colour adjustments to your manipulations, especially if you are using images taken under different conditions. Use the options in the Image>Adjustments menu, such as Hue/Saturation.

Layers Photomanipulations can live or die by layer management, so make sure you call up the Layers palette (go to the View menu if it isn't showing) and place all your elements on their own layer.

Blending modes Nestled in the Layers palette, these let you merge elements and get creative effects.

Tools of the trade

Photomanipulation

Twist and turn your images into something new

Essentials

YOUR EXPERT

Jo Cole

ON THE DISC

Learn more about the photomanipulation tools with the video on the CD

It's a strange path that leads a person to photomanipulation. Usually it begins with something jovial, such as using a photo of a friend and making them do something unlikely like stand in a group photo next to the president.

Pretty soon, that person realises that you can 'Photoshop' absolutely anything to create absolutely anything, and that's when Photoshop can become truly addictive. While we would try and steer you away from pretending that you have dined with heads of state, the fact remains that the art of photomanipulation opens up a wide world of creative possibility. Photoshop gives you all the tools you need to select parts of a photo, add them to another document, give everything a bit of spit and polish and create a whole new image. You can quite literally bend a photo to fit in with your creative vision and do a whole lot more besides.

In this chapter we will look at a few nifty tricks to get you started on your own photomanipulation journey. We'll show you how to use layers to store all of the elements used in an image, as well as revealing what selection tools are and how they work. You'll discover how blending modes are a dream when it comes to assembling separate parts and be shown how ordinary objects can be transformed into something different. Photomanipulation is the magical part of Photoshop, where nothing is quite as it seems. Read on to find out about the tools you'll be using and then get ready to give your imagination a workout!

Multiple images This picture was made up of different pictures but all brought together using the blending modes.

 Tool of the trade

LAYERS
Keep them organised

The Layers palette is your best friend in any sort of photomanipulation project, so it pays to get to know it very well. If you put each element of the project on a separate layer, you will be able to keep everything to hand should you need to make any more adjustments. It's good practice to name your layers as you go, just so you know where everything is. To do so, simply double-click on the existing layer name and then type. You can even choose to group layers in folders to help keep things organised.

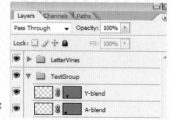

Tool of the trade

MAGIC WAND
Click and select

If you have simple objects to select, the Magic Wand is the quickest and easiest option. With this you can click on an area and select all other parts of the image that are the same as that area. You can use the Tolerance setting to decide how small a selection is. For example, if you clicked to select the blue of the sky, a low Tolerance level would just target pixels that shared the same properties as the colour you clicked on. A high Tolerance level would pick up all the blues.

Blending modes You will find the blending modes at the top of the Layers palette. They work from a drop-down menu.

Photo manipulation tutorial on the CD

Layer stack Blending modes can take a bit of getting used to if you are dealing with multiple layers. They alter layers below the selected one, so keep that in mind when applying them. They also differ according to the colours in an image. The best way of choosing a blending mode is to go through the list and try them all!

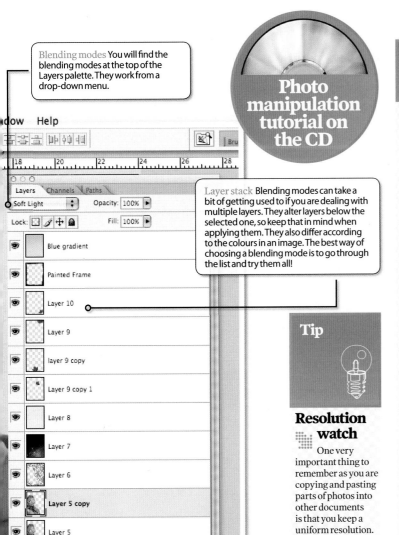

Tip

Resolution watch

One very important thing to remember as you are copying and pasting parts of photos into other documents is that you keep a uniform resolution. You can find an image's resolution by going to Edit>Image Size. Have a check and if you need to alter the size, you can do so from the Image Size dialog.

TRANSFORM TOOLS
Resize, skew and distort your photos

As you set about building up photo composites or manipulating areas of an image, you'll find yourself heading to the Transform tools more and more. Found under the Edit>Transform menu, they allow you to alter the size, shape and orientation of a layer or selection

Scale
Scale it down (or up) With the Scale option, you can make an object larger or smaller than it starts out. Once enabled, the Scale option allows you to drag corner handles to make the edit. Beware that this can distort your image if you just start dragging. If you want to make the scale proportionate, hold down Shift as you drag in or out.

Rotate
Spin me right round The name says it all with this one! The Rotate option allows you to make a rotation of a layer or selection by moving the mouse in the direction you want the rotation to go. You can rotate by eye if you know what you need, or if you hold down Shift you can constrain the rotation to 15-degree increments.

Skew
Twist and turn The Skew command brings up a bounding box with handles in the corner and in the middle. If you move the corner handles, you can expand or contract from that point (slant it). Move the middle handles to alter the angles. This can lead to some great effects if you are creating a photo collage project, for example.

Distort
Distort your vision The Distort option also works using a bounding box and series of handles, just like the Skew command previously. This time, if you move a corner handle you can stretch or retract the image, while dragging a middle handle will alter the angle of view, giving a sort of 3D effect to your image, which again can be very effective.

Perspective
Gain some perspective Choosing Perspective will allow you to alter your object and keep the perspective. This is achieved using the familiar bounding box and handles, and you can drag in any direction, which can help a lot if you need to correct images with perspective distortion before using them in your photomanipulation projects.

FEATHERING SELECTIONS
Avoid harsh cutouts

If you are selecting parts of a photo to add to a different composition, you might find that you want a softer edge to your selections than using the default Photoshop settings to help it blend in better. This is achieved using the Feathering command at the top of the screen. Feathering blurs the edges between your selected object and the surrounding area. If you go too far it will lead to loss of detail but a small amount can help give you a far smoother transition.

Photoshop's Selection tools

To show or not to show? Either way, Photoshop has got just the right Selection tool for the job

All the great artists understood that the purpose of their art was not just recreating real life. Their art strove to present things and concepts as they saw them. To do that, they had to choose what to show on their canvases. While the tools have changed with time, the basic practice of selecting the seen and unseen continues to this day.

Today, Photoshop has replaced the need for cumbersome cut-out masks, expensive pre-cut templates and toxic masking fluids. Although these certainly still have their uses, for the digital artist, Photoshop's native Selection tools are more than adequate. Once mastered, these allow users to edit their images by removing or hiding unwanted areas with masks, leaving only the selected portion visible. This practice, combined with other advanced techniques such as painting and filters, allows the proficient Photoshop artist to weave together stunning images with relative ease.

> "Today, Photoshop has replaced the need for cumbersome cut-out masks, expensive pre-cut templates and toxic masking fluids"

For new users, the ever-expanding toolchest can seem mind-boggling at first. To make things less daunting we've prepared this little primer to explain the various Selection tools available in Photoshop.

For classification's sake, we've sorted most of the tools into three easy-to-decipher categories: Marquees, Lassos and Pens. In the following pages we'll explain the tools within each family, and tell you how they work. We'll talk about where and how best to use them, and illustrate the tools in action. Towards the end, we'll dive into the more complex Pen tool and take you through a short tutorial to get you used to the asset.

Once you get comfortable with Photoshop's Selection tools, the possibilities are endless. Advanced users can take their art a step further by combining Selection tools with masks and brushes to create intricate details.

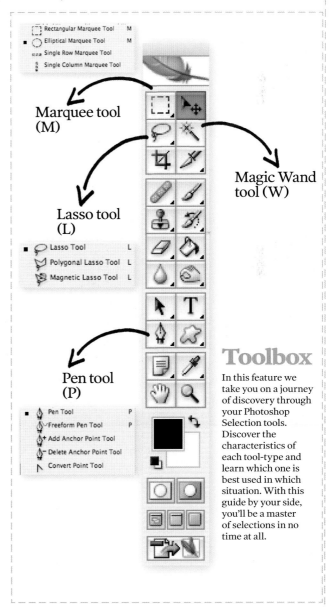

Toolbox

In this feature we take you on a journey of discovery through your Photoshop Selection tools. Discover the characteristics of each tool-type and learn which one is best used in which situation. With this guide by your side, you'll be a master of selections in no time at all.

Marquee tools

Photoshop's Marquee and Magic Wand are its most basic Selection tools. These are perfect for beginners – it doesn't take much effort to get a feel for them and even master their uses.

The Marquee tool family consists of four members: Rectangular marquee, Elliptical marquee, Single Row marquee and Single Column marquee. Marquees are excellent for creating simple rectangular or oval selections. They can also be modified with certain modifier keys (see the box on the right) to alter their shapes somewhat. The main drawback to marquees is that because of their simple nature, they are usually not very good for creating more organic selections. On the other hand, they are excellent when images need to be constrained within a defined shape – for instance, a web banner.

The Magic Wand tool works on a completely different principle, but is still very easy to use. The 'wand' creates a selection based on a selected colour. To choose that colour, you simply need to click on your artwork with the tool. It's good for making quick selections of irregular shapes, particularly if the shape in question is uniformly coloured. The Magic Wand doesn't do so well with objects that have many shades of colour.

Modifier keys

Apart from choosing the Selection tools on-screen, you can also modify them for use with special keys on your keypad. Hold down Shift while using the Rectangular or Elliptical Selection tool to make square or circle selections respectively. Holding Shift while using any Marquee or Lasso tool also allows you to add to any active selections. The pointer will have a tiny '+' sign next to it. Hold Shift, click and drag to create additional selections. If you want to deselect a portion of an active selection, hold down Ctrl. The pointer now sports a little '-'. Hold Ctrl, click and drag to deselect extra portions. If you want to select everything on a layer, hit Select>All or Ctrl+A. To deselect everything, choose Select>Deselect or hit Ctrl+D.

Magic Wand tool

The Magic Wand tool is a special Selection tool that automatically creates a selection for you. All you have to do is pick a colour, and the tool will automatically select that, plus similar adjacent colours for you. Choosing the Magic Wand tool will load its options in the top menu bar. Increasing the Tolerance value will enable you to select a greater range of colours; however, the selection may become less accurate. Anti-alias softens the edges of the selection. Contiguous constrains the selection only to adjacent colours, but if you want to select everything of the same colour, uncheck this option for some rapid selection magic! Sample All Layers will select everything of your chosen colour across all your layers. This is helpful, but if you have many layers it can severely slow your system. If you're a beginner, it's best to leave this box unchecked.

Elliptical marquee

The Elliptical marquee creates oval-shaped selections. If you cannot see the tool, click and hold down on the Rectangular Marquee button – this will call up the Marquee family menu. The Elliptical marquee options are the same as that of its Rectangular sibling, but you have the option of choosing Anti-alias. Unchecking Anti-alias will produce an oval-shaped selection with rough, pixelated edges. Occasionally this proves useful (when making transparent GIFs, for example), but otherwise it's better to leave the Anti-alias option selected.

Rectangular marquee

The Rectangular marquee lets you create rectangular selections by clicking and dragging the tool across the wanted area. As with all selections, the boundaries are represented by flashing, dotted lines. The selected image is always contained within these flashing dotted lines. Selecting the Rectangular Marquee tool will load its options to the top menu bar. Here you can change its Feather settings (the default is '0') to create a selection with a softer edge. You can also select one of three styles – Normal, Fixed Aspect Ratio and Fixed Size.

Single Column marquee

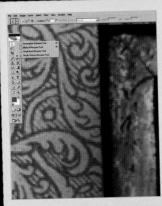

The Single Column marquee is exactly the same as the Single Row marquee except it creates a 1-pixel thick selection that spans the height of the canvas. Although you can choose to alter the Feather settings for both Single Row tools, you won't be able to select a thing if you do. Be sure to set Feather to '0' before using either tool.

Single Row marquee

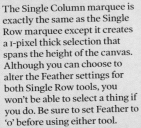

The Single Row marquee creates a very fine selection that is only 1 pixel high but is as long as your canvas. This delicate Selection tool is very specialised, but when there is a use for it, it proves to be a real time-saver. Simply click on your artwork to use this tool; there is no need to drag to make a selection.

Marquees are excellent for creating simple rectangular or oval selections. They can also be modified with certain keys to alter their shapes"

Lasso tools

Marquees are fine when you need to make selections of regular geometric shapes. However, quite often objects of interest do not come in the form of rectangles or ovals. While you can still use the Magic Wand tool for irregularly shaped objects, it can be cumbersome to use, and it's quite likely you'll end up with an unsatisfactory selection if your image happens to have a lot of colours.

The next set of tools are designed specially to make up for the lack of flexibility of the former. The Lasso tool family consists of three members – the Lasso, Polygonal Lasso and Magnetic Lasso tools. All of these are Selection tools with greater precision than Marquee tools and the Magic Wand tool. They are great for creating general selections for irregular shaped objects, and with a bit of practice you should become fairly proficient in using them.

Photoshop CS3 and CS4 users can also take advantage of the Quick Selection tool. This awesome tool combines the advantages of the Magic Wand and Lasso tools, and since it acts more like a brush, it should be ideal for users who prefer a more organic approach to working.

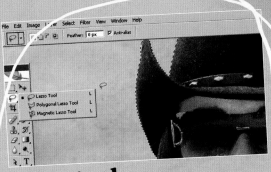

Lasso tool

The Lasso tool is the first tool in the Lasso toolset. It allows you to trace out the bits you want to select. To use it, select the tool, click and drag it across your artwork. Release your mouse button to create the selection borders. You can also hold down the Shift button to continue dragging your tool to add to your selection. Or you can hold down the Ctrl button and click and drag to deselect unwanted areas.

Magnetic Lasso tool

The Magnetic Lasso tool is a smart tool that 'senses' the edges of an object by its colour contrast. Click and drag (you don't have to hold down the mouse) around the portion you wish to select, and the lasso will automatically 'stick' to the shape. The pointer will have a little 'o' when you return to the start point. Click the start point again to close the selection. You can adjust the tool's sensitivity by tweaking its Width and Edge Contrast settings in the top menu bar.

Quick Selection tool

The Quick Selection tool was introduced in Photoshop CS3, and is a cross between a brush and the Magic Wand. Actually, it even replaced the Magic Wand tool in priority (click and hold down the Quick Selection tool to expand it to find the Magic Wand). The Quick Selection tool enables you to easily make selections by 'painting' the area you want to select. The tool automatically expands and finds defined edges of the image. The tool's sensitivity can be adjusted by its top menu options. The Brush drop-down lets you customise its size, shape and feel. Stylus users can also take advantage of its pressure-sensitive capabilities by selecting Pen Pressure from the Size drop-down. Check off Auto-enhance to have the tool automatically smooth out your selection. Or, for more fine-tuning, use the Refine Edge button and adjust the sliders in order to optimise the selection.

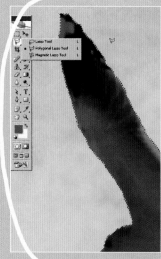

Polygonal Lasso tool

The Polygonal Lasso tool works best when creating selections of irregular shapes with straight edges. Click on the start point of the selection (no need to hold the mouse button). Drag the tool to the next convenient point, and click again. Continue to click around the area you want to select. Once you get back to the starting point, the pointer will have a little 'o' next to it. Click again to close the selection and generate the selection boundaries.

Start images

After

How to save and load your selections in Photoshop

Sometimes you may want to save your selections to reuse later. To do so, make use of the Select>Save Selections function. You can save the selection within the current document or on a new file, but the former is usually better. Give the selection a name and hit OK. Saved selections are stored in the Channels palette (Window>Channels). To load a selection, go to Select>Load Selection if you can remember its name. Otherwise, look for the right selection in the Channels palette and click it. This may make your artwork turn into a black and white splodge, but don't fret. Hold down Ctrl and click on the selection layer to load it. Now look for the RGB channel (or CMYK, if you're working in that mode). Click that to restore your image to the way it looked.

The Pen tool

The Pen tool is the most precise Selection tool in Photoshop. It is also perceived to be the most complex, because it behaves rather differently from the way other Selection tools do.

The Pen tool works by creating a series of dots called 'anchor points'. These are similar to the points of a Polygonal Lasso, but differ greatly in two aspects: firstly, these points can create straight lines or curves. The Polygonal Lasso can only create straight edges. Secondly, the points are editable, allowing users to add, remove or tweak a point after it's been created.

The Pen tool also does not create selection boundaries like the other Selection tools. Instead of flashing dotted lines, you'll see a thin grey line. The reason is that the tool is actually drawing out a path. This is stored in the Paths palette (if you

can't see it, hit Window>Paths), usually as Work Path.

To work with the Pen as a Selection tool, select it and make sure the Paths icon is depressed in the top menu. Click your image to begin your path. To make a straight edge, simply click at the next convenient point. To make a curved line, click, hold down and drag. You'll see a line protrude from the anchor point. These lines are the direction lines that control the extent of the curve. Continue drawing until you return to the start point. Mouse over the first anchor point to see the Pen icon have a little 'o' beside it. Click to close the path.

In the Paths palette, click the top right button and hit Make Selection. Leave Feather at 'o' and choose New Selection. The path will change to a selection with the usual flashing dotted line borders.

Before

"The Pen tool is the most precise Selection tool in Photoshop – as well as the most complex"

01 **Configuring the Pen tool for selections** Open up the file 'hair.jpg' from the CD. If you want to use this exact image then go to www.istock.com and enter image code 3221590. Choose the Pen tool. In the top menu bar, ensure the tool is set to Paths. Also check that the Add to Path Area option is selected.

02 **Drawing the general outline** Use the Pen tool to carefully trace the outline of the girl, and the larger parts of her hair. Try to get everything in one general shape – we can worry about the details later. Click and drag to create curves. When you're done, your path should look something like the above.

03 **Adding details** With the general outline in place, you can start adding in the details. Make sure Add to Path Area is selected in the top menu. Continue working with the Pen tool to select the wispy bits of hair. Try to get enough bits in to suggest the fineness of the hair.

04 **Remove selected areas** Now select the Subtract From Path option in the top menu bar. This changes how the Pen tool works – from here on, the paths you draw will remove the areas enclosed within. Now use your Pen tool to remove the additional bits of blue trapped between the hair.

05 **Load the selection and mask** In the Paths palette, click on your path, then click the top right palette button. Select Make Selection, leave the settings alone and hit OK. In the Layers palette, hit Add Layer Mask to mask the girl. Reuse the selection on a new layer in order to make some white graphic elements.

Top 5 tips

1: Combining Selection tools

Try mixing Selection tools to create complex selections. By holding down the Shift and Ctrl keys, you can add or subtract selections to get the details you require.

2: Magnetic Lasso tricks

You can fiddle with the tool's options to make it more sensitive, or use the Image> Adjustments> Brightness/ Contrast function to increase the contrast of your image.

3: Looking closely

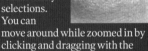

Use the Zoom tool to get in really close, to nail tricky selections. You can move around while zoomed in by clicking and dragging with the Hand tool.

4: Deleting and reloading your selections

You are able to cancel any active selection by hitting Select> Deselect. If you accidentally cancel your selection, you can get it back by going to Select>Reselect.

5: Transform selections

Use Select> Transform Selection to reshape your selection. You can scale, rotate, sheer and even warp your selection, and manually input coordinates for precision placement on your canvas.

Give photos a 3D effect

Create the illusion of 3D with coral and fish swimming off the page

Essentials

TIME TAKEN

1.5 hours

YOUR EXPERT

Giles Angel

ON THE DISC

All the source files

Key Photoshop Skills Covered
What you'll learn

MAKING SELECTIONS

SCALING OBJECTS

MASKING

REVEALING SELECTIONS

Have you ever wanted to give your compositions the illusion of 3D? Well, now you can with this sub-aqua tutorial. We'll start with a series of underwater elements: coral, fish, a diver and nature's most important element – water.

Each of these elements will be scaled and blended into a seamless composition. To heighten the sense of depth and three dimensions, some of the fish and coral will be isolated and scaled to flow outside the composition itself. This not only makes the image more lifelike, but gives the picture a more organic feel by breaking up the straight edges.

The Free Transform tool will be used to magnify foreground elements for a wide-angled close-up look. The diver element in the composite will be shrunk to further the feel of distance between him and the foreground elements. We will also make extensive use of masks on many of the layers to partially hide and reveal content and smooth out any sharp edges. In addition, small watery areas will be copied and stretched to build up the sea in the background.

Thanks to Jenny Huang for the use of her images
www.flickr.com/photos/ diverslog/216639520/in/photostream/

PHOTOSHOP CS3 | **WORKS WITH**

Tip

Keep an eye on the light

When making an image composite, try and use elements that are taken in the same lighting conditions otherwise they won't marry together effectively. In this case the photography is all front-flashed so the elements work well side by side. Mixing an element that's taken in bright sun with another on a dull day, for example, wouldn't look very realistic.

FISHY BUSINESS
Begin to create your virtual aquarium

01 Set the scene Open 'frame.psd'. Open 'blue_fish.jpeg', pick the Move tool, drag and drop onto frame.psd. Pick Free Transform, hold Shift+Alt/Opt, and pull on a corner of the bounding box to scale the image up. Release the buttons, move the cursor to the corner, rotate the image to adjust the angle.

02 Isolate the fish Select the Pen tool (P), add points around the blue fish until the path is complete. Right-click/click and hold and pick Make Selection. Use a Feather of 1 pixel. With the selection active, click Add a Layer Mask at the bottom of the Layers palette. This hides background material and isolates the fish.

Tip

Consider visual hierarchy

When bringing all your elements together think about how you can create a visual hierarchy. This can be achieved by making elements larger or smaller over others, and through the use of blurring to soften elements which can simulate a shallow depth of field setting on a standard camera lens. Colour desaturation can also help to highlight one area over another.

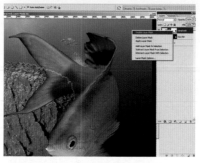

03 Add red coral Open 'coral_red. jpeg' and drag and drop onto the comp image. Position the image behind the fish. Now Ctrl/Cmd-click on the fish mask in the Layers palette to load as a selection. Press Ctrl/Cmd+Shift+I to invert the selection. With the coral layer selected, click on the Add Layer Mask icon to create another mask.

04 Hide the tail – part 1 Now we'll make a selection of the coral and use this to mask out the fish tail behind it. Right-click/ click and hold on the coral mask and hit Disable Mask. This hides the fish and allows a path to be made. Make a new path around the coral, then Ctrl-click/click and hold on the mask and enable the mask again.

05 Hide the tail – part 2 Load the new path as a selection (Feather 1 pixel), select the coral mask on the red coral layer and pick the Brush tool (B) with white as the foreground in the Color picker on the main Tools palette picker (press D to reset to black and white, and X to toggle the background and foreground colours). Paint inside the selection to reveal the coral in front of the tail.

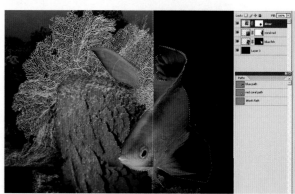

06 Tidy edges Select the Marquee tool (M) and draw a rectangle around the edge of the guide as shown in the image reference. Select black as the foreground and paint on the coral mask to hide the coral sea area and make the fish spill off the page.

07 Add the diver Open 'diver.jpeg', drag it onto the composition and position it above the blue fish and red coral layer. Now reload the blue fish path as a selection and invert it, then click the Add Layer Mask icon to reveal the tail again. Reload the coral path selection and paint in black on the mask to reveal the red coral again.

3D MAGIC
Create a spectacular effect

08 Add yellow coral Open 'yellow_coral.psd'. This has been cut out to save you time. Drag the cut-out layer to the composite image and position in place. Load the red coral path as a selection. Now invert the selection and load a layer mask on the yellow coral layer to make the red coral stand out in front.

09 Add more red coral Next, open 'coral_red2.psd'. Drag this layer onto the composite image and use the Move tool to position it in the foreground in front of the yellow coral.

Creating that 3D look

Although the composite is made entirely from two-dimensional imagery, by allowing elements to spill outside the main content this breaks up the straight edges and creates an impression of depth. This is further emphasized by exaggerating the scale of the foreground imagery. The diver is greatly outsized by the coral and the fish – this helps draw your eye into the image. How the elements are lit is very important for creating a 3D look. In this case the brightly lit foreground elements frame the darker background elements lit by ambient light.

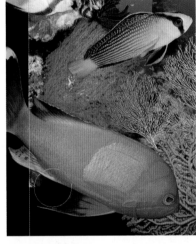

11 Purple and yellow coral Open 'purple_coral.psd' and 'coral_left.jpeg'; drag onto the composite between the fish/diver layers. Free Transform yellow_coral.psd, making it smaller. Add a layer mask: 'yellow coral 2'. With the Brush tool (foreground set to black), paint on the mask to reveal the purple layer. Add a layer mask; remove unwanted coral under the red fish.

10 Add more fish Open 'red_fish.psd' and drag the red fish layer onto the comp document. Drag this layer to the top of the layer stack so it's positioned in front of the red coral. Use the Free Transform tool to scale the fish up in size. Now open 'yellow_fish_01.psd' and 'yellow_fish_02.psd' and dag and drop onto the composite. Scale and rotate the fishes as before, so they look large and in the foreground.

12 Scale the diver Select the diver layer and unlink the layer image thumbnail with the mask by clicking on the link icon between them. Free Transform the diver image and scale it down. Hold down Shift and drag inwards from the top left-hand corner, so the top edge matches with the guide.

13 Stretch! Pick the Marquee tool and select a vertical slice of sea on the diver layer without the diver. Hit Ctrl/Cmd+J to copy/paste to a new layer. Free Transform the layer and stretch it left to cover the sea. Hold Alt/Opt to distort corners. Add a layer mask, use a soft brush and blend the edges with the background sea. Repeat for the yellow coral layer.

14 Adding ripples and finishing off Marquee select some ripples on the yellow coral 2 layer and copy and paste onto a new layer above, then add a layer mask. Now select the Gradient tool. With the mask selected, draw a vertical gradient on the mask to blend out the hard edge. Press Ctrl/Cmd+Shift+Alt/Opt+E to merge the layers onto a new layer. Now use the Clone tool and Healing brush to smooth out stretch marks in the sea.

The spotlight effect

Key Photoshop Skills Covered
What you'll learn

LAYER MASKS
GAUSSIAN BLUR
CHANNELS
CURVES
BLENDING MODES
LAYER MASKS
LEVELS
HUE/ SATURATION

Essentials

TIME TAKEN
90 minutes

YOUR EXPERT
Matthew Henry

ON THE DISC
spotlightbefore. jpg

Spotlighting is a popular effect that adds a bit of wow to any image. Re-create it here!

Spotlighting owes its origins to the theatre, but it has steadily made its way into the world of photography.

At first, identical tungsten light sources to those in the theatre and cinema were used, but purpose-built spot attachments for flash heads, or flash units with focusable lenses to enable movement from spot to flood have replaced them. Whatever the equipment, the purpose is the same – to pick out and highlight a subject in a larger area, or to pick out a specific part of a subject, using a circular pool of light.

The spotlight becomes the brightest source and main focus of attention, so all light outside the spot field can be considered ambient lighting. There may be enough ambient lighting to reveal detail outside the spot, or everything outside the spot field may be black. Imagine an actor crouching centre stage for his final speech, lit by a single beam while the stage around him is barely visible.

If you don't have the equipment to produce such atmospheric effects, fear not, there's a way to get close with Photoshop. All you need is an image with fairly even lighting, or one that's lit face on.

FROM THIS

TO THIS

CREATE YOUR SPOTLIGHT USING CURVES
Unleash the power of the layer mask for the spotlight effect

01 **Draw a spotlight circle** Start with a well exposed image and select the Elliptical Marquee tool (Shift+M to cycle through to it). Hold down Shift to constrain proportions to a circle and draw your spotlight area. Click and drag from the middle to reposition if necessary.

02 **Darken ambient lighting** Now use Shift+Ctrl/Cmd+I to invert your selection and add a Curves adjustment layer via the icon at the bottom of the Layers palette. Place one point in the centre and drag the curve downwards to darken the area outside the spotlight. Now set the blending mode to Luminosity.

03 **Feather spotlight edge** Go to Filter>Blur>Gaussian Blur and drag the Radius slider rightwards to feather the edge of the spotlight. The defined edge of the spotlight will bend where it meets a non-flat surface, so we need to attempt to recreate this movement.

SECRETS BEHIND OUR SPOTLIGHT
The techniques that created the effect

Hair We don't touch the fine detailed edges of the hair until the very end, where we work over with Dodge and Burn tools at only 25%.

Levels We can see here how things look after the Levels change has been applied. Shadows have been darkened and highlights lightened.

Skin The skin shows good separation from the background. We can darken this easily to black using the Burn tool.

Dodge and Burn Despite being somewhat darker than the subject clothing, we decide to Dodge the background and Burn the subject, as the skin itself is dark.

Clothing The clothing has little separation from the background in terms of tone, so we need to work carefully with each tool to bring out the contrast.

04 **Plan your subject mask** To do this, we need to make a mask of our subject. Use your preferred method, be it painting in Quick Mask mode (hit Q and paint with a black brush) or cutting out with the Pen tool (Lasso if you really must). A quick solution we used here is the Channels method.

05 **Choose your channel** The Channels method is great for cutting out subjects against plain backgrounds. Turn off Visibility for the Curves layer. Navigate to the Channels palette and choose the Red, Green or Blue channel, whichever provides the best contrast between subject and background.

PHOTOSHOP 7 AND ABOVE | **WORKS WITH**

Controlling the balance

It might take a little time to get the balance right between the ambient lighting and the spotlight. You can darken ambient light by double-clicking the Curves layer to re-open the dialog, dropping the curve further. To lighten the ambient light, drop the opacity of the layer in the Layers palette. The same principles can be applied to the levels layer that brightens the spotlight: move the White slider in further, or drop the layer opacity.

Choice of subject

Ideally you want to use a subject against a flat, plain background for this technique. A studio backdrop is ideal, but an interior wall is fine as well. Your subject needs to appear fairly close to the background too, or the spotlight circle will have to appear different in size on subject and background. Pick a subject that has been lit fairly evenly or, ideally, has been lit face on.

06 Work the alpha channel Drag this channel to the Create New Channel button at the bottom of the palette. A new alpha channel appears. Go to Image>Adjust>Levels and drag the Black slider rightwards to darken shadows, but not so much as to kill important midtone detail in subtle areas such as hair.

07 Dodge and Burn Do the same with the White slider, again being careful not to go too hard. Now take the Burn tool and set it to Shadows at 100% and work over the subject or background area, whichever is the darker of the two. Do the reverse with the Dodge tool set to Highlights. Avoid fine hair edges at this stage.

08 Finish the mask Keep going until subject and background are separated. Use black and white hard-edge brushes to fill in central areas away from the outline. Finish by working over the hair edges once with Dodge and Burn, each set to 25%. Your selection is done, so click the RGB channel. Turn the Curves layer on.

09 Spherize Ctrl/Cmd-click the alpha channel, leaving RGB as the active channel. A selection should load up around the subject. Invert if necessary with Ctrl/Cmd+Shift+I. Select the layer mask on the spotlight Curves layer and go to Filter>Distort>Spherize. Choose +35%.

10 Re-create spotlight contrast A spotlight is quite a harsh light source, so contrast will be quite strong. As the original lighting in this image is fairly soft, we're going to boost contrast for the spotlight area. Start by Ctrl/Cmd-clicking the layer mask on the Curves layer.

11 Manipulate the curve A selection will be loaded based on the layer mask. Invert this selection with Shift+Ctrl/Cmd+I. Now add another Curves layer and produce an S curve, lightening the highlights and darkening the shadows. We pulled the shadow point right to the base here, to really deepen the blacks.

12 Prevent saturation changes The contrast increase will increase saturation, so we can prevent this by changing the layer mode to Luminosity. Spotlights tend to be hottest nearest the centre, so we'll try to create this look. Start by adding a new Curves adjustment layer and raise the curve slightly before inverting the layer mask with Ctrl/Cmd+I.

13 Create centre brightness Now take a white brush with 0% Hardness and resize it with the bracket keys until it's about half the size of the spotlight circle. Make sure the layer mask is still selected and click three of four times in the centre of the circle. Now run Gaussian Blur hard to feather this edge.

FINISH THE EFFECT AND ADD SOME WALL DETAILS
When the light is perfected, it's time to have some fun!

14 Brighten spotlight If the spotlight still doesn't look bright enough, Ctrl/Cmd-click the layer mask on the contrast-boosting layer to load it as a selection and add a Levels adjustment layer. Drag the White slider left to clip the highlights slightly and lighten overall.

15 Reload spotlight selection We can also tinge the spotlight area with a little yellow to simulate the warm colour balance of a tungsten spotlight. If the necessary selection isn't already still active, Ctrl/Cmd-click either the contrast curves or levels layer to load it up.

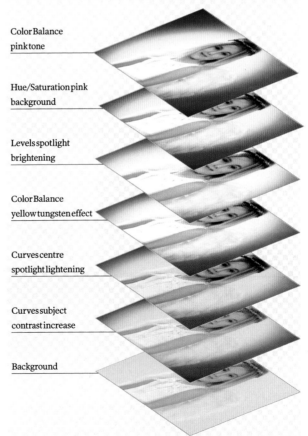

16 Spotlight colouring Now add a Color Balance adjustment layer and move the Yellow/Blue slider about 5 to 10 points towards yellow with the Midtones button selected. Deselect when you're done with Ctrl/Cmd+D. All done here, so now it's time to have a little fun!

17 Reload the person selection We're going to start by colouring our background. First Ctrl/Cmd-click the alpha channel selection we made of our subject to load it as a selection. Invert the selection with Ctrl/Cmd+Shift+I so everything around the subject is selected instead. Add a Hue/Saturation adjustment layer at the top of the stack.

18 Colour the background Check the Colorize box. Now move the Hue slider to the 0 value, and the Saturation slider to the 40 value. This gives us a nice pink tone. Any background colour will also contaminate a foreground subject, so we need to add a pinkish tone to our subject.

LAYER STRUCTURE
Under the spotlight...

Color Balance pink tone

Hue/Saturation pink background

Levels spotlight brightening

Color Balance yellow tungsten effect

Curves centre spotlight lightening

Curves subject contrast increase

Background

19 Colour the subject Ctrl/Cmd-click the Hue/Saturation layer mask, then invert the selection using Ctrl/Cmd+Shift+I. With the Midtones button selected, set the Red/Cyan slider to +30 red and -6 magenta. This gives our subject a realistic pinkish hue.

20 Alter values to finish When everything is finished we can step back and have a good look at our overall image, and then decide which of the layers need altering, if any. Here we chose to feather the spotlight further and drop the original Curves layer to further darken the background.

Kitchen robot

Create your very own robot from the everyday kitchenware found around your house

Essentials

TIME TAKEN
3 hours

YOUR EXPERT
Giles Angel

ON THE DISC
All the images you will need

In this tutorial we're going to do something a little different – so open up your kitchen cupboards and pull out those saucepans and cheese graters!

We're going to make a metallic robot from common kitchenware found around the house. We'll be taking you through the entire process from start to finish: sourcing materials, arranging the objects, photographing them and then manipulating the images into a montage.

You'll learn tips on how to photograph shiny objects, including ways to combat flare from studio flashes and use reflections to enhance form and maximise impact.

We'll then take all the elements into Photoshop for manipulation. Isolation will be hot on the agenda to remove the backgrounds from the objects. A number of isolation techniques will be covered, which will be

invaluable future. We'll scale and blend the objects together, using masks before creating a composite.

We'll then create a grounding shadow from the merged composite, and distort and blur it to get a softer,

> ## "A number of isolation techniques will be covered, which will be invaluable in future"

more realistic look. We'll also apply some simple colour and tonal adjustments to reduce colour casts, and increase contrast and saturation.

SOURCING RAW MATERIALS
What's in your kitchen cupboard?

Key Photoshop Skills Covered
What you'll learn

STUDIO LIGHTING TIPS

ISOLATING OBJECTS USING PATHS, MAGIC WAND TOOL AND CHANNELS

TRANSFORM TOOL

MASKING

ADJUSTMENT LAYERS

CREATING SHADOWS

01 Getting started First gather a pile of kitchen objects for selection. Any objects will work, but bear in mind the shape of the object and what part of the body it could represent. We've chosen metallic objects, but you could work with plastic or wooden materials.

02 Selection and visualisation Once you've found enough materials to work with, lay the objects on a flat surface in the arrangement you want. In this case, thinner objects have been selected for arms and legs, and larger items for the main body. This may change later, but it will help you visualise how the elements can fit together.

WORKS WITH | PHOTOSHOP 7 AND ABOVE

03 **Setting up** Once you've selected the objects, they need to be photographed at the right angle to aid compositing in Photoshop. Set up a clear, plain white table top surface, then set up the lights. Three lights were used here, one overhead and one from each side. Perspex was used to help diffuse the light and minimise reflections.

Tip

Lighting setup

Photographing shiny surfaces can be particularly problematic, as they have a tendency to reflect everything around them. The trick is to house the object(s) in an enclosed space and use pieces of opal perspex between the lights and the subject. This will help diffuse the light, spreading it across the surface. By moving the perspex closer or further from the light source, this will affect the amount the perspex is reflected into the object. Controlling the reflection will help shape your object and make it look more metallic. Silver foil can also be used to fill shadows and sculpt reflections further.

CREATIVE KITCHEN-CRAFT
Design your robot and prepare it for its moment in the spotlight

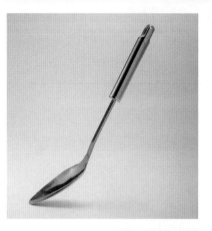

04 Shooting begins
Once the lighting has been set up, arrange the objects for the camera. Some larger ones will stand up, but others may need to be suspended using fishing line to minimise reflections. Some elements can be balanced on top of one another at the photograph stage to speed things up.

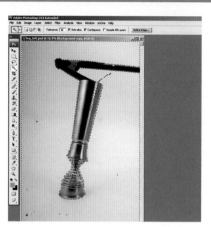

05 Select the leg
Open 'leg1.jpeg', select the Magic Wand tool (W) and set Tolerance in the Options bar at the top to 15. Click on the background of the image to select it. Hold down Shift and keep clicking on any unselected areas. The selection should look similar to the image on the left.

06 Quick Mask leg1
Press Q to enter the Quick Mask tool. We need to paint out the area where the clamp is and paint in the highlight area of the pepper grinder. Select the Paintbrush tool, with white as the foreground colour and Opacity at 100%, and paint out the red area where the clamp is, and the dust at the bottom.

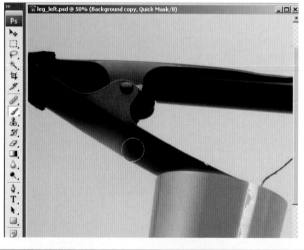

07 Floating selection
Press X on the keyboard to flip the foreground to black, and paint in the highlight areas on the pepper grinder. Now press Q to exit Quick Mask and convert to a selection. Press Ctrl/Cmd+Shift+I to inverse the selection, then press Ctrl/Cmd+J to copy/paste to a new layer and float the selection.

ISOLATED PEPPER GRINDERS AND PANS
Preparing the parts for assembly

08 Isolate the leg
Open 'leg2.jpeg'. Repeat steps 5-7 using the Magic Wand and Quick Masking, and copy/paste to a new layer. Be sure to Shift-click the selection while using the Wand on the gaps between the springs. You can tidy up the selection using Paths.

09 Isolate shoulders part 1
Open 'shoulder1.jpeg'. Select the Pen and zoom into the edge of the object 200%. Start adding points around it. To draw a curve, add a point on one side, click the other holding the mouse, then pull to create the curve. Hold Alt/Opt and click on the point to reset the anchor.

10 Isolate shoulders part 2
Carry on adding points until the path is complete. Now pick Make a Selection in the Paths menu palette, with a Feather Radius of 1.5. Hit Ctrl/Cmd+J to copy/paste onto a new layer. Repeat with 'shoulder2.jpeg'. See steps 11 and 12 for an alternative masking technique.

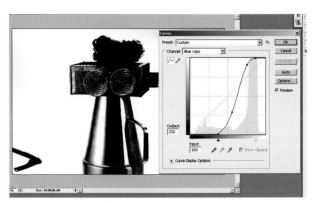

11 **Isolating head and neck** Open 'head.jpeg'. This time we'll use another technique for isolation. Click on the Channels tab. Select the most contrasty channel – in this case the blue one – and click Duplicate Channel from the Channel Options menu. With the Blue channel copy selected and the eye icon turned off on the other channels, press Cmd/Ctrl+M to enter Curves. Move Highlights and Shadows in to exaggerate the contrast.

12 **Floating selection of head and neck** Using a black brush, paint in the highlight areas. Paint in white over the clamp and background. To get a crisp edge, draw some paths and fill with black or white accordingly. Ctrl/Cmd-click on the mask to load as a selection. Now hit Ctrl/Cmd+Shift+I to invert the selection. With the RGB channel and the main layer selected, press Ctrl/Cmd+J to float the selection onto a new layer.

13 **Gather the pieces** Using all the techniques, carry on isolating the rest of the objects: 'body.jpeg', 'shoulder 1.jpeg'/'2.jpeg' and 'hips.jpeg'. Now create a document roughly A4 in size at 300dpi. Open all the object cutouts and drag and drop onto this document. Scale down any objects that are too big using Free Transform, Ctrl/Cmd+T, and place roughly in the right position. Open 'layout.psd' if you want to start from this point.

14 **Assemble the shoulders** Open 'layout.psd'. Uncheck the eye icon on all layers except shoulders and body. Pick the shoulder1 layer, move into place. Hit Add Layer Mask (bottom of Layers palette). Pick the white box (mask) next to the layer, and with a black brush and low opacity paint on the canvas to reveal the body at the join. Use gradual strokes for a fused metal look. Repeat with shoulder2.

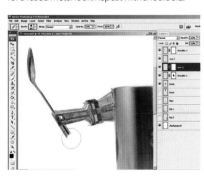

15 **Assemble arms** Move the arm1 layer into place with the Move tool. Add a layer mask and paint out the extraneous handle using a black paintbrush and low opacity. If you make a mistake, press X; this flips the foreground colour to white and you can paint the mask back in. Paint on the shoulder mask to help blending. Repeat for arm2.

HANDY TECHNIQUES
Make the most of your metallic monster

Selections Load and float selections onto a new layer from channels and masks.

Getting ahead Isolate the head by using Channel masks and Curve adjustments.

Diffuse the light Use white opal diffusion materials between the light and the subject when photographing shiny objects.

Scale to size Scale objects using the Free Transform tool.

In isolation Isolate the legs using the Magic Wand and Quick Mask.

Tip

An eye on white balance

If you're using studio flash, it's a good idea to set your camera's white balance to Flash mode to prevent unwanted colour casts. Shooting in Raw format will also give you more flexibility for subtle adjustments in colour temperature. The Camera Raw converter in Bridge is a useful tool for this. For metallic silver objects such as these, reducing the colour saturation in Photoshop will also help create a more neutral silver look.

PUT THE PARTS TOGETHER
Start the robot assembly line

LAYER STRUCTURE
Our robot dissected

16 **Adding the hips and legs** Turn on the hips layer and move it up so it sits on the bottom of the body layer. Drag the legs layers above the hips and then add a layer mask as before and start the blending process. You'll need to add a layer mask to the hips layer too, so you can blend back and forth.

17 **Adding the head** Turn on the head layer and drag it down behind the body layer. Add a layer mask to the head layer and paint on the mask. Again, you will need to paint on the body layer to help blending.

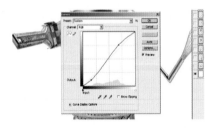

18 **Merging and tonal adjustments** Turn off the background layer, select all the other layers and press Ctrl/Cmd+Shift+ Alt/Opt+E. This is the shortcut to merge and copy onto a new layer. Now click the Adjustment Layer icon at the bottom of the Layers palette and choose Curves. Add and drag points to make an 'S' shape like the one in the picture to increase contrast and saturation.

19 **Add shadow part 1** Add another adjustment layer under the Curves layer. Hit Hue/Saturation and type -84 in the Saturation box. This will strip out much of the colour and make the robot appear more silver. Select the merged layer, hold Ctrl/Cmd and click to load as a selection. Click Add New Layer and fill with black using the Paintbucket.

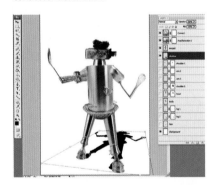

20 **Add shadow part 2** Name this layer 'Shadow', and place under the merged layer. Press Ctrl/Cmd+T to enter Free Transform. Hold down the Alt/Opt key and drag on the corners of the selection to distort the shadow, and then make the Opacity 25%. Now duplicate the layer and go to Filter>Gaussian Blur 40%.

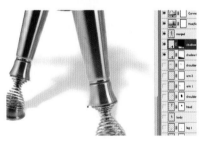

21 **Finish off** Blur the other shadow layer by 5% and add a mask on each shadow layer. Set the foreground colour to black and white (D) and draw a gradient across each mask from the feet going away from the body. Select the 5% Blur shadow mask and press Ctrl+I to invert. This gives a sharper shadow, falling off to a blurred one behind. Finally, adjust the opacity and clone out the bluetak on the body, and any other blemishes.

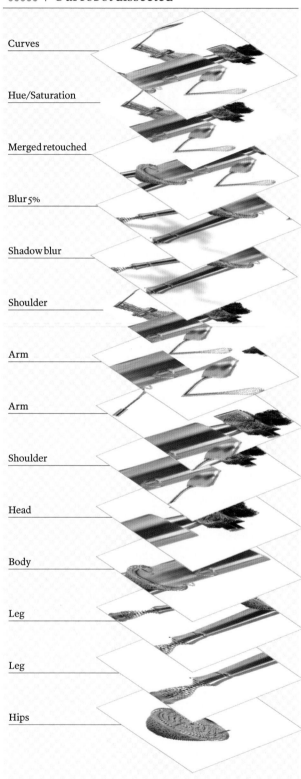

Curves

Hue/Saturation

Merged retouched

Blur 5%

Shadow blur

Shoulder

Arm

Arm

Shoulder

Head

Body

Leg

Leg

Hips

Transform an object's shape

BEFORE

Creating a square apple requires more than a trip to Hogwarts – the Liquify filter beats any magic wand!

Part of Photoshop's charm for many people is its ability to take a familiar object and turn it completely on its head.

This could take many formats – maybe a colour change that goes against nature, or placing items in environments they would never usually occur. This type of image editing can be a lot of fun, and produce images that wouldn't look out of place in a clever advertising campaign.

For this tutorial we're going to take the humble apple and give it a new spin by turning it square. Turning a round object square is no easy task, particularly if there's texture that can get warped, stretched and distorted to give away the game. The apple we worked on here contains an incredible amount of lines, swirls and spots in its texture that can easily begin to look unreal if the natural shape is noticeably altered. Much of the hard work then, isn't in the physical reshaping of the object's proportions but in maintaining the detail while this reshaping takes place.

As with any Photoshop task, there are a number of different methods that could be used to achieve this effect, but the Liquify filter certainly produces the most lifelike result in the shortest length of time. It's marvellous at this sort of thing when used with care – there's a real art to selecting which bits to drag at which brush size, to prevent rather unsightly stretch marks. But the great thing about fruit is that it's not a uniform size and contains many imperfections. You're actually better off having slightly wonky edges than having them all perfectly square. Which is a good thing, because perfectly square is not something the Liquify filter does particularly well!

It might possibly seem something of an exercise in futility, but there's more than the fun factor in this application. If you are able to get the hang of preserving detail while changing the fundamental properties of a shape, you will have mastered the Liquify filter and realised just how powerful a tool it really is. It's certainly one of Photoshop's most underrated features!

Key Photoshop Skills Covered
What you'll learn

LIQUIFY FILTER
BRUSH CONTROL
BLUR
USING QUICK MASKS

Essentials

TIME TAKEN
1 hour

YOUR EXPERT
Matthew Henry

ON THE DISC
square_fruit.jpg

WORKS WITH | PHOTOSHOP CS AND ABOVE

IT'S HIP TO BE SQUARE
Have fun with nature

01 Set horizontal positioning It's more accurate to make a square out of an apple that's properly horizontal, so Select All Ctrl+A (PC) or Apple+A (Mac), then use Edit>Transform>Rotate to square things up a little if needs be. Use Ctrl/Apple+D in order to deselect.

02 Duplicate background layer It's good practice when working on any image to duplicate the background layer. That way, if you mess up you've still got the original to go back to. Either select Layer>Duplicate Layer, or drag the layer to the Create a New Layer symbol at the base of the Layers palette.

Tool School

Liquify max brush size

The maximum size brush that the Liquify filter can use is 600 pixels, which is a little underpowered for pushing about objects shots on today's mammoth megapixel cameras. It works best on an image of around 1000 x 1000 pixels, as this allows large drag movements. For bigger images you'll have to make do with a number of smaller movements to achieve the same effect – which requires that little bit of extra patience and precision.

03 Fire up the Liquify filter Make sure the background copy layer is selected, then select Filter>Liquify. Select the biggest brush size you can, using the slider or the] key. Divide the apple into four sections in your head, and drag each upwards and outwards.

04 Work the corners more Next, take the brush size down a third or so and pull outwards and upwards again, this time starting a little closer to the corners – though not at the corner tips. If necessary, move the brush further inwards to another spot and pull to prevent overstretching a specific area.

05 And some more Take the brush size down a third again, and tease the corners out a little more. You're aiming to square them off to reduce the rounded effect, but avoid going too far because we still want some corner rounding.

06 Correct edge bow You'll probably find now that the left, right and bottom edges of the apple are beginning to look like they're bowing slightly. Take a large brush and then bring them back in line, so the edges look relatively flush.

07 Straighten things up After all this pushing and pulling, you may find the apple appears a little wonky, so take a large brush and pull at the four sections again so the apple looks relatively horizontal and symmetrical.

ADVANCED FEATHER
Get some real-time feathering action!

When it comes to feathering a selection, forget Select> Feather – it doesn't give you any sense of what's going on. Instead, make a selection, hit Q for Quick Mask mode, then Filter>Blur>Gaussian Blur. Zoom in or out to see your selection, then move the slider to see real-time feathering!

01 Make the selection
Use the Freehand Lasso tool to make your selection rather than Polygonal, as the results are more natural. Bear in mind that feathering is going to bring in information from outside the selection as well, so make the selection smaller in order to compensate if needs be.

02 Enter Quick Mask mode
Hit Q to enter Quick Mask mode. You'll notice that everything selected remains normal, and everything not selected has gone a shade of red. The buttons to toggle Quick Mask mode can be found under the foreground/ background colours on the Tools palette.

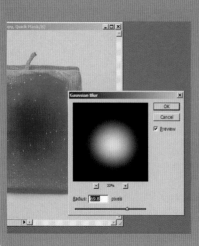

03 Feather with Gaussian Blur
Next, go to Filter> Blur>Gaussian Blur and zoom in or out with the Percentage slider until you can see the whole of your selection. Move the Radius slider up and down to change the amount of feathering. After application, hit Q in order to bring back your newly feathered selection.

THE FINE DETAILS
Make sure it all lines up

08 Fine-tune corners
With a relatively small brush, we're now going to fine-tune our corners. First, click and drag at the centre edge of each corner. Next, do the same thing at the corner's topmost point as it turns into the straight line, and then do the same again at the bottom point.

09 Reshape texture detail
At this stage, there's probably a fair amount of detail that looks a little stretched further in from the corners. The white circles are a good give-away on this particular apple. Use a small brush to push and pull several points to bring things back into line.

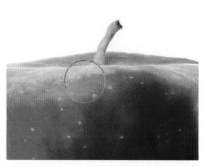

10 Straighten the top edge
The top edge of the apple front side now needs flattening a little to make it look a bit more like a cube. Start with a medium-sized brush, and move areas up or down to square it off, varying brush size where necessary.

11 Add depth realism
The line behind the apple core stem needs extending to give the appearance of cubic depth, so we're going to use a small brush to continually stretch the top line outwards until it extends to the edges of the shape.

SHADY BEHAVIOUR
Give the apple some presence

12 Check Mesh
At this point it's a good idea to check the Show Mesh box in the View Options section of the Filter dialog. This shows you exactly what you've pushed and pulled so far with reference to the original, and can help you visualise what needs tidying up with a little more tweaking.

13 Cut out the shadow
Next, we need to sort the shadow, as it doesn't quite reflect the new apple shape. Use a Polygonal Lasso tool to cut around the shadow. Don't worry about the edge of the other side of the apple. When you've finished, hit Ctrl/Apple+J to float the selection to a new layer.

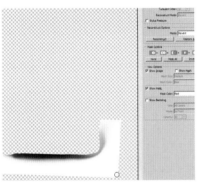

14 Liquify shadow
Now go back to the beloved Liquify filter and use suitable brush sizes (try 24 at 50% Density) to shape the shadow edges so they appear squarer, without removing the corner curvature.

15 Mask out any debris
You may have stretched the shadow into the apple after using Liquify, so add a layer mask with Layer>Layer Mask>Reveal All. Next, make sure the mask is selected, then take a small brush at 90% Opacity and paint black into the areas of the apple that have been affected by shadow.

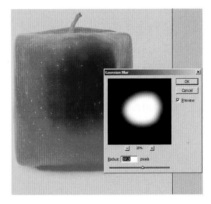

16 Select the centre bulge
The apple's upper centre still seems to bulge towards the camera. We can fix this with a little 'Pinch'. Use the Freehand Lasso to draw a rough circle around the bulging area, and hit Q for Quick Mask mode. Use Filter>Blur>Gaussian Blur to feather the selection edges.

LAYER STRUCTURE
Slicing through the apple

17 Use a little Pinch
Hit Q again to exit Quick Mask mode, and the red overlay disappears, leaving you with the selection marching ants. Go to Filter>Distort>Pinch, zoom outwards so you can see the whole apple, and play around with the + settings on the slider until you achieve the desired result. Finally, flatten your image with Layer>Flatten Image and SAVE it!!

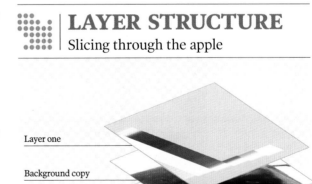

Layer one

Background copy

Background (original)

Before

Vintage effect

Give a nod to nostalgia and head back to yesteryear by turning a modern image into a vintage, timeworn classic

Essentials

TIME TAKEN

60 minutes

YOUR EXPERT

Matthew Henry

ON THE DISC

vintage_before. jpg

A handful of your grandparents' old photographs will tell you enough about how that vintage timeworn effect should look.

You're not only viewing something captured with antiquated technology, you're also seeing how the finished product has degraded over time. In your grandparents' day these images would have displayed far more punch and polish, despite the relative infancy of camera technology.

Sepia toning was a popular finish at the time, so it's always a great starting point once you've converted to black and white. After this, it's a matter of adding film grain, which is no longer present with digital technology, and then degrading the image to recreate the

aged effect. Yellowing of the highlights is a common problem, and easily recreated. Fading can be done relatively easily as well, although it's important to remember that it is rarely uniform across an image, so we've added some greater fade in the corner for good measure.

Old photos also frequently show missing, blotchy areas that can have been caused by physical damage, or more likely by uneven development at the processing and printing stage. We have a clever method for accurately recreating this effect. The final vintage topping comes in the form of a torn corner – again a frequent problem with brittle vintage paper stocks that didn't sport the longevity technology we have today.

Key Photoshop Skills Covered
What you'll learn

BLACK AND WHITE CONVERSION

SEPIA TONING

FILM GRAIN

USING LEVELS TO CREATE FADE

USING THE GRADIENT TOOL WITH MASKS FOR LOCAL FADE

COLOR BALANCE

HANDWRITING WITH THE TEXT TOOL

CREATING DAMAGE SPOTS WITH THRESHOLD

TRANSFORM YOUR PIC WITH SEPIA TONING
Sepia toning is the best starting point for a truly vintage look

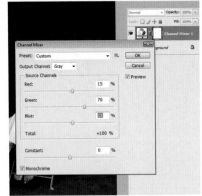

01 **Black and white CS3** We're going to start by converting our colour image to monochrome. CS3 users and up can navigate to the Layers palette and choose the Black and White adjustment layer. The Green filter setting from the drop-down menu works well for most images, particularly with people shots.

02 **Black and white pre-CS3** If you're using an early version of Photoshop, you can achieve the same effect with the Channel Mixer. Select a Channel Mixer adjustment layer from the Layers palette base. Now check the Monochrome box and push Green to 70% and Red and Blue each to 15%.

03 **Sepia toning** Now we want to add a sepia tone to give that vintage, aged feel. We first make sure the top layer is selected and then add a Color Balance adjustment layer from the Layers palette so it appears at the top of the stack. We then set the Cyan/Red slider 30 points toward Red and the Blue/Yellow slider the same to Yellow.

WORKS WITH | PHOTOSHOP 7 ONWARDS

Lucy writing in her diary aged 10

ADD FILM GRAIN, AND FADE THE IMAGE
Destroy detail and apply a fade for maximum realism

04 Add neutral overlay
Now make sure the top layer is selected again, hold down Alt/Option and click the Create a New Layer button. When the dialog box appears, change the blending mode to Overlay and check the box underneath to fill with an overlay-neutral colour.

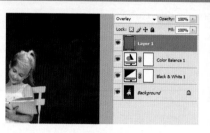

05 Add film grain
With this Overlay layer selected, go to Filter>Noise>Add Noise and select the Monochrome and Gaussian options. Choose an amount of 20% – we can always drop the layer opacity at a later stage if this is too much. Now go to Filter>Blur>Gaussian Blur and run a 1-pixel Radius blur.

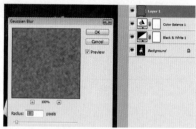

06 Blur grain
The noise added in Photoshop is quite sharp and doesn't resemble film grain as it stands. To make it realistic, we need to add a touch of Gaussian Blur. With the noise layer active, go to Filter>Blur>Gaussian Blur and add a 1.0 Radius blur.

07 Discard detail
Now we're going to try and degrade the image. Add a Levels adjustment layer via the button at the bottom of the palette and drag the black and white Input sliders inwards to discard detail in the shadows and highlights. Don't go too hard on the highlights.

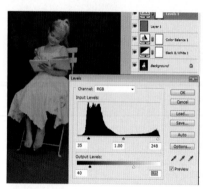

08 Fade image
We can use the same Levels dialog to fade the image. In the Output sliders section underneath the histogram set the black to 40 and the white to 175. This weakens the blacks and the whites to reduce overall contrast and give that time-faded look.

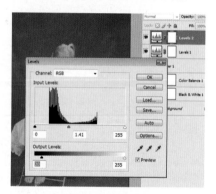

09 Levels for fade
We're now going to attempt to simulate gradual fade. Add another Levels adjustment layer and move the middle Input slider leftwards to lighten the image. Drag the black Output slider at the bottom of the dialog inwards to about 20.

FADING AWAY
Using Levels to produce fade

We've made use of a Levels adjustment layer as the crux of our vintage, faded look. The first step involves dragging the Input sliders inwards past the detail at both sides of the histogram. What we're effectively doing here is turning all the nice detail in the shadows and highlights into pure blacks and whites. Photography was something of a hit and miss affair in the early years, and the film emulsion technologies were not as advanced, so rarely was the full range of tones captured. Photographs also fade naturally over time, so to recreate this general fade we turned to the Photoshop Output sliders. By moving these inwards, we can wash out all the very dark areas and the light areas, reducing contrast to produce a sense of fade. The detail has already been lost through the Input sliders, so won't be rescued by our work here.

10 Set the gradient
Now press 'G' to select the Gradient tool. Make sure Linear Gradient is selected in the Tool Options bar, and Foreground to Background also selected via the drop-down Gradient Editor. Now press 'D' to reset the colour palette to black and white.

11 Gradient for gradual fade
Next, with white as your foreground colour and black as your background, draw a point from any corner or edge to near the centre of the frame in order to replicate a gradual fade. It's best to experiment with this a few times until you get it right.

YELLOWING, WRITING, A BORDER AND AGE DAMAGE
It's these small finishing touches that emphasise the antique feel

12 Yellow fade Next, we want to add a bit of yellowing to the highlights to suggest yellow fade, which is common to aged photographs. Add a Color Balance adjustment layer, select Highlights in the dialog and set the Blue/Yellow slider to -15.

13 Add handwriting Now press 'T' to select the Text tool and then select a handwriting font, choose an appropriate font size and change Anti-aliasing from Sharp to Smooth. Click somewhere and start typing a sentence or two. Use the spacebar and Return to line things up as you wish.

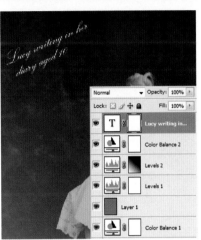

14 Position writing Highlight the text by clicking and dragging, then hold down the Ctrl/Cmd key until handles appear around your text. Drag one of the corners to rotate the text. Click on the text to deselect, then click outside the text and drag to move.

15 Fade writing Next, drop the Opacity of the text layer to 65% so it looks a little faded, and change any paragraph characteristics via Windows>Character if necessary. Add a layer mask, pick a black soft-edged brush at 30% and brush over areas of the text to fade them a little.

16 Add a border Press 'C' to access the Crop tool. Draw a crop around the entire image, release the mouse button, then drag the crop outside the image to extend the canvas each side. The previous adjustment layers will ensure the border is yellow and faded.

LAYER STRUCTURE
Travelling back in time

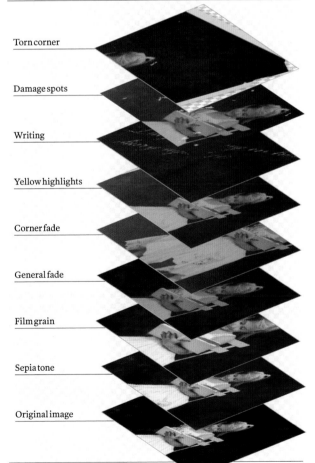

Torn corner

Damage spots

Writing

Yellow highlights

Corner fade

General fade

Film grain

Sepia tone

Original image

17 Add damage marks To recreate damage marks, add a new layer then press 'D' and go to Filter>Render>Clouds. Change the blending mode to Lighten. Go to Image>Adjustments>Threshold and move the slider rightwards until a few white specks are visible. Drop Layer Opacity to 60%.

18 Corner tear Finish with a small corner tear. Add a new layer, hold down Alt/Option and select Merge Visible from the Layer menu. Turn off all layers below. Select a small corner with the Lasso tool then hit Delete. Right-click the layer, choose Blending Options and play with the Drop Shadow settings to suit.

Grayscale solarization techniques

ORIGINAL PHOTO

USING CURVES

Learn two great ways to solarize your photos without resorting to Photoshop's Solarize filter

The Solarization technique (termed the 'Sabatier Effect') was first described in a letter from William Jackson in 1857. Though it was practised right through the 19th Century, it wasn't until Man Ray and Lee Miller breathed new life into the technique in the 1920s and 30s that it became popular.

Other photographers who experimented with this technique were Maurice Tabard, Helen Muspratt, Francis Bruguiere, Konrad Cramer and Wynn Bullock. Even Ansel Adams used Solarization in his toolbox of techniques. Part of its appeal is no doubt the spectacular haunting effect it creates. The images become stark negative inversions with surreal glows. Objects that could never cast light in the

real world become light sources under Solarization's spell.

'Solarization' and the 'Sabatier Effect' are used interchangeably, but they are two separate processes that produce a similar result. Solarization is the result of extreme overexposure of the film. The Sabatier effect occurs when film or paper is partially developed then treated to a dose of white light. The result is a partial inversion of the image's tonal range. This also creates glowing outlines (Mackie lines) along distinct edges. Technically, what we've come to know as Solarization is actually the Sabatier effect.

These processes are easily reproduced in Photoshop. Here we show you two ways to solarize your black and white images.

WITH GLOW APPLIED

Essentials

TIME TAKEN

▦ Approximately
10 minutes

YOUR EXPERT

▦ Rob Anselmi

ON THE DISC

▦ Starter file
and solarization
actions

Key Photoshop Skills Covered
What you'll learn

EXCLUSION
BLEND MODE

GRAYSCALE
COLOR MODE

LEVEL AND
CURVES
ADJUSTMENT
LAYERS

TAKE A JOURNEY THROUGH THE SOLAR SYSTEM
Go from humdrum to humdinger

More Resources

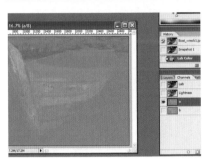

01 Convert the image modes
Open the starter file on the CD, then convert the image into Lab Color mode (Image>Mode>Lab Color). Now click on the Channels palette and delete the 'A' channel. Once this is done, convert your image to Grayscale (Image>Mode>Grayscale).

02 Create a duplicated Exclusion layer
Create a duplicate layer and set its blend mode to Exclusion. This blend mode is one of the main keys to creating a convincing solarization effect. Think of Exclusion as a lighter form of the Difference blend mode – which is a mode that partially inverts the image with the layer underneath.

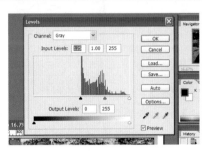

03 Merge, invert and level it out
Merge both layers together (Ctrl/Cmd+E), and then invert the Layer (Ctrl/Cmd+I). Apply Levels (Image>Adjustments>Levels), and move the left Input slider (Shadow slider) to the right until it lines up with the leftmost bar of the histogram. In the example above, that was Input level 125. The solarization is starting to take shape.

Exploring solarization
For more on Solarization, see William L Jolly's article, Solarization Demystified (1997), at www.cchem. berkeley.edu/ wljeme/SOUTLINE. html. For info on the person responsible for the resurgence of Solarization, Man Ray, visit www.man ray-photo.com/cat alog/index.php, which has a gallery of his work. Finding books on Man Ray may be hard, but try searching www. amazon.com or www.taschen.com.

04 Duplicate, exclude and adjust
Repeat step two, creating a duplicate Exclusion layer over the image. Add a Levels adjustment layer, and move the right Input slider (Highlight slider) a little left of the rightmost bar of the histogram (140 here). If the effect is too strong, move the slider anywhere between 130-255.

05 Apply the glow
Select the Exclusion layer and apply a heavy blur of about 30 pixels (Filter>Blur>Gaussian Blur). This enhances the haunting effect and diffuses the Sabatier lines you have produced along the high contrast edges. The effect is now complete.

06 Alternative adjustable process
For an alternative process, start over at the beginning with the original image. Create a new Channel Mixer adjustment layer, checking the Monochrome checkbox. If you wish, adjust the Red, Green and Blue mix using the sliders to gain a better Grayscale balance.

Expert Tip

Introducing colour into your solarization
You're not confined to black and white images – explore the Adjustable Curve technique on a colour image. By using the Channel drop-down in the Curves dialog, you can target specific colour channels in your image and apply the Solarization curve to them, creating some very sophisticated solarization effects. You can also save these curves for later use.

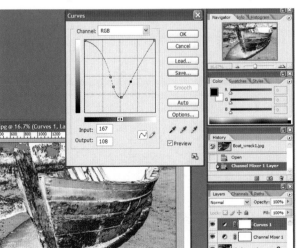

07 Add a Curves adjustment
Add a Curves adjustment layer to the top of the layer stack. In the Curves dialog, create a U or V-shaped curve, as shown on the left. If you wish, you can click the Load button and navigate to the Curves supplied on the CD. There are two solarization curves available for you to use.

08 Blur the image layer
Optionally, apply a Gaussian blur of between 1 and 2 pixels to the main image layer at the bottom of the layer stack (Filter>Blur>Gaussian Blur). This diffuses and softens the main image slightly.

Start image

Flower baby

Draw inspiration from your garden and dress up your baby with Photoshop

It's time to put down your gardening gloves and grab the computer mouse for the ultimate baby dressage tutorial. As the theme is gardening, a potting shed is the setting for creating our 'flower baby' – and you don't even need to get your hands dirty!

We'll start with a gorgeous picture of a baby on a chair, kindly donated by Jaroslaw Wojcik from iStockphoto. First, the baby will be magically lifted off the chair and into a flowerpot. We'll then scale and blend the two images together to form a brand new composite. To finish off , an extra detail will be added in the way of a lily flower, carefully balanced on the baby's head.

You will learn how to isolate specific areas of an image using the Pen tool, and reveal and hide selections using layer masks. Some layer masks will be painted on directly using the Brush tool to reveal parts of a layer underneath. The Free Transform tool will also be used on selected objects such as the flower to adjust the proportions to fit the background. We'll add grounding shadows to the baby's hands and

underneath the flower to help integrate them with the flowerpot and the forehead.

We'll also be using levels and blending modes in order to reduce highlights in unwanted areas that show no obvious light source. Adjustment layers will be used for subtle contrast and brightness

> ## "Put down your gloves and grab the computer mouse for the ultimate baby dressage tutorial"

corrections – some of these adjustments will be clipped to individual layers underneath and so prevent the changes affecting all of the layers below.

Essentials

TIME TAKEN
3 hours

YOUR EXPERT
Giles Angel

ON THE DISC
All the files you need to complete this tutorial

Key Photoshop Skills Covered
What you'll learn

CHANNELS
PEN TOOL
MASKS
ADJUSTMENT LAYERS
SCALING
ADDING SHADOWS
CLIPPING LAYERS
DARKER COLOUR BLEND MODE
WHITE POINT ADJUSTMENT

PREPARE THE SCENE FOR THE POTTING SHED
Lift the baby from the chair

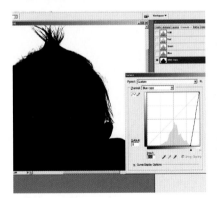

01 Isolating the background – 1 First we'll lift the baby from its background. Open the 'baby' image and and then choose Channels. Select the Blue channel from the Channel options list (top right), then select Duplicate Channel. With the channel selected, press Ctrl/Cmd+M to enter Curves. Click on the bottom left of the histogram and drag to the right.

02 Isolating the background – 2 This is darkening the area for use as a mask. With the channel still selected, use the Brush tool (B) and paint in black over the whites of the eyes and over some of the edges of the hands. Next, Ctrl/Cmd-click the channel to load it as a selection. Go to Select>Inverse to invert the selection.

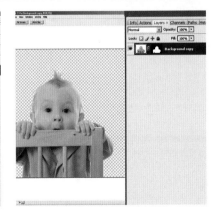

03 Creating the mask Now select the RGB channel in the channels layers, go back to Layers and double-click on the background layer. The dialog box pops up; name this layer 'Baby' and press Enter. With the selection still active, click on the Add Layer Mask icon (circle and square icon) at the bottom of the Layers palette.

Tip

Shadows
If adding shadows to an object, note direction and intensity of the light. If it's very bright and close to the object, the shadows will be harder and shorter. Further away, they'll be softer and longer. Time of day can also be a factor outdoors.

KEEP AN EYE ON DETAILS
Create harmony and a realistic blend

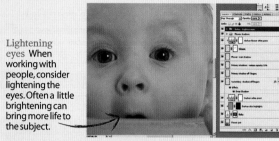

Lightening eyes When working with people, consider lightening the eyes. Often a little brightening can bring more life to the subject.

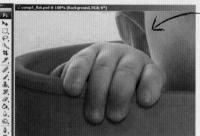

Multiple shadows Depending on the lighting, many objects cast more than one shadow. Consider primary and secondary shadows.

Quality of scale Consider photographing each object close up for the best quality – they can be scaled down in Photoshop afterwards.

Direction of light Pay attention to the angle and direction of light when using images from different sources.

Balancing the light Check if highlights and shadows balance with the background. It's often necessary to lighten/darken.

CHANGE UNWANTED PROPS
Hide the chair from view

04 **Isolate the chair** Zoom in (Z) and select the Pen tool (P). Carefully add points around the arms, fingers and along the top of the chair until you reach the other side. Zoom out and complete the path by adding further points outside the canvas. Now double-click on the workpath layer in the Paths palette and name it 'Chair'.

05 **Hide the chair** Choose Make Selection from the Options menu at the top right of the Paths palette and select a Feather Radius of 0.5. Select the mask in the Layers palette by clicking on it and then choose the Paintbucket tool (G). Now fill inside the selection with black. This should hide the chair from view.

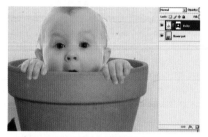

06 **Introduce the flowerpot** Open 'flower_pot.jpg', select the Move tool (V) and drag it onto the baby file. Drag the layer beneath the Baby layer. Using the arrow keys, move the flowerpot into position at the mouth. Select Image>Canvas Size and extend the image downwards. Select the Baby layer and go to Edit>Transform>Flip Horizontal.

07 **Tidy the edges** Select the baby layer mask and choose a black brush (B). Paint around the the baby edges to hide unwanted sleeves and skin. Now Ctrl/Cmd-click the mask, select the baby icon on the same layer and press Ctrl/Cmd+J to copy and paste onto a new layer.

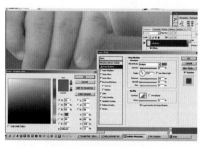

08 **Add secondary shadows under fingers** Name the new layer 'Shadows' and double-click the layer to bring up Layer Styles. Tick the Drop Shadow box , select the title to enter the options. Now click on the Color box and use the Eyedropper to sample on the flowerpot. Enter the following settings: Opacity about 8%, Distance 38 pixels, Spread 0% and Size 9 pixels. Uncheck Global Light.

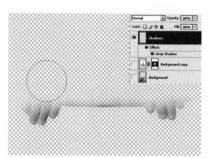

09 **Remove unwanted shadows** Select the Shadows layer and make the other layers invisible by holding down Opt and clicking on the eye icon. Next, using the Eraser tool (E) remove all the face until just the fingers and the finger areas remain. Now turn back to all the other layers. Select the Baby layer and erase any other white left behind.

BLEND BABY AND THE POT
Refine the shadow areas

10 **Add primary shadows under fingers** Duplicate the Secondary Shadows layer and double-click the Drop Shadow settings box. Now enter the following settings: Opacity about 47%, Distance 8 pixels, Spread 7% and Size 6 pixels. Uncheck Global Light. Next, Cmd/right-click on the Fx icon and then select Create Layer to render the effects as pixels.

11 **Darken the face highlights** Select the Baby layer then go to Layer>New Adjustment Layer>Levels, and move the white slider to the left to 237 and click Enter. This darkens the face by moving the white point. Now select the Eyedropper tool (I) and select the brick red from the pot. Select G and fill this layer with red.

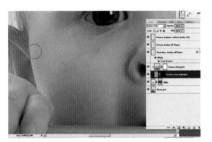

12 **Paint out the face highlights** Select Darken as the layer blend mode, hold down the Opt/Alt key and click on the Add Layer Mask icon. Paint in white on the layer mask over the cheek to reduce highlights. Hold down the Alt key and click between the Baby layer to clip it to the baby. Repeat this step with the Levels adjustment layer above.

13 **Introduce the flower** Open 'flower.psd' and drag it onto the baby document. Use Edit>Free Transform to scale and rotate it into position. Select the Pen tool (P) and draw a path around the front two petals to make a selection. Click the Layer Mask icon to hide these petals. Load the selection and invert it. Now, with a soft brush and low opacity, paint a subtle shadow under the flower.

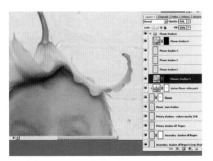

14 **Flower shadows** Create further new layers and gradually build up the shadow. Vary opacity and blend modes such as Difference and Multiply to further blend in the darker areas. Introduce a little pink on the forehead to simulate the cast from the petals. Add another clipped Levels adjustment layer on the flower and darken the white point.

15 **Finishing off** With a little patience the shadows should build up to form a reasonable cast on the forehead. Finish off with some overall contrast adjustments, and touch up on spots and mask fringes.

LAYER STRUCTURE
Our cute baby creation

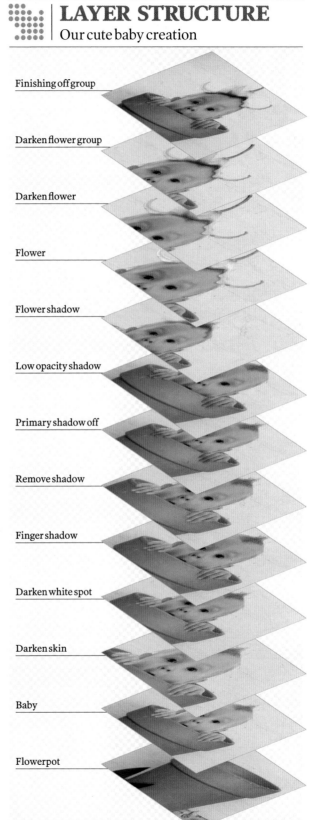

Finishing off group

Darken flower group

Darken flower

Flower

Flower shadow

Low opacity shadow

Primary shadow off

Remove shadow

Finger shadow

Darken white spot

Darken skin

Baby

Flowerpot

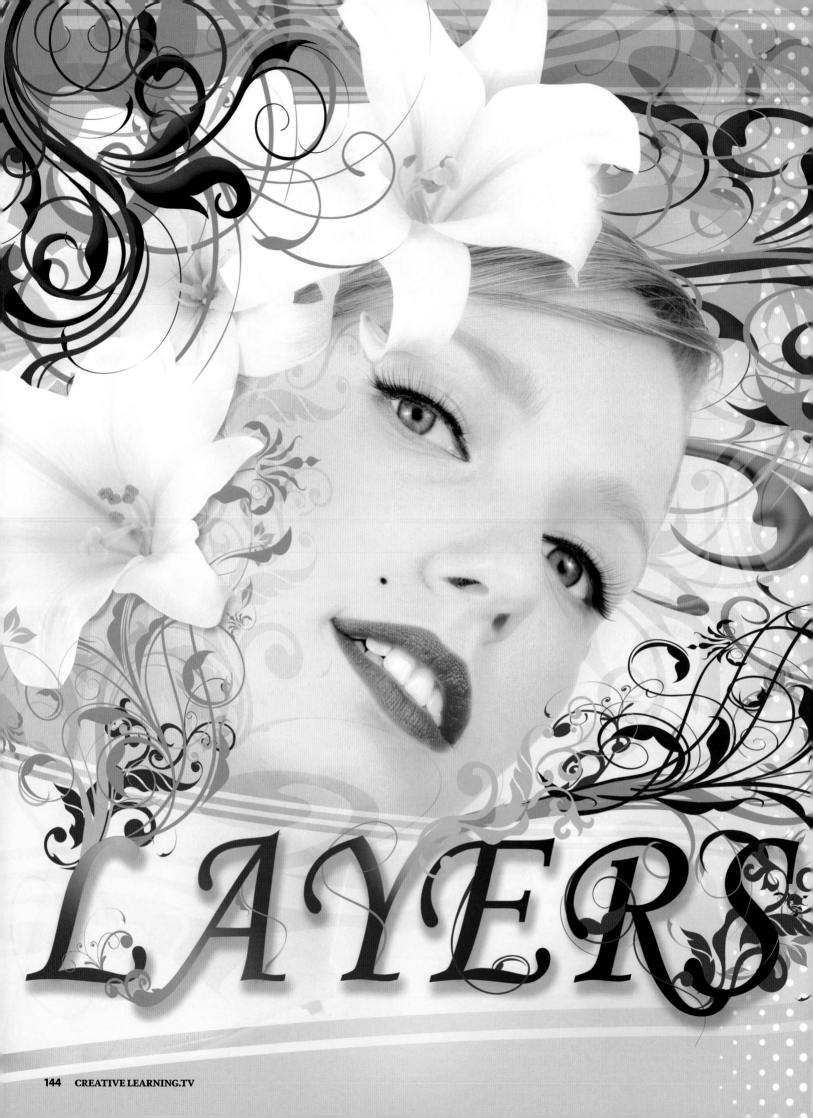

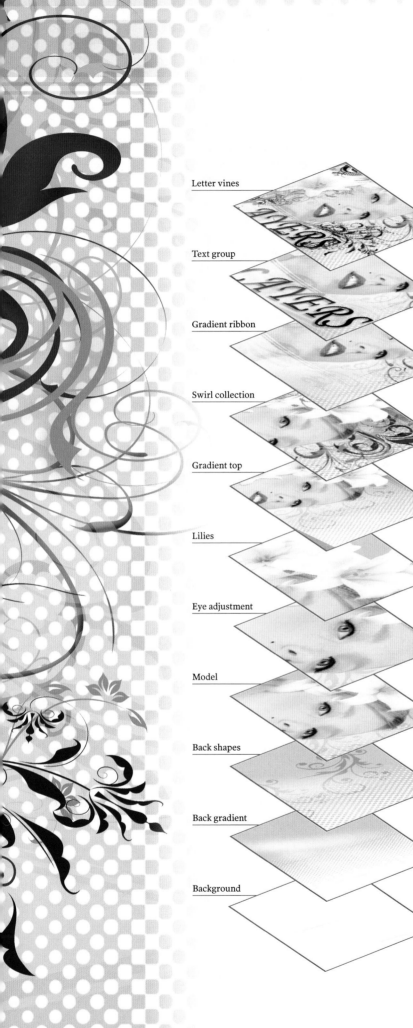

Letter vines

Text group

Gradient ribbon

Swirl collection

Gradient top

Lilies

Eye adjustment

Model

Back shapes

Back gradient

Background

If Photoshop gave up Layers, most of us would give up Photoshop. Learn more about this fundamental feature that makes Photoshop such a powerhouse...

When you hear the word 'layers', what immediately springs to mind? Perhaps a wedding cake or an enormous sandwich? Maybe it conjures up childhood memories of chilly mornings with your mother reminding you to always 'dress in layers' – as if there were any other option for how to clothe yourself. Or it's quite possible that you're like us, and the utterance of that word brings your thoughts to Photoshop. The ability to divide a composition into layers is arguably the most powerful feature of this remarkable program.

Over the next six pages we'll dissect the artwork you see here and discuss how it was developed by using layers of all shapes, types and sizes. If you're new to Photoshop, you don't want to miss this. Learning how to use layers effectively is an essential skill that must not be ignored. If you're a grizzled old Adobe veteran who remembers what Photoshop was like before it even had layers, stick around anyway – you might pick up a few tricks you'd forgotten about.

Layering isn't a new feature in Photoshop: it's been around since version 3.0 was released in 1994. The very concept of stacking up individual pieces of a drawing goes back even further. It's how the first animation studios back in the 1920s streamlined their workflow. The animators would separate artwork onto transparent pieces of celluloid that could be stacked, or layered, to form the whole picture. This approach enabled an individual element to be changed without affecting the rest of the composition. The technique allowed for objects and characters to be separate from backgrounds, so the landscape wouldn't need to be redrawn for every frame of animation.

Even though we're working with digital pixels, not ink on thin sheets of plastic, this still remains one of the best analogies for how the concept of layers works in Photoshop. The inherent power of layers comes from the flexibility they provide by isolating different elements of the composition. But the fun doesn't stop there – Photoshop offers many more features to complement the brilliance of layers. Vector masks, adjustment layers, clipping masks, layer styles and blending modes are all techniques that are designed to enhance the usefulness of layering.

Take a close look at the adjoining artwork. Notice how the swirls wrap around one another and the flowers curl through the text. See how the background fades into a halftone pattern. Take note of how some swirls appear to be colourless but enhance the colour of whatever lies beneath them. These are all effects that were accomplished by utilising some of the many layer tools available in Photoshop.

Layers palette

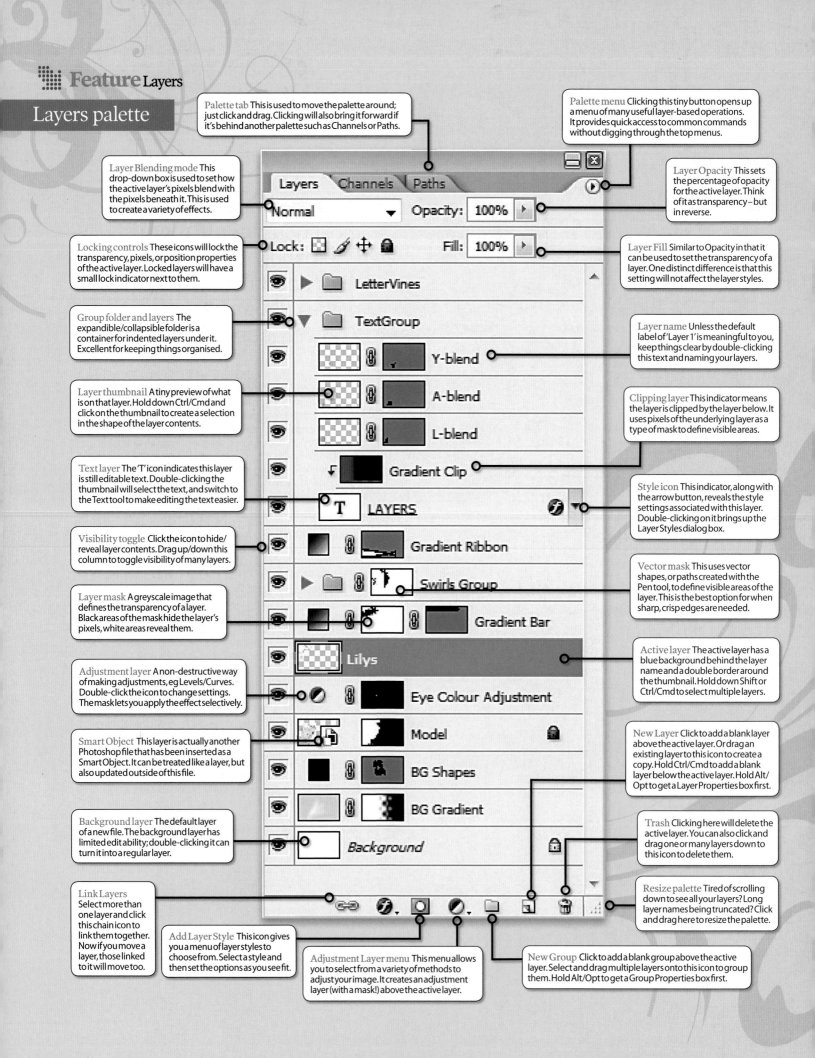

Palette tab This is used to move the palette around; just click and drag. Clicking will also bring it forward if it's behind another palette such as Channels or Paths.

Palette menu Clicking this tiny button opens up a menu of many useful layer-based operations. It provides quick access to common commands without digging through the top menus.

Layer Blending mode This drop-down box is used to set how the active layer's pixels blend with the pixels beneath it. This is used to create a variety of effects.

Layer Opacity This sets the percentage of opacity for the active layer. Think of it as transparency – but in reverse.

Locking controls These icons will lock the transparency, pixels, or position properties of the active layer. Locked layers will have a small lock indicator next to them.

Layer Fill Similar to Opacity in that it can be used to set the transparency of a layer. One distinct difference is that this setting will not affect the layer styles.

Group folder and layers The expandible/collapsible folder is a container for indented layers under it. Excellent for keeping things organised.

Layer name Unless the default label of 'Layer 1' is meaningful to you, keep things clear by double-clicking this text and naming your layers.

Layer thumbnail A tiny preview of what is on that layer. Hold down Ctrl/Cmd and click on the thumbnail to create a selection in the shape of the layer contents.

Clipping layer This indicator means the layer is clipped by the layer below. It uses pixels of the underlying layer as a type of mask to define visible areas.

Text layer The 'T' icon indicates this layer is still editable text. Double-clicking the thumbnail will select the text, and switch to the Text tool to make editing the text easier.

Style icon This indicator, along with the arrow button, reveals the style settings associated with this layer. Double-clicking on it brings up the Layer Styles dialog box.

Visibility toggle Click the icon to hide/reveal layer contents. Drag up/down this column to toggle visibility of many layers.

Vector mask This uses vector shapes, or paths created with the Pen tool, to define visible areas of the layer. This is the best option for when sharp, crisp edges are needed.

Layer mask A greyscale image that defines the transparency of a layer. Black areas of the mask hide the layer's pixels, white areas reveal them.

Active layer The active layer has a blue background behind the layer name and a double border around the thumbnail. Hold down Shift or Ctrl/Cmd to select multiple layers.

Adjustment layer A non-destructive way of making adjustments, eg Levels/Curves. Double-click the icon to change settings. The mask lets you apply the effect selectively.

Smart Object This layer is actually another Photoshop file that has been inserted as a Smart Object. It can be treated like a layer, but also updated outside of this file.

New Layer Click to add a blank layer above the active layer. Or drag an existing layer to this icon to create a copy. Hold Ctrl/Cmd to add a blank layer below the active layer. Hold Alt/Opt to get a Layer Properties box first.

Background layer The default layer of a new file. The background layer has limited edit ability; double-clicking it can turn it into a regular layer.

Trash Clicking here will delete the active layer. You can also click and drag one or many layers down to this icon to delete them.

Link Layers Select more than one layer and click this chain icon to link them together. Now if you move a layer, those linked to it will move too.

Add Layer Style This icon gives you a menu of layer styles to choose from. Select a style and then set the options as you see fit.

Adjustment Layer menu This menu allows you to select from a variety of methods to adjust your image. It creates an adjustment layer (with a mask!) above the active layer.

New Group Click to add a blank group above the active layer. Select and drag multiple layers onto this icon to group them. Hold Alt/Opt to get a Group Properties box first.

Resize palette Tired of scrolling down to see all your layers? Long layer names being truncated? Click and drag here to resize the palette.

Layers palette

If you look to the far right of the Layers tab you'll find a small, inconspicuous black triangle inside a circle. Clicking it reveals the Layers Palette menu. This gives quick access to many frequently used layer functions. Although these functions can be accessed through the regular menus, it's handy to have them available right here in the Layers palette where we find a good portion of our work being accomplished.

In our example image, the source photo of our model was cropped a bit too tight. We used several layers to extend her face, neck, hair and flowers. We added a gradient that matched her skin tone, then used the Smudge brush to blend it in, increasing her neck area to give more to work with. Extending her hair involved a good bit of using the Clone Stamp, as did some of the flower petals. The image of our model included many layers that

weren't crucial to the composition, so we selected them and used the Group Into New Smart Object command in the Palette menu. This created a separate Photoshop file containing the layers used to alter the model, but combined them into one layer. We could then treat the entire model image as one layer for things like colour adjustments and masking, but by having the layers in a separate file we can still make changes.

The beautiful swirls were created mostly as vector art in Illustrator. They were pasted into Photoshop as shape layers. Once all basic shapes were present, it was fairly simple to duplicate, scale, change colours and use the Pen tools to edit the shapes. This resulted in dozens of shape layers cluttering up the Layers palette. We didn't want to lose flexibility by merging them all, so we used the New Group From Layers command to put them into a tidy little folder.

Here the model photo has been extended and grouped into a Smart Object. The swirls have been pasted in from illustrator and grouped. The Swirls Group has a mask, to place the model in the midst of them.

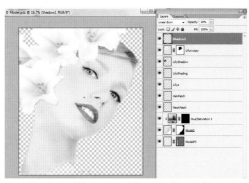

Extending the model pic meant adding several layers. They weren't important, but we didn't feel right merging them and sacrificing flexibility. Grouping them into a Smart Object was the ideal solution.

Hide behind a mask

Giving the user the power to separate an image into layers is sweet indeed, but the ability to use masks is the frosting on the Layers cake. Masks are what allow layer pixels to be transparent without being deleted. Sometimes a layer needs to appear to be in front of and behind another layer at the same time (like a vine wrapped around a letter). One solution would be to duplicate the vine layer, move the duplicate behind the text and select and delete the appropriate  pixels. By using a mask we achieve the same effect with a single layer and we don't destroy any pixels in the process. Notice how the vine is wrapped around the 'Y' – observe how the black part of the mask hides the vine pixels and makes it appear to be behind the text layer.

Layer masks
These use greyscale values to define amounts of transparency. Masks can be treated like greyscale layers and receive features used on regular layers. They can be painted on, use adjustments or even filters. Here we used a combination of the Gradient tool and Halftone feature to produce our image's background. Alt/Opt-click the mask thumbnail to see the greyscale pic.

Paths Vector masks define visible pixels by using paths drawn with the Pen, created by the  Shape tool or imported from another program. In this case, most swirls and vines were created in Illustrator and pasted in Photoshop as a shape layer, which uses vector masks. This way the paths were editable with the Pen and Direct Selection tools.

Layers Palette menu

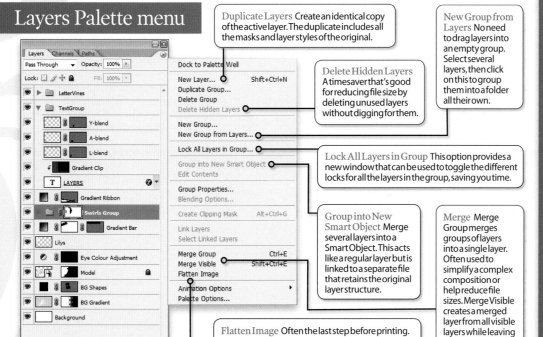

Duplicate Layers Create an identical copy of the active layer. The duplicate includes all the masks and layer styles of the original.

New Group from Layers No need to drag layers into an empty group. Select several layers, then click on this to group them into a folder all their own.

Delete Hidden Layers A timesaver that's good for reducing file size by deleting unused layers without digging for them.

Lock All Layers in Group This option provides a new window that can be used to toggle the different locks for all the layers in the group, saving you time.

Group into New Smart Object Merge several layers into a Smart Object. This acts like a regular layer but is linked to a separate file that retains the original layer structure.

Merge Merge Group merges groups of layers into a single layer. Often used to simplify a complex composition or help reduce file sizes. Merge Visible creates a merged layer from all visible layers while leaving all the hidden layers untouched.

Flatten Image Often the last step before printing. Combines the entire design into a single layer. Be cautious with this function as it destroys all layer info.

Add Layer Style

If masks are the frosting on the Layers cake, then Layer Styles would be the decorative candles on top. Styles provide an easy menu-driven method of creating a variety of effects that would be difficult to produce otherwise. Complex effects such as Bevel and Emboss are just a checkbox away. These styles all come with several options and slider bars, so you can tweak and customise to your heart's content! Not only that, but styles are also non-destructive so they can easily be altered again or removed completely.

In our main piece we used two very popular layer styles: Drop Shadow and Bevel & Emboss. You can see the Drop Shadow effect on the main text in the artwork. We softened the effect by decreasing the opacity and increasing the size and distance. The green swirl near the top left has the Bevel and Emboss style, but highly customised. The Size and Soften values were increased to give a rounded appearance to the vine, then Gloss Contour was altered to change the way the lighting fell on the shape. Finally, the Highlight and Shadow opacities were lowered to make the effect softer and more subtle.

We also used Layer Styles to change the blending modes to Overlay for the black swirls and then lowered the opacities to produce those interesting swirls that appear colourless except for enhancing the colour beneath them.

Right-clicking the Styles icon in the Layers palette produces a menu with even more functionality. This let us copy/paste Style settings from the green swirl to the tan swirl on the model's right. Photoshop makes it all so easy!

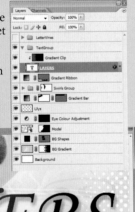

Drop Shadow is one of the most useful styles, but very overused. The trick is to use it to make a layer pop off the page without drawing attention to itself. Here, a soft, subtle shadow did the best job.

Layer Style menu

Style checkbox The checkmarks indicate which styles have been activated. This provides an easy method of toggling the styles on and off.

Blend mode The Style blend mode works the same way as the Layer blending mode. In this case the Shadow blend is set to Multiply to darken the pixels underneath the shadow.

Colour swatch Want your drop shadow to be red instead of black? No problem! Clicking this swatch enables you to change the colour of the effect.

New Style button If you have a setting you're particularly happy with and you know you'll want to use it again in a future work, click this button to save it as a preset.

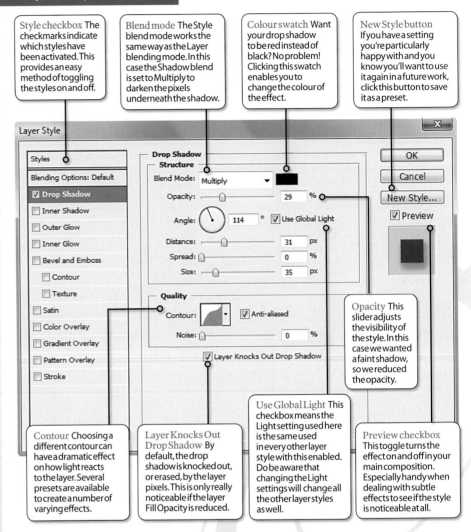

Contour Choosing a different contour can have a dramatic effect on how light reacts to the layer. Several presets are available to create a number of varying effects.

Layer Knocks Out Drop Shadow By default, the drop shadow is knocked out, or erased, by the layer pixels. This is only really noticeable if the layer Fill Opacity is reduced.

Use Global Light This checkbox means the Light setting used here is the same used in every other layer style with this enabled. Do be aware that changing the Light settings will change all the other layer styles as well.

Preview checkbox This toggle turns the effect on and off in your main composition. Especially handy when dealing with subtle effects to see if the style is noticeable at all.

Opacity This slider adjusts the visibility of the style. In this case we wanted a faint shadow, so we reduced the opacity.

Layer Style tips and tricks

Fill Opacity This reduces visibility of layer contents but doesn't affect the layer styles. To draw an easy circle, create a round shape with the Ellipse, add a Stroke layer style and drop the Fill Opacity. The shape's gone but the stroke remains!

Blend If This creates transparency based on the Black to White slider. To remove black pixels, slide the black handle into the centre. To remove white ones, slide the white handle in. Hold Alt/Opt to split the handle and create a smoother transition.

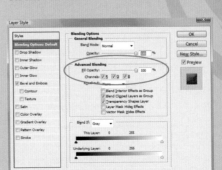

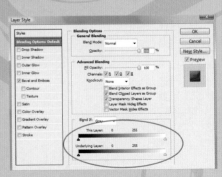

New Adjustment Layer

Adjustment layers provide yet another flexible means of making changes to an image without destroying the pixels. The adjustment's settings are held and can be re-edited at any time. Having these adjustments represented as a layer form also provides the advantage of being able to move them up and down in the layer stack, thereby changing the elements they affect. Another bonus is that these adjustment layers can be copied into other files, so you can easily use the same settings. They also come pre-fitted with a mask so you're able to restrict the adjustments to the elements you want.

The New Adjustment Layer menu gives many of the expected options such as Curves, Hue/Saturation and Levels. But there are also a couple there that might surprise you, such as Gradient Map, Photo Filter and Posterize. While not the most commonly used features, some of these can

produce very nice effects quickly and with a great deal of control.

In our design we used an adjustment layer to pop the model's eye colour. You didn't really think her eyes were that blue, did you? We added a Hue/Saturation adjustment layer on top of the model layer. We filled the mask with black to hide the effect completely and used a soft white brush to reveal the adjustment only on the irises. This technique then allowed us to tweak the eye colour to match with the blue swirls we used in the rest of the design.

While there's really much more to be said about Photoshop's layers (entire books have been written on the subject), we hope this brief rundown has at least revealed the usefulness of this primary function in our favourite pixel processor.

If you have any questions or comments, pop by at www.photoshopcreative.co.uk and you will find some friendly ears to talk to.

Merging layers

Sometimes you just start drowning in layers and need to combine them for any number of reasons. Yet if you flatten the image you lose all that wonderful flexibility you used Layers for in the first place! What's an artist to do? There's a 'secret' feature that will merge all visible layers into a new layer but leave the original layers untouched. It's called 'Stamp Visible' and it's not found in the menus. You have to use a hand-cramping hotkey to get it. On a PC hit Ctrl+Alt+Shift+E, and on a Mac hit Cmd+Opt+Shift+E. But remember, shhhh! It's a secret!

We utilised an adjustment layer of Hue/Saturation to enhance the blue of the model's eyes. The mask was used to restrict the effect to only her eyes and not the entire image. Making this change with an adjustment layer allowed us the flexibility to easily tweak the blue shade later on to match the blue in the swirls.

Layer Mask Hides Effects Ever have a drop shadow on a layer with a gradient mask? Ever wondered why it looks so awful? It's because the style is ignoring your mask by default. Click this inconspicuous checkbox to make the troubles go away.

Interactive shadow placement Don't fiddle with the angle and distance adjustments. There's an easier way! With the Layer Styles box still open, simply go to your design and then click and drag the shadow to where you want it.

Glowing shadow Want a shadow that radiates evenly? Use the Outer Glow style but change the glow colour to black and the blend mode to Multiply. It works the other way too. Change the drop shadow colour to white, and the mode to Screen to get a Drop Glow.

Add styles to Adjustment Layers A not-so-obvious advantage of having an adjustment in the form of a layer is the ability to add layer styles. Experiment with different combinations in order to achieve some very interesting and varied results!

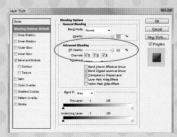

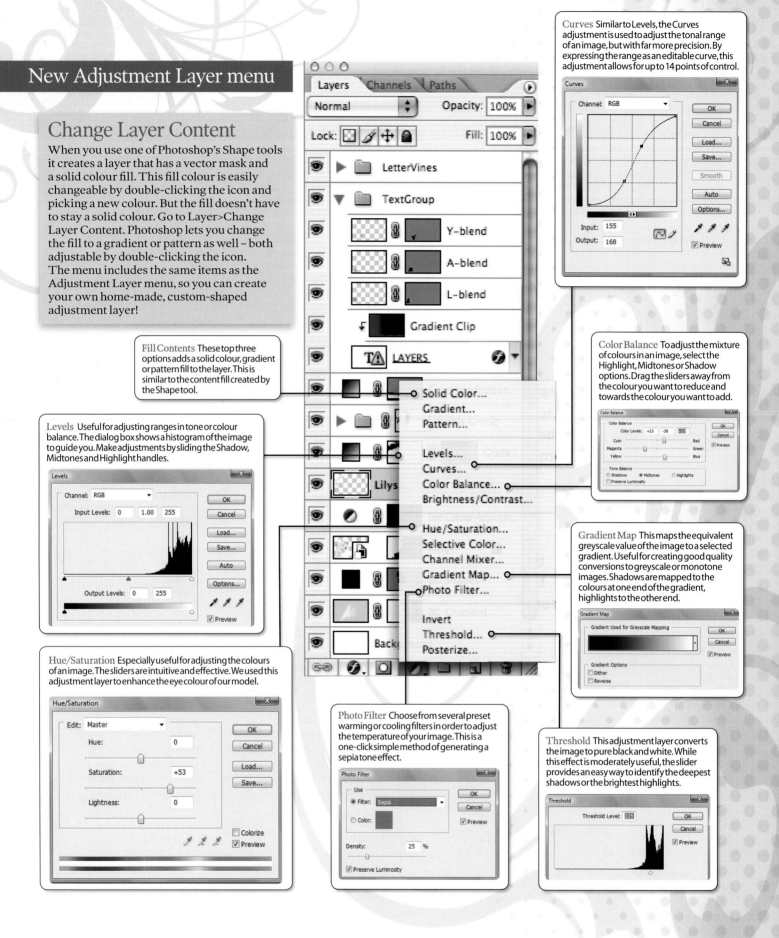

New Adjustment Layer menu

Change Layer Content

When you use one of Photoshop's Shape tools it creates a layer that has a vector mask and a solid colour fill. This fill colour is easily changeable by double-clicking the icon and picking a new colour. But the fill doesn't have to stay a solid colour. Go to Layer>Change Layer Content. Photoshop lets you change the fill to a gradient or pattern as well – both adjustable by double-clicking the icon. The menu includes the same items as the Adjustment Layer menu, so you can create your own home-made, custom-shaped adjustment layer!

Curves Similar to Levels, the Curves adjustment is used to adjust the tonal range of an image, but with far more precision. By expressing the range as an editable curve, this adjustment allows for up to 14 points of control.

Fill Contents These top three options adds a solid colour, gradient or pattern fill to the layer. This is similar to the content fill created by the Shape tool.

Color Balance To adjust the mixture of colours in an image, select the Highlight, Midtones or Shadow options. Drag the sliders away from the colour you want to reduce and towards the colour you want to add.

Levels Useful for adjusting ranges in tone or colour balance. The dialog box shows a histogram of the image to guide you. Make adjustments by sliding the Shadow, Midtones and Highlight handles.

Gradient Map This maps the equivalent greyscale value of the image to a selected gradient. Useful for creating good quality conversions to greyscale or monotone images. Shadows are mapped to the colours at one end of the gradient, highlights to the other end.

Hue/Saturation Especially useful for adjusting the colours of an image. The sliders are intuitive and effective. We used this adjustment layer to enhance the eye colour of our model.

Photo Filter Choose from several preset warming or cooling filters in order to adjust the temperature of your image. This is a one-click simple method of generating a sepia tone effect.

Threshold This adjustment layer converts the image to pure black and white. While this effect is moderately useful, the slider provides an easy way to identify the deepest shadows or the brightest highlights.

Blending mode portrait

Essentials

TIME TAKEN
35 minutes

YOUR EXPERT
Lora Barnes

ON THE DISC
Canvas Roll.psd
Brilliant
Sunset.jpg
Script.psd
Blk&Wh
pattern.psd
Stardust.tif
Cream
material.psd

With the help of Photoshop's amazing blend modes, creating a collaged portrait image couldn't be easier. The possibilities are endless!

Blending modes have to be one of the most revolutionary and powerful options to come with Photoshop. They allow layers to interact with one another and simply do what the name suggests – blend.

Usually you would work on each layer independently, and once you've placed a new layer on top of an existing one, you'd start to cover up what lies beneath. But with blending modes you can mix and merge the top layer with all those underneath it. Of course, you can change every layer's mode if you like and it doesn't matter where it sits in the layer stack, its effect will only interact with the ones below it and not the layers above it.

There's an enormous choice of blend modes, and each one makes a layer act in a different way. Some will make its dark pixels darker, for example Multiply, Darken and Color Burn. Others, such as Screen and Soft Light, will have the opposite effect. So we aren't just talking about making a layer see-through – blend modes have magical powers (well kind of!). The possibilities are endless and

you will find yourself being tempted to try each and every one of them on every layer.

However, the trick is to use them when you need to, and not to throw every mode at an image just because you can. Blending modes are a godsend to many an imaging problem, but if you over-use them things can start to look a little shocking, so beware!

> "The trick is to use them when you need to, and not to throw every mode at an image just because you can"

Please feel free to use your own portrait photo and textures, and to have a play around with the different modes as you follow the steps. It's all good fun!

GETTING STARTED
Setting the scene

Key Photoshop Skills Covered
What you'll learn

BLENDING MODES
ERASER TOOL
LASSO TOOL
MAGIC WAND
CHANNEL MIXER
GRADIENTS

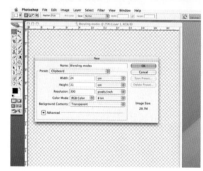

01 **Document setup** Create a new document by going to File>New. Change the dimensions to 24cm wide by 31cm high. Make the Resolution 300dpi, but make sure the Resample Image box is checked so this doesn't change the physical size of the document, and then choose RGB for the Color mode.

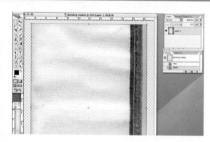

02 **Background texture** Open the 'Canvas Roll' image from the CD. Hit Select All and copy/paste the entire image into the new document. To make the image bleed right to the edges, go to Edit>Transform>Scale. While holding down Shift to keep the scale in proportion, drag the corner nodes out to the edges of the document. Make sure the texture fills the entire area then either hit Return or the Commit tick icon on the Properties bar.

03 **First splash of colour** Your next step is to open the 'Brilliant Sunset' image and, as before, click Select All then copy and paste the image into the new document and scale to fit the entire canvas area. Check the step picture above for a positional guide. Now the blending mode fun begins! Change this layer's mode to Multiply and watch the canvas texture show through.

WORKS WITH | PHOTOSHOP 7 ONWARDS

COMPOSITE CRAZY
Layer it up

04 Dampen down the hues Create a layer above the existing two and pick purple (R=130, G=24, B=78) for the foreground and a creamy yellow (R=249, G=248, B173) for the background. With the Gradient tool click-drag in a central line from the bottom to the top. Change this layer's Opacity to 64%. This will help with the final colour choice once the other layers are on top.

05 Another dimension To add a different kind of interest and texture to the image, open the 'Script' image from the CD and, as before, copy it over and scale it to fit. Now change the blending mode to Overlay. This allows the darker areas on this active layer to become even darker, and the midtones to fade back and become lighter, intermixing with the pixels beneath them.

06 Main focal point Time to add the focal point. We chose an iStock photo Ref no: iStock_000000877103XX, but you can use the shot on the disc or one of your own. As we're going for a collage/scrapbook look, don't worry about neatness when cutting out. Pick the Lasso tool, feather it by about 18px and roughly trace round the edges of your model. Copy/paste the selection into the main document.

07 Softening the edges Look at the main image for reference to position your model in the right place, and then choose the Eraser tool with the Airbrush Soft Round 300px brush selected. Use this to soften the edges of the woman around the hair, getting rid of as much background colour and as many hard edges as possible. Then change this layer's mode to Luminosity.

08 Detail Open the 'black and white pattern' file. Copy/paste and scale the image, then change its layer mode to Color Burn. This lets this layer take on the colours in the pixels below. As you can see, the black pattern has picked up the reds and pinks. With the same eraser as before, erase the pattern area covering the woman. Leave a few bits round the bottom/sides of her blouse. Do this on the script layer too.

09 Sprinkle some stardust Open the 'Stardust' file, hit Select All and copy the image over to the main document. We're going to add a painterly texture here, so once you've scaled up the image using Transform, change this layer blend mode to Soft Light. This will lighten the white areas and merge in the midtones so they become less visible.

10 Brighten it up Things are starting to get a bit murky, so to brighten the place up a bit, open the last of the files from the CD ('Cream material') and copy/paste it in at the top of the layer stack. Transform it to size and change the mode to Overlay. This will lighten the lightest colours beneath it.

FINAL FINESSE
Start to add the finishing touches

11 Autumnal leaves Now that you have a nice sandwich of different textures that work as a background, why not add a few additional aspects to the foreground? And as the colour theme in this piece is quite autumnal, we downloaded, for free, a beautiful photo of a red maple leaf from Stock exchange **www.sxc.hu** image ref: 869368_70810911. If you have your own leaf image, you can use that instead.

12 Leaf it out Open the leaf image in Photoshop, and using the Magic Wand tool select the black background and then go to Select>Inverse so you end up with the leaf selected. If you're using your own photo, cut out the leaf before copying and pasting it into the blending mode document.

13 Positional guide To begin, Transform> Scale the leaf so it's a bit smaller. Now, still using Transform, rotate the leaf so the stork is pointing slightly to the bottom right of the picture. Hit Return on your keyboard when you're happy with the angle and move the leaf up to the top right-hand corner so it's partially cropped off at the top.

14 Falling leaves Now to give the impression of leaves falling down the page, duplicate this layer and rotate this copy so the stalk is pointing to the bottom left-hand corner of the image (see the final artwork for a guide). Using Transform>Scale, reduce the size of this leaf a touch so it's smaller than the top leaf. Now duplicate the top leaf layer again and move this leaf copy to the bottom of the image.

15 A merger All the leaf layers' blend modes have been left on Normal so they look like they're on top of the background design. To add a different look and help merge the leaf motifs with the rest of the image, copy the smaller leaf and change its blend mode to Screen. Go to Transform>Horizontal Flip, move it to the bottom right corner and watch the white stems shine and the darker background pattern show through.

BRILLIANT COLOUR
Make the most of blending modes

Color Burn This blending mode will up the contrast and deepen the colours directly below the active layer by 'burning in' the pattern's darker pixels.

Overlay This is one of Photoshop's Light modes and will darken the darkest colours and lighten the lightest colours. With the script layer this resulted in the background colour fading and the writing becoming visibly stronger.

Screen Turning the leaf layer to Screen resulted in the layers underneath becoming lighter. It also made the leaf itself almost illuminated.

Multiply This blending mode is probably the most useful and most used mode in image compositing. It enables the darker areas of images/layers to combine. So this is great for making an image look like it's on a texture.

Erase the effect Use the Eraser tool set as the Heavy Smear Wax Crayon at an Opacity of 50%, and lightly rub out this area on the brilliant sunset layer to bring back a lighter yellow for more colour diversity in the image.

COLOUR CORRECT AND FRAME YOUR ARTWORK
With everything in place, finish it off with a bit of definition and a painterly frame

16 Pick the right tools for the job
Create a new layer at the top of the layer stack. Now choose the Brush tool, and in your Brush Preset picker click the little arrow at the top right and choose to append your list with the Dry Media brushes from the drop-down menu.

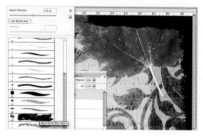

17 Paint in the frame To frame off the edges of your image, pick the Heavy Smear Wax Crayon brush and change its size to 100px. Before you start painting, Press 'D' on your keyboard to bring back the black and white default colours in your toolbar. With the brush loaded with black, brush in the frame lines around the outside edge. Don't worry about being neat.

18 Darken the mood
The image looks a bit washed out, so to get back a bit of contrast, make a new layer at the top of the stack, choose a foreground blue of R=120, G=197, B=255 and a background blue of R=173, G=244, B=255. Select the Gradient tool and click-drag from the top of the image to the bottom, then let go. Change this layer's blend mode to Color Burn.

19 Contrast on the face and hair
You could leave this image at this stage, as everything is working well together, but to show you how to vary the colour of a layer that's been blended, here's a quick variation to try. Duplicate the woman layer and place it above the original. Now change the mode to Soft Light and the layer's Opacity to 64%.

20 Mix it up Go to Image>Adjustments> Channel Mixer. Choose Red for the Output channel, and for the Source channels change Red to +42, Green to -74, Blue +20 and the Constant to +36, adding darker tones to shadows and green to yellows, for contrast. You can erase around the edges of the hair to soften the colour change. Also, go through the layers and erase areas of texture to break up the symmetry.

LAYER STRUCTURE
The making of a portrait

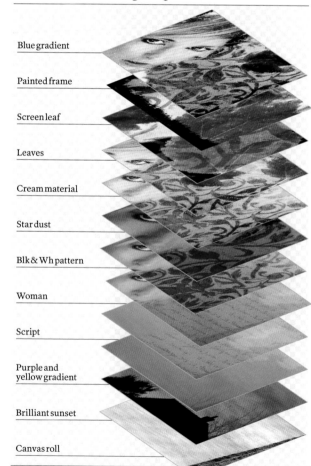

Blue gradient

Painted frame

Screen leaf

Leaves

Cream material

Star dust

Blk & Wh pattern

Woman

Script

Purple and yellow gradient

Brilliant sunset

Canvas roll

Watch and learn with CREATIVE LEARNING TV

Photoshop for beginners

Watch these videos and **YOU** can become a Photoshop master

90 minutes of video tutorials

Learn vital Photoshop skills such as these…

- Navigate the Photoshop interface
- Open files and make simple edits
- Clone out unwanted objects
- Adjust and boost colour
- Retouch old photos
- Use the selection tools
- Work with layers
- Print images like a pro

90 minutes of video tutorials for **£19.99** available from

www.creativelearning.tv

IMAGINE PUBLISHING

BEFORE

USING THE
PEN TOOL
FINE-TUNING
PATHS
ADVANCED
SELECTIONS
CREATING
MOTION BLUR

Create some dramatic motion blur effects

Set a static aircraft soaring into battle using Photoshop's selection, compositing and motion blur-creating techniques

Essentials

TIME TAKEN

60 minutes

YOUR EXPERT
George Cairns

ON THE DISC

PlaneBefore.jpg
Background.jpg
AttackPlane.psd

Our dramatic aerial dogfight would be a nightmare to try and shoot for real (especially as it's decades since these vintage aircraft last took to the skies).

Shooting any fast moving objects, whether planes or cars, can be a challenge for a variety of reasons. For starters you'll be lucky to capture the whole of your erratically moving vehicle in the frame, let alone spend time creating a perfect composition.

If you use a fast shutter speed setting on your camera, you'll freeze the moving object in time and lose the natural blur that adds a sense of movement to the vehicle. By using a slower shutter speed, you'll get plenty of motion blur but you'll lose valuable details on

the subject's surface. By adding motion blur to a static object in Photoshop, you can create the perfect balance between capturing a sense of movement and preserving important details.

The beauty of shooting a static object is that you can spend time setting up your shot to create a dramatic well-framed composition. We'll show you how to free our vintage warplane from the confines of a museum using a combination of selection and compositing techniques to place it in a more exciting scene. We'll then show you how to bring the shot to life by adding a variety of motion blur effects to the aircraft.

So, it's chocks away as we reach for the skies – as well as the Blur filters!

REACH FOR THE SKY
Free your subject from its background with help from the Pen tool

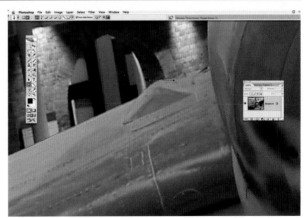

01 Choose your weapon As our source image has a very busy background, it makes sense to use the powerful Pen tool to select it. Hit P to activate the Pen tool. Before you start using it, pop up to the Options bar and make sure that the Paths icon has been selected.

02 Place points Go to the top of the wing and click to place your first anchor point. Place another point further along the wing. A path line will join the two anchor points together. You can select long straight shapes like the top of the wing with a few clicks.

03 Curve path When you get to a curved section of the plane's outline, keep the mouse held down after you place your latest anchor point. By dragging the cursor you can curve the path line between two anchor points. This is a powerful way to select curved shapes quickly.

PHOTOSHOP 7 ONWARDS | **WORKS WITH**

PERFECT PATHS
Fine-tune your path to make a perfect selection

Perfect paths

The more confident you get with the Pen tool, the fewer points you'll need to place to draw a path around objects like our aircraft. This enables you to isolate complex shapes from a busy background with ease. You can access your saved path at any time, even after closing then reopening the file. This means you can quickly generate a selection marquee at any stage in your project.

04 Complete the path Continue clicking anchor points around the plane's outline. Don't worry if the points aren't creating a perfect path, as you can fine-tune it later. To complete the path, click to place the last anchor point on top of the first. The path will turn into a solid line.

05 Edit the path Grab the Direct Selection tool from the toolbar (A). Click on the path and the anchor points will re-appear. You can use the Direct Selection tool to reposition the points to improve the shape of the path. You can also drag a point's Bezier curve handles to tidy curved path lines.

06 Missing the point? If the path still needs help selecting parts of the aircraft's outline, hold down the mouse over the Pen tool's section of the toolbar. A selection of Pen tool variants will pop up. Grab the Add Anchor Point tool. Click on any part of the path to add an extra point or two.

07 Paths palette Once you're happy with your path, go to the Paths palette. You'll see a thumbnail featuring a white plane-shaped workpath against a grey background. This is a temporary workpath. Click on the palette's pop-up menu icon and choose Save Path. Label it 'Plane Path'.

08 Copy... To turn the path into a selection, click on the Paths palette's pop-up menu icon and choose Make Selection. Choose a Feather Radius of 1 pixel and click OK. The 'marching ants' selection marquee will appear. Choose Edit>Copy to copy the selection into your computer's clipboard.

09 ...and paste Open the file 'Background.jpg'. Edit>Paste the selected aircraft into its new home. Press M to select the Move tool and position the plane as shown. To help manage your project efficiently, label the layer 'Main Plane'. Labelling your layers makes it easier to find specific components once the project gets more complex.

THE RADIAL BLUR DIALOG
Get to know the interface

Amount This slider lets you increase the amount of blur applied to your selection. It's easy to go over the top and blur an image beyond recognition.

Blur method The Spin blur is great for adding motion to car wheels (or propellers). Zoom makes the object blur dramatically towards the viewer.

Quality You'll get the smoothest blur effects by clicking the Best button, though the effect will take longer to render. Draft creates a quick but noisy-looking blur.

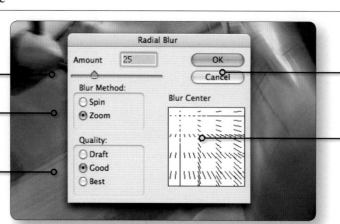

Reset If you want to start from square one, hold down the Alt key. The Cancel button will change to a Reset button. This will restore the dialog box to its default settings.

Perspective For a successful motion blur effect, click and drag here in order to change the angle and perspective of the blurred pixels so that they match the source image.

BRILLIANT BLURS
Add a sense of motion using a variety of blur effects

10 **Clone** The supporting cables on the wings betray the fact that the plane is really hanging in a museum. Press S to select the Clone Stamp tool. Alt-click to sample a clear patch of wing next to the cable. Click to spray the sampled pixels over the unwanted cable.

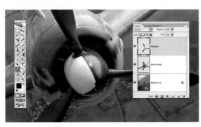

11 **Duplicate the propeller** Use the Pen tool (P) to draw a rough and ready path around the propeller. Right-click inside the path and pick Make>Selection from the pop-up menu. A marquee will appear. Go to Layer>New>Layer Via Copy. This will place the propeller on a layer of its own. Label the layer 'Propeller Blur'.

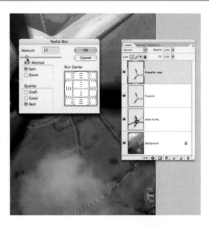

12 **Radial blur** Use the Elliptical Marquee (M) to make a circular selection round the duplicated propeller. In Filter>Blur>Radial Blur set Amount to 13, Blur Method to Spin, Quality to Best. Hit OK to add rotating motion blur. Emphasise this by dragging the Propeller layer thumbnail to the Create a New Layer icon to duplicate it.

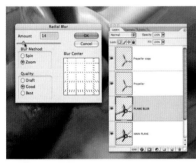

13 **Duplicate the plane** Now add some motion blur to the aircraft's fuselage. Drag the Main Plane thumbnail onto the Create a New Layer icon to create a copy. Label the copy 'Plane Blur.' Draw a rectangular marquee around the plane. Go to Filter>Blur>Radial Blur. Push the Blur Center up and left to make the blur match the position of the plane. Set Blur Method to Zoom. Finally, click OK.

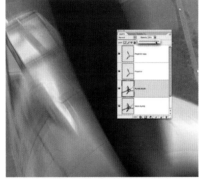

14 **Blend the blur** The Zoom blur obscures the texture detail on the plane's fuselage. Target the Plane Blur layer in the Layers palette and reduce its Opacity to 85%. This enables you to create a balance between motion blur and original texture details. Like most special effects, digital motion blur works best if it's subtle and not over the top.

15 **Selective erasing** Some sections of the aircraft will still be obscured by the motion blur layer. Grab the Eraser tool (E), set its Opacity to 33% and gently spray out some of the blur to reveal details like the engine air intake and cockpit. This helps restore details without losing the sense of speed.

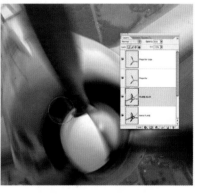

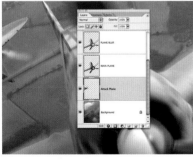

16 **On the attack** Now copy the pursuing plane from the file 'AttackPlane. psd' on your CD and paste it into the main project as a new layer. In the Layers palette, drag the Attack Plane layer's thumbnail below the Main Plane layer so that it appears to be flying behind the foreground aircraft.

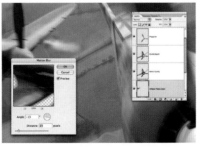

17 **Motion blur** Duplicate the Attack Plane layer. Go to Filter>Render>Motion Blur. Set the Blur Angle to -13 to make it follow the direction that the plane is flying in. Set Distance to 23 pixels to create a dramatic motion blur effect. Click OK. You can then erase sections of the blur layer to reveal details such as the bursts of machine gun fire on the layer beneath.

LAYER STRUCTURE
How we staged our dogfight

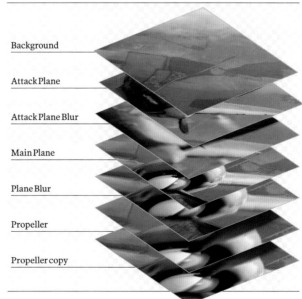

Background

Attack Plane

Attack Plane Blur

Main Plane

Plane Blur

Propeller

Propeller copy

Beginner's **Photoshop** **Photomanipulation**

ORIGINAL IMAGE

Photoshop atop a skyscraper

Re-create this classic Ebbets photograph using yourself, your family and your friends

If you have even seen the famous photograph by Charles Ebbets entitled 'Lunchtime atop a Skyscraper', you've probably been amazed at the apparent courage of the 11 men casually enjoying lunch while perched precariously hundreds of metres above the streets of New York.

If you viewed the photo in a public place, it's also likely that you heard somebody claim to be related to one of the men: "The second guy from the right is my great-great-uncle…" While this claim is almost impossible to verify, we thought we'd do one better and use Photoshop to place ourselves and friends in a photo of our own.

Over the next few pages you'll learn how to take these photographs of your friends and family (all safely on the ground) and place them into a similar shot of 1930s New York. Then we'll show you how to age the photo so it appears to actually be 70 years old.

So grab your digital camera and a willing group of family members – and let's start recreating this awe-inspiring scene.

Essentials

TIME TAKEN
1.5 hours

YOUR EXPERT
Kirk Nelson

ON THE DISC
CityBackDrop.jpg
BeamSource.jpg
Cutouts.jpg

JOIN THIS GROUP OF FEARLESS WORKERS
But don't risk life and limb to do so!

01 **A few good friends** Grab as many willing members of your family and friends as you can. You'll need a bench for them to sit on and a raised position to place your camera. The angle is rather important, because the background we'll use has already determined a high angle shot looking downward at the subject. Try to use a tripod and take several shots so you'll have plenty of material to work with. (Or if you want to use the same elements as we did here, we've included them in a single, easy to select file called 'Cutouts.jpg' on the CD.)

02 **Cut and paste** Open 'CityBackDrop.jpg' from the CD. Also open up the photos you've chosen from your photoshoot (or the 'Cutouts.jpg' we've supplied for you). With the Polygonal Lasso tool, roughly draw a selection around the elements you want. Copy and paste them into the background image as new layers. Don't fret over making the selection perfect – this is just to get the rough shapes into the composition. We'll tighten things up later.

03 **Heavy metal** We need an iron girder for the family to sit on. We created one using rectangular selections and the Gradient tool. You can try this for yourself or use ours, which is called 'BeamSource.jpg' on the CD. Once you have the beam, use the Perspective tool (Edit>Transform>Perspective) to line it up with the bench from the photos. After you've applied the transformation, move the beam layer below the layers with the family.

Key Photoshop Skills Covered
What you'll learn

SELECTION TECHNIQUES

VECTOR AND LAYER MASKS

GRADIENT MAP ADJUSTMENT LAYER

USING FILTERS TO AGE A PHOTOGRAPH

PHOTOSHOP CS AND ABOVE | **WORKS WITH**

Photoshoot

Although we provide you with the source images to recreate this project, we encourage you to snap your own pics of family and friends to use. Have your subjects remove modern items such as cell phones. Props like random tools, a lunchbox and food will help sell the illusion. We want the image to appear to be a candid 'moment in time' sort of shot, so make sure your friends aren't smiling at the camera!

Research

About the photographer

Charles C. Ebbets' most famous photos are of workers on a steel beam during the construction of Rockefeller Center in New York City. The image we used is the most famous. The pic of 11 men casually sharing lunch in such a precarious position has fascinated viewers for decades. Another photo in the series shows them napping on the same girder! To learn more about Ebbets' work, check out www.ebbetsphoto-graphics.com.

DON'T LOOK DOWN!
Your lunch break will never be the same again

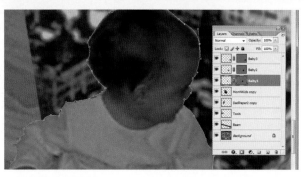

04 **The mighty Pen** Select the Pen tool and click the Path icon in the Options bar. For each person's layer use the Pen tool to create a path around that individual. Take your time and keep it tight. When you complete a path, go to Layer>Vector Mask>Current Path to use that path as a mask to cut the person out of their background. Feel free to use the Direct Selection tool to adjust the path as needed after you've applied the mask.

05 **One big happy family** When you're satisfied with the masking, select all the individual family layers by holding down Shift as you click on each thumbnail. Hit Ctrl+E (Cmd+E) to merge the layers together and name this new layer 'FamilyonBeam.'

06 **Black and white** There's one big thing that keeps the family layer from looking like it belongs in the pic: colour! One way to turn a colour layer into a black and white one is the Gradient Map. Go to Layer>New Adjustment Layer>Gradient Map. In the New Layer options hit Clipping Mask. In the Gradient Map options select a black to white gradient. This technique allows you to go back and fine-tune the gradient.

07 **Removing detail** Every modern digicam can capture details that eluded Ebbets and his equipment in the 1930s. Blurring the photo removes detail unilaterally; we want to remove some, but not all. With the FamilyonBeam layer selected, go to Filter>Other>Maximum. Give a Radius of 1 pixel and note how this blooms the light pixels, obscures fine details and even helps with the edge of the layer.

08 **Edge treatment** Right now, the edge is still too sharp to look natural. Use the Blur tool and a soft-edged brush to soften the edge. Use the Eraser tool with a small, fine brush to remove unwanted areas that the masking process missed.

09 **Growing hair** Notice how even with the blur, the areas around the hair still appear cut out? We can treat this by drawing in a few pieces of hair to break up that contour edge. A 1-pixel wide brush does the job nicely. If you don't have a tablet, open the Brushes palette and set the Size control to Fade at 50.

10 **Look at those curves** Let's add a Curves adjustment layer, the same way we added the Gradient Map back in step 6 (Layer>New Adjustment Layer> Curves). Be sure it's clipped to the FamilyonBeam layer too. Adjust the curve into a gentle 'S' shape to help pop the black and white shades.

SPEED UP TIME IN PHOTOSHOP

No need to wait decades for a photo to age – Photoshop can do that for you

11 Creating shadows Create
a 'Shadows' layer between the
Background and Family layers. Select a soft-
edged brush about 20 pixels wide and black
paint. Now gently paint in the shadows that fall
onto the beam.

12 Burning up Next, select the Burn
tool and then go to the FamilyonBeam
layer. Grab the same soft-edged brush and use
this tool to create shadows and darkened areas on
the family members. This is also a good method
of eliminating any pesky edge glow that you
might be experiencing.

13 Adding texture The beam is looking rather plain, even for an
old chunk of steel. Let's add some texture to it so the stark clean
shapes won't be distracting. Add a new layer just over the Beam layer
and name it 'BeamTexture.' Make sure your colours are set to the default
black and white and go to Filter>Render>Clouds. Now go to Filter>Brush
Strokes>Spatter. We used a Spray Radius of 15 and Smoothness of 6. Set this
layer's blending mode to Overlay. Clip this Texture layer to the Beam layer by
holding down Alt/Opt and clicking between the layer thumbnails.

14 Highlights Add a 'Highlights' layer
to the top of the stack. Hold down
Ctrl/Cmd+Shift, then click the thumbnails for the
Family and Beam layers. This creates a selection
in the shape of the two layers. Hit the Add Layer
Mask icon in the Layers palette to create a layer
mask in this shape. Use a soft brush and white
paint to add highlights to the edges of the people
and beam. The mask lets you easily paint only on
the foreground elements, so use the brush just
outside the edges, letting the rim apply the paint.

TURNING BACK TIME

The secrets behind the illusion

15 White glow Add a 'WhiteHalo'
layer just above the background layer.
Reduce the layer Opacity to around 45%. Now
using a large (about 200 pixels) white brush with
a soft edge, paint in a subtle halo around the
foreground elements. This contrast will help to
visually set them off from the background.

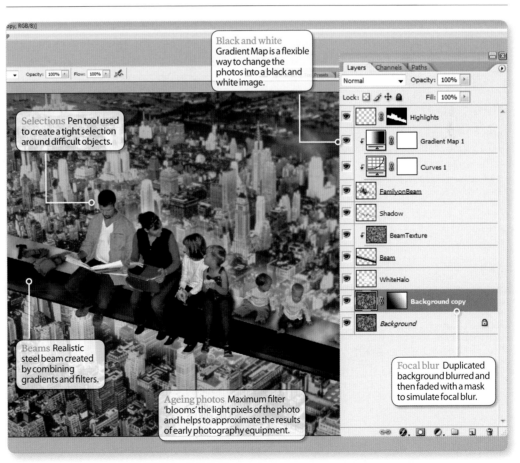

Black and white
Gradient Map is a flexible
way to change the
photos into a black and
white image.

Selections Pen tool used
to create a tight selection
around difficult objects.

Beams Realistic
steel beam created
by combining
gradients and filters.

Ageing photos Maximum filter
'blooms' the light pixels of the photo
and helps to approximate the results
of early photography equipment.

Focal blur Duplicated
background blurred and
then faded with a mask
to simulate focal blur.

FINISH UP THIS ICONIC SHOT
But find a safer place to take your break!

16 **Background blur** Now let's fade a background blur along the image. Click on the background layer and hit Ctrl+J (Cmd+J) to duplicate it. Go to Filter>Blur>Gaussian Blur and set it to 4 pixels. Add a mask to this layer and use the Gradient tool on the mask to fade the Blur layer, so the further away the buildings are, the more blurred they appear.

17 **Age the photo** To get the aged look, you could print the pic and leave it in a drawer for 60 years – or use a few Photoshop filters. Create a 'BGSmudge' layer just above the background copy layer. Set your foreground and background colours to a light and dark shade of mid-level grey. Go Filter>Render>Clouds. Follow with Filter>Noise>Add Noise and use 8% as the setting, then Filter>Other>Maximum set at 1px. Change the blend mode to Hard Light, add a layer mask and use the Gradient tool to vertically fade this layer in towards the centre of the image.

18 **Add film grain** At the top of the layer stack, add another layer and name it 'Grain.' With your colours set to the default again, go to Filter>Render>Fibers – the default settings should work just fine. Set this layer's blending mode to Soft Light to add an aged film grain effect to the image.

19 **Antique colours** Click the Create New Fill Layer icon at the foot of the Layers palette and select Gradient. From the Gradient menu, select the Copper option and click OK. Now change the blending mode to Color and reduce the Opacity to around 40% to give the image an antique sepia tone.

20 **Photo vignette** Select the top layer and hit Ctrl+Shift+Alt+E (or Cmd+Opt+Shift+E) to merge the layers at the top of the stack. Make sure this new layer is active and go to Filter>Distort>Lens Correction. In the dialog, set Vignette Amount to +53, and make sure the edge is set to Transparency. Hit OK and you're done!

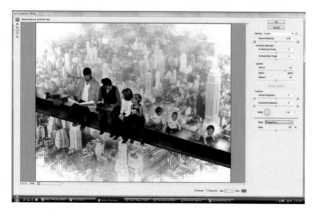

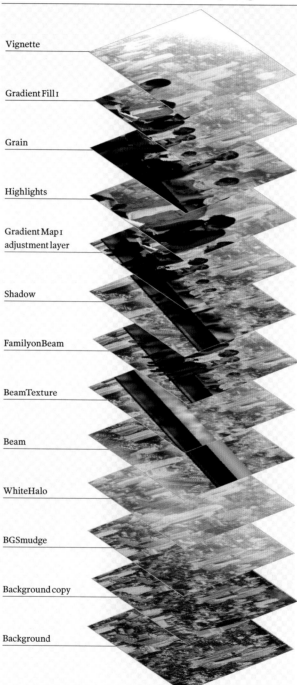

Vignette

Gradient Fill 1

Grain

Highlights

Gradient Map 1 adjustment layer

Shadow

FamilyonBeam

BeamTexture

Beam

WhiteHalo

BGSmudge

Background copy

Background

Free stuff!

Photoshop Daily is a new site dedicated to bringing the latest news, gossip and inspiration to the Photoshop community. Oh, and did we also mention that there's free stuff too?!

Visit today!

Photoshop Daily news updates
Get the latest stories for Photoshop users

Features
Read about Photoshop techniques and other creative skills

Reviews
Find out about the best Photoshop peripherals

Get involved!
Leave your comments and suggestions

Free video tutorials
Learn essential Photoshop skills with the help of regular video tutorials

Daily freebies
Download free Photoshop resources, such as brushes, texture packs, royalty-free stock photos and desktops

Podcasts
Interviews with Photoshop masters

www.photoshopdaily.co.uk

Chapter 4
Retouch your photos

Give your portraits a polished sheen

Tip

Small bites

For general retouches, you'll find that you get the best results from retouching techniques if you use a lot of tools at small amounts. A touch of sharpening here, a bit of cloning there – it will all add up to a perfectly edited image.

Quick-start retouching tutorial on the CD

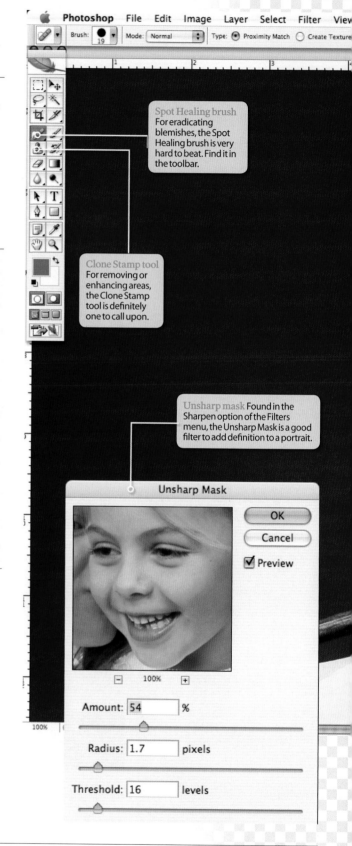

Spot Healing brush For eradicating blemishes, the Spot Healing brush is very hard to beat. Find it in the toolbar.

Clone Stamp tool For removing or enhancing areas, the Clone Stamp tool is definitely one to call upon.

Unsharp mask Found in the Sharpen option of the Filters menu, the Unsharp Mask is a good filter to add definition to a portrait.

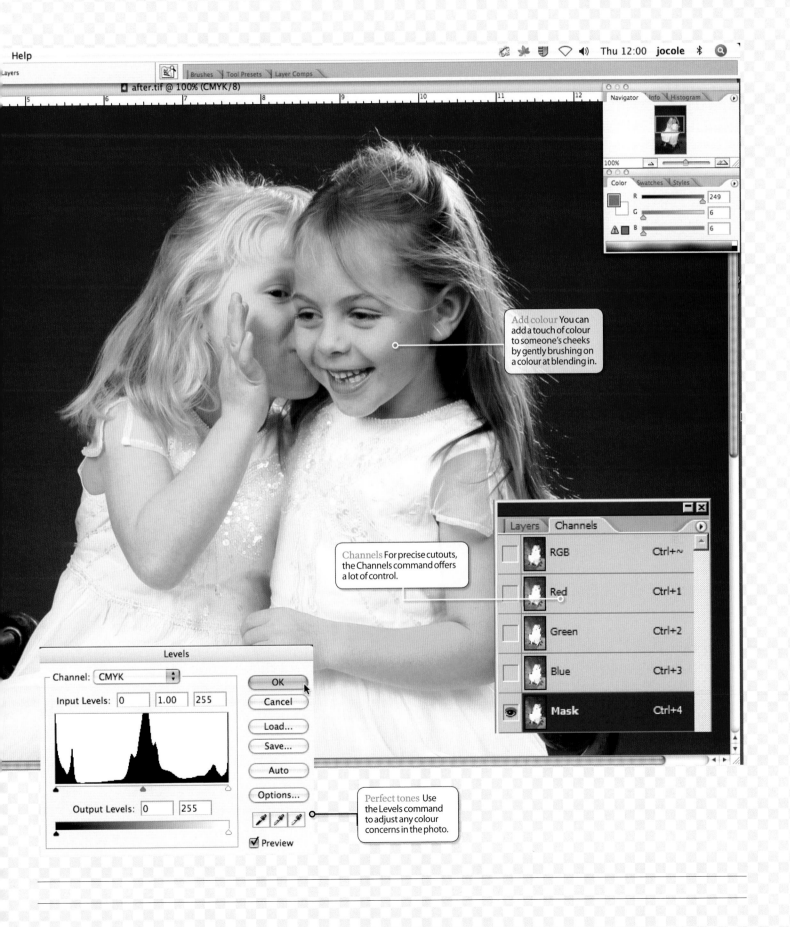

Add colour You can add a touch of colour to someone's cheeks by gently brushing on a colour at blending in.

Channels For precise cutouts, the Channels command offers a lot of control.

Perfect tones Use the Levels command to adjust any colour concerns in the photo.

Retouching photos

Add a professional touch to your portraits

Essentials

YOUR EXPERT
Jo Cole

ON THE DISC
Quick-start guide to retouching tools on the CD

The art of retouching photos has received a hard press, but the truth is we all want to look our best and a few edits here and there can work wonders for the ego!

Photoshop is obviously the tool of choice for professional retouchers and there is nothing to stop you using the same tools as the pros to give your portrait shots a desirable veneer.

Before you flick past in horror, we aren't going to suggest you spend your life airbrushing through your family photos. Even five-minute edits can suddenly bring a portrait to life and Photoshop Elements users will find a lot of automated options for retouching tasks. However, we're going to look at the manual tools here and show you how easy it is to create the maximum impact.

Common retouching tasks will focus on the face, whether it's smoothing out skin or doing a touch of spot and blemish removal. Whitening the eyes or teeth is another easy edit that can really make a difference, as can a simple colour correction command. There's no reason why you can't also employ a touch of Hollywood glamour by creating a subtle soft focus effect.

We're going to look at all of these tasks in this chapter, in addition to a few other essential tricks. The most important thing to remember, though, is keep it subtle. Like it or not, wrinkles and wobbly bits give us character and if you wade in with a virtual plastic surgeon's knife, you won't improve an image. A light touch here and there is all you need for the best results.

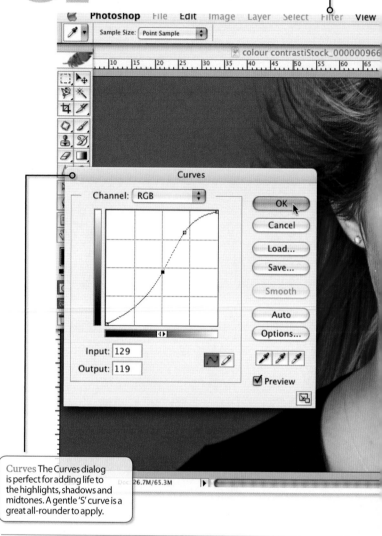

Curves The Curves dialog is perfect for adding life to the highlights, shadows and midtones. A gentle 'S' curve is a great all-rounder to apply.

 ## RED EYE TOOL
Cast out the demon eye!

Even with fancy camera settings, red eye is a really common problem that is thankfully very easy to fix. Red eye is caused by a camera's flash reflecting in a person's retina and makes the subject look as though they have just stepped out of a horror movie. Photoshop has a useful tool for the job in the guide of the Red Eye tool. Simply pick the tool from the toolbar, place it over the offending eye and click. If the red eye puts up a fight and refuses to

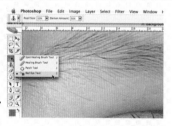

move, simply undo the edit and then use the Pupil Size and Darken Pupil settings to make adjustments.

 ## WHITEN TEETH AND EYES
Less is definitely more

No doubt you have all seen celebrity pictures where the eyes and teeth are so white they practically glow. This is definitely not a look to go for! The best way to make these sorts of edits is by using the Curves command. That way you have plenty of control over what it is you are doing. Simply select the white area of the eye or the teeth, open up the Curves dialog, pick highlights and then lighten the areas. If you aren't

confident with selecting areas, you could also use the Dodge tool and paint over the areas to lighten.

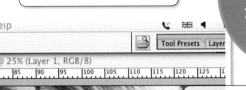

Edge contrast The Unsharp Mask command is worth applying to a portrait, even if it's just at a small amount. It helps to define features.

Quick-start retouching tutorial on the CD

Before and after Here you can see how the image has improved from the original. By employing obvious tools in addition to some sneaky additions, it's possible to turn flat portraits into something far more dramatic.

Tip

Soft focus effects

When done correctly, a small amount of blur can improve the right kind of image. Before you scoot up to the Blur filters menu, though, try out the Blur tool from the toolbar. This allows you to 'paint' on the blur, which is perfect for making sure you only affect the parts that you want.

SPOT HEALING BRUSH
Remove blemishes the easy way

Did an unwelcome spot ruin your prom photo? No need to fear, the Spot Healing Brush tool lives up to its name by quickly removing blemishes and other imperfections. Here's how it works...

Pick a brush size
Introducing... The Spot Healing Brush tool is found in the toolbox, nestled with the Healing Brush, Patch and Red Eye tools. Once selected, pick a brush size that's slightly larger than the area to be edited from the brush options at the top of the workspace area. This lets you perform a one-click fix, which will ultimately give you the most accurate results.

The options
Set the tool to suit If you are working on a photo with noise or film grain, make sure that you choose Replace. The Proximity Match option uses pixels from around the edge of a selection to use as a patch. The Create Texture option uses all the pixels in the selection to fix the area. Experiment with the different options to get the most from the tool.

All layers
Using the lot You will achieve the best results if you select the Use All Layers option in the Options bar at the top of the screen, as this uses information found throughout the image and not just on the individual layer that you have selected at the time. Finally, to make the fix, click over the area that you want to sort out and the tool will work its magic. Simple!

TRANSFORM AND LIQUIFY
Digital cosmetic surgery

The Transform tools are usually called upon when dealing with photomanipulations, as you can scale, distort and twist a selection with ease, though they have their uses here too. The Liquify filter is normally used in making a subject look like a caricature of themselves, with bulgy eyes or exaggerated features. It might seem odd to mention them as retouching tools, but they are fantastic for sucking areas in,

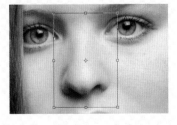

making other areas more pronounced and basically performing a touch of minor Photoshop surgery!

ADVANCED SELECTIONS
Precision counts

We have already touched upon the various many selection methods in other chapters throughout this book, but when it comes to photo retouching, you need the delta force of selection methods. For this, the Channels palette is hard to beat and is actually quite easy to do once you get used to using it for selections. With just a bit of patience, you can isolate tricky objects such as flyaway hair and then make what adjustments need to be

made without spending hours trying to cut out individual strands with the Pen tool, for example.

Quick route to retouching

A professional style makeover is only 60 minutes away with a bit of basic knowledge and a willing subject!

In this tutorial we've got a speedy makeover for this lucky young lady, and the principles that we'll utilise here can really be applied to any portrait subject.

It will take you around an hour to complete – at least if you're reasonably au fait with Photoshop's keyboard shortcuts and the basics of non-destructive edits.

We say 'non-destructive' because what we achieve here is done through using adjustment layers, blank layers in the case of some tools, and duplicates of areas of the background layer, rather than working directly on the background layer with our tools and image adjustments.

This might perhaps seem to contradict our pledge for a miraculously quick makeover, but if you're familiar with adjustment layers, you'll already have realised that working any other way is false economy. With a job like this, mistakes are inevitable, and as the History palette only contains a limited number of steps to undo, you'll quickly find yourself having to correct mistakes that you can't go back on.

If you haven't yet quite grasped the principles behind adjustment layers, this is the perfect time to start learning – and you'll find them very quickly by clicking the half-black, half-white circle at the bottom of the Layers palette.

BEFORE

AFTER

Key Photoshop Skills Covered

What you'll learn

CURVES
LEVELS
ADJUSTMENT LAYERS
SPOT HEALING BRUSH
CLONE STAMP
SELECTIONS
PATCH TOOL

Essentials

TIME TAKEN
1 hour

YOUR EXPERT
Matthew Smith

ON THE DISC
Starter.jpg

WORKS WITH | PHOTOSHOP CS AND ABOVE

QUICK COLOUR CORRECTION
Get the basics sorted

01 Levels contrast
Open up the 'starter.jpg' file from the CD. The image looks a little flat, so beef things up a bit by setting the white and black points using the Levels dialog. Hold down Alt (PC) or Option (Mac) and move the black slider inwards until you see colour appear, then move it back so it just disappears. Now do the same with the white slider.

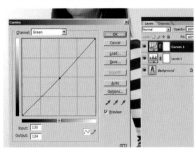

02 Curves for colour The image also has a slight green colour cast, so we add a Curves adjustment layer and select Green from the drop-down menu instead of RGB. Using the mid-point on the Curves line, we drag downwards very slightly to reduce green and increase magenta, until the cast looks neutralised.

Expert Tip

Eye wrinkle removal
Circle an area underneath the wrinkles (and bigger than the wrinkles) with the Freehand Lasso. Hit Q to enter Quick Mask mode and soften the edges heavily with Gaussian Blur. Hit Q again. Select the background layer and float the selection with Ctrl/Apple+J. Hit V for the Move tool and move the new skin over the wrinkles. Take a big soft black brush and slowly work away at the edges of the new skin area until only the wrinkles are covered.

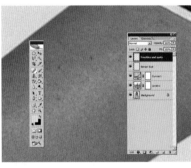

03 Sensor dust An initial inspection reveals there is some sensor dust on the image that needs removing. We create a new layer, and select the Spot Healing brush (Healing brush if you have an early version of Photoshop). We select Sample All Layers in the Tool Options bar, and then slowly remove the dust bit by bit.

04 Clone required Some sensor dust is found on areas with changing contrast and colour. The Spot Healing brush brings blue into the white area of the top, so instead we select the area with the Polygonal Lasso to protect the edges, and use the Clone Stamp on the same layer (also set to Sample All Layers).

05 Freckles and spots Now we're going to create another new layer, name it appropriately and perform the same Spot Healing brush and Clone Stamp work with freckles and spots, and we can also do any neck lines this way.

Alert!

Be subtle
The art of retouching is to make an image look beautiful but unretouched! The corrections we've made here might even be too strong for some people's tastes. In particular, avoid over-whitening eyes and teeth, and don't use the Healing and Patch tools repeatedly. If it doesn't look good, undo and try again – don't keep working on the same area or you'll kill detail! If an area does look overly smooth, throw some noise in with Add Noise at 2-3px Radius.

06 Lazy eye
Notice the right eye is slightly lazy – there's too much of the white eye showing, making the girl look a little cross-eyed. The solution is to copy the left eye across. Use the Marquee tool to make a rough selection of the left eye, make sure the background layer is selected and then hit Ctrl/Apple+J for Layer via Copy.

07 Masking the new eye Rename the new layer, and hit V to access the Move tool. Drag the new eye across so it sits over the lazy eye. Next, add a layer mask by clicking the Add Layer Mask icon in the Layers palette, click Ctrl/Apple+I to invert it and paint only the eye centre back in with a soft black brush.

SEE TO THE EYES
The all-important sparkle factor

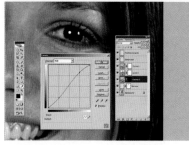

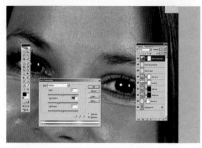

08 Eye work Next, we're going to do some work on the eyes. Make a selection around the right eye with a Polygonal Lasso, or freehand if you've a steady hand – making sure not to include any of the eyelid or eye bag. Next, Select>Feather about 3 pixels.

09 Eye boost Now we've got our selection, we select a Curves adjustment layer from the Layers palette which we'll later rename 'Right Eye'. As the eye was selected, the layer is loaded with a layer mask, which means our adjustment works only on the eye. We darken shadows a touch, and boost highlights a little more.

10 Red-eye We do the same with the left eye. The right eye still has a bit of redness showing, so we add a Hue/Saturation adjustment layer, select red from the drop-down menu, and drop Saturation to -30. We then select the layer mask on the Hue/Saturation layer, invert it (Ctrl/Cmd+I) and paint in just the red area with a soft white brush.

KEY AREAS
Focus on the eyes, teeth, crease lines and specular highlights

Whenever you open up a portrait, there are certain key areas that once improved will make the photo a gazillion times better. Eyes, wrinkles, glare and teeth are always a good starting point, so here's a look at how we went about editing our lady.

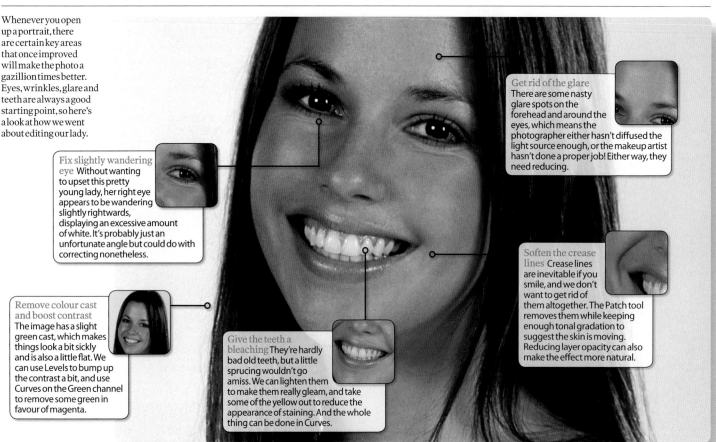

Get rid of the glare There are some nasty glare spots on the forehead and around the eyes, which means the photographer either hasn't diffused the light source enough, or the makeup artist hasn't done a proper job! Either way, they need reducing.

Fix slightly wandering eye Without wanting to upset this pretty young lady, her right eye appears to be wandering slightly rightwards, displaying an excessive amount of white. It's probably just an unfortunate angle but could do with correcting nonetheless.

Remove colour cast and boost contrast The image has a slight green cast, which makes things look a bit sickly and is also a little flat. We can use Levels to bump up the contrast a bit, and use Curves on the Green channel to remove some green in favour of magenta.

Give the teeth a bleaching They're hardly bad old teeth, but a little sprucing wouldn't go amiss. We can lighten them to make them really gleam, and take some of the yellow out to reduce the appearance of staining. And the whole thing can be done in Curves.

Soften the crease lines Crease lines are inevitable if you smile, and we don't want to get rid of them altogether. The Patch tool removes them while keeping enough tonal gradation to suggest the skin is moving. Reducing layer opacity can also make the effect more natural.

IRON OUT THE CREASES
Putting the Patch tool to work

11 Floating the face
Next, we're going to use the Patch tool to soften the crease lines from the smile a little. The Patch tool can't be used with Sample All Layers, so we select the background layer, marquee the face off and float it to a new layer with Ctrl/Apple+J for Layer via Copy.

12 Crease line removal Draw around a crease line with the Patch tool, leaving space around the edges, then move the Patch tool inside the selection and drag it outwards to a piece of clean skin. The crease line disappears! Do the same for each wrinkle. You can lower the layer opacity if you want to reduce the effect.

13 Glare removal We now want to get rid of some of the nasty specular highlights on the face. We marquee the face, select the background layer and Ctrl/Apple+J again, so that we've got separate control over the crease lines. We use the Patch tool again for the smaller areas on the cheeks and chin.

14 Forehead glare The bigger areas on the forehead are too big for the Patch tool. Instead, select the soft-edged brush, set to Darken, and 10% Opacity. Sample from a colour outside of the glare using the Alt /Option-click method, and paint slowly over the glare. Sample another colour and repeat. Keep repeating until finished.

15 Polishing teeth Add a Curves adjustment layer, and take up the highlights while fixing the shadows in place so they don't move. Select blue from the drop-down menu and increase it slightly to take out the yellow. Select the layer mask and Ctrl/Apple+I to invert it, then brush the teeth back in with a soft white brush.

TOOL TIP
Patch tool strategies

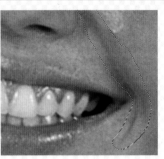

If you want to use the Patch tool on larger areas but there's a conflicting colour close by, you'll get some colour in between the two. The way to avoid this is to make a selection that avoids the contrasting colour but includes the wrinkle and enough clean info to sample from. Float the selection to a new layer (Ctrl/Apple+J) and apply the Patch tool from there.

THE LAYER STRUCTURE
Makeover secrets revealed

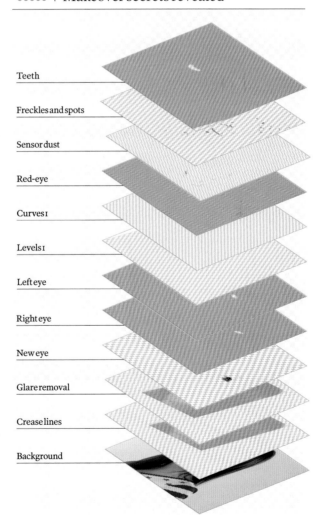

Teeth

Freckles and spots

Sensor dust

Red-eye

Curves 1

Levels 1

Left eye

Right eye

New eye

Glare removal

Crease lines

Background

Accentuate your subject's eyes

The eyes deserve some careful retouch work. They're the windows to your portrait and can make or break an image!

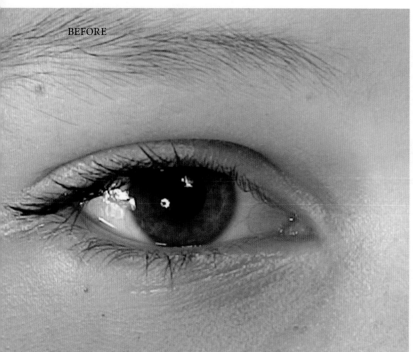

BEFORE

AFTER

Essentials

TIME TAKEN
Approximately 20 minutes

YOUR EXPERT
Matthew Smith

ON THE DISC
eye before.tif

Whenever we meet or greet an individual, the first thing we look at is his or her eyes. This is a primitive instinct, and one that none of us can shake. The same habit is extended to portraits – show anyone a picture portrait, photograph or otherwise, and the first thing they'll be drawn to is the eyes. Only then will they glance around the rest of the portrait, taking in other aspects of the person such as the clothes, hair and teeth, and the background to the shot.

It's for this reason that it's important to make the most of the eyes in our portraits, because although the surrounding area is, of course, also important, that initial glance will produce the sort of subconscious judgement that will make the viewer feel warm or cool towards your image. Present the viewer with open, sparkling, colourful eyes, and they're more likely to appreciate the portrait as a whole.

That's not to say that fantastic eyes can make up for an otherwise poorly composed, badly retouched image, but

it certainly gives you a head start and can help a good-looking image be perceived as a great-looking one.

The technique we've got for you here is an altogether thorough one, and covers pretty much every single aspect of the eye, paying attention to each individually, and giving each its own adjustment layer so the effects can be knocked back individually at a later stage with layer opacity if necessary.

If you're not used to using adjustment layers, don't panic. It's little different from applying adjustments such as curves in the usual way. You just click the half-black, half-white circle at the bottom of the Layers palette and select your adjustment. You'll get a new layer that affects layers with image information below (not other adjustment layers). Every layer comes with its own layer mask, which is the white rectangle to the right of the main adjustment icon, and you simply click it to select it. By double-clicking the layer icon itself, you can get back into the adjustment dialog and alter your adjustments. Genius.

WORKS WITH | PHOTOSHOP 7.0 AND ABOVE

THE GENERAL CLEAN-UP
Tidy up around the edges

Tip

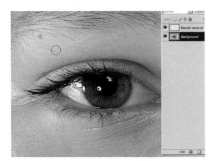

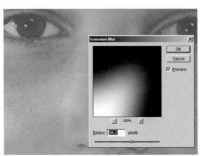

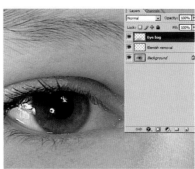

01 Spotting out blemishes We'll start with a little clean-up around the eyes to spot any small marks or freckles. The Spot Healing brush is the best choice for this unless you're close to any drastic changes in lightness or colour information, in which case use the Clone Stamp. Use both on a new layer with the Sample All Layers box checked in the Tool Options bar.

02 Selecting wrinkle-free skin Next, we want to remove the eye bags and wrinkles. They're too close to the eye to use Healing brushes, so we're going to make a Polygonal Lasso (L) selection around a clean area of skin underneath the eye. Press Q to enter Quick Mask mode and use Gaussian Blur to feather this selection quite strongly.

03 Floating and moving Press Q to get back to Normal mode and then Ctrl/Apple+J to float the selection to a new layer. Next, hit V to access the Move tool, and click and drag the feathered patch of skin over the eye bag, lining up the centres.

Mesmerising eyes
If you're more concerned with impact than maintaining realism, try increasing the Lightness in the Hue/Saturation adjustment instead of decreasing it. You can use this trick whether or not you're changing eye colour. The lighter shade of brown, blue or green eyes can produce a sort of mesmerising wolf-eye effect. A small number of people actually do have eyes this striking, so it can still look realistic if done subtly.

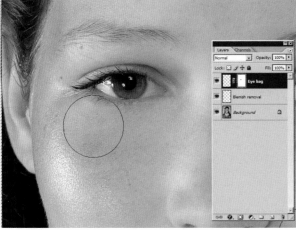

04 Blending new info Click the Add Layer Mask icon at the bottom of the Layers palette, then take a large black brush at 0% Hardness and use the very outer reach of the brush to remove any excess information from the bottom and sides so it blends nicely with the information below.

05 Painting the eye back in Now take a smaller, harder black brush, and paint any information out that has strayed into the eye itself. It's important that the new information blends well, so if it doesn't, try setting the layer blending mode to Luminosity, and/or dropping the layer opacity a little bit.

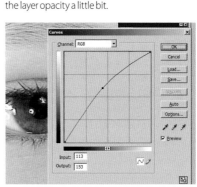

06 Producing an eye-socket Darkening the area a little can help show a natural eye socket. Use a Levels adjustment layer set to Luminosity mode, and move the slider slightly right to darken. Now select the mask and use Ctrl/Apple+I to invert it, then paint over the newly clean area to darken it ever so slightly.

07 Whitening with curves Now we're going to lighten the whites of the eye a little. We add a Curves adjustment layer, and push up the curve with a single point – it doesn't matter where it's placed. We then select the layer mask and use Ctrl/Apple+I to invert it.

EYE TECHNIQUES
We've used mostly basics, with little nuggets thrown in

IT'S ALL WHITE
Gleaming eyeballs are a moment away

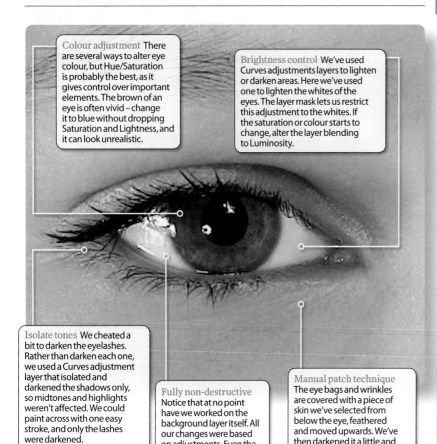

Colour adjustment There are several ways to alter eye colour, but Hue/Saturation is probably the best, as it gives control over important elements. The brown of an eye is often vivid – change it to blue without dropping Saturation and Lightness, and it can look unrealistic.

Brightness control We've used Curves adjustments layers to lighten or darken areas. Here we've used one to lighten the whites of the eyes. The layer mask lets us restrict this adjustment to the whites. If the saturation or colour starts to change, alter the layer blending to Luminosity.

Isolate tones We cheated a bit to darken the eyelashes. Rather than darken each one, we used a Curves adjustment layer that isolated and darkened the shadows only, so midtones and highlights weren't affected. We could paint across with one easy stroke, and only the lashes were darkened.

Fully non-destructive Notice that at no point have we worked on the background layer itself. All our changes were based on adjustments. Even the cloning out of veins in the eye was achieved using a separate layer, and setting the Clone Stamp tool to Sample All Layers.

Manual patch technique The eye bags and wrinkles are covered with a piece of skin we've selected from below the eye, feathered and moved upwards. We've then darkened it a little and dropped its opacity for a more realistic blend. Because of the proximity of the eye itself, the Healing tools are not a sensible option.

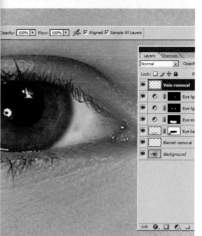

08 **Painting in the curve** We then zoom in with Ctrl/ Apple and+ and use a white brush set to 90% Hardness and 100% Opacity on the layer mask to paint the brightness increase into the whites of the eye only. If the inner white is a bit darker, add another Curves layer and boost this a little separately.

09 **Cloning out the veins** Now we want to remove the evidence of any veins in the eye. Add a new layer and take the Clone Stamp tool (S) set to Lighten mode and Sample All Layers. Sample carefully and regularly with Alt/ Option either side of the veins to ensure that no pattern is replicated, and click to remove the veins.

10 **Brushing out the veins** If the veins are very prominent and there's not enough of a clean area to clone from, we can use the Brush tool instead on the same newly created layer. We set the Brush tool to Lighten and about 30% Opacity, then sample a clean area of colour with Alt/Option and brush carefully over the veins.

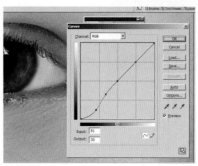

11 **Clever curves for eyelashes** Now we want to give a little more prominence to the eyelashes. We add another Curves adjustment layer, and fix points at the highlight and midtones so they don't move. We drop the shadows point and watch carefully to see if the skin around the eyelashes is affected.

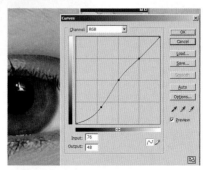

12 **Tweaking our clever curves** If the skin is darkened as well as the eyelashes, we need to divide the shadow area into two with another point, moving our new point upwards a little and manipulating our lower point to ensure the eyelashes are still darkened.

THE BIG FINISH
Making the eyes sparkle

13 Accentuate the eyelashes
Now select the layer mask and use Ctrl/Apple+I to invert it. Take a white brush at around 60% Hardness and 100% Opacity, and brush over the eyelashes at the top and bottom of the eye. The skin below should remain unaffected.

EXPERT TIP
The whole picture

Pay lots of attention to the contrast of surrounding information. If you have quite a flat-looking image with fairly low contrast, then an eye with bright whites, dark pupils and dark eyelashes is definitely going to stand out – but a little too much. It's just not going to look real. Either knock the effects back with the Layer Opacity function, or adjust the contrast of the rest of the image to suit.

EYE ON THE PRIZE
How your layers should look

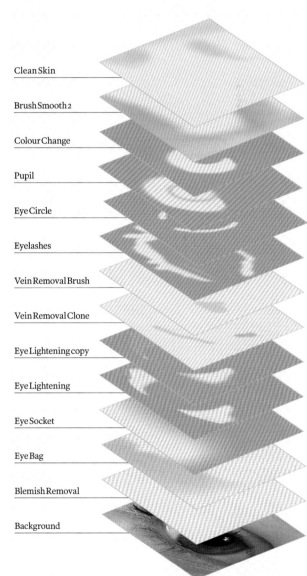

Clean Skin
Brush Smooth 2
Colour Change
Pupil
Eye Circle
Eyelashes
Vein Removal Brush
Vein Removal Clone
Eye Lightening copy
Eye Lightening
Eye Socket
Eye Bag
Blemish Removal
Background

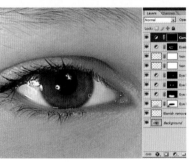

14 Boosting eye impact
Now we'll use a further Curves adjustment layer with a very subtle amount of darkening, with a similar setup so only shadows are affected. Invert the layer mask again, and this time use a white brush at 70% Hardness to paint over the thin circle line that separates the iris from the white of the eye.

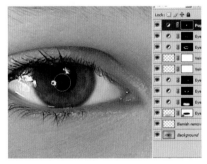

15 The pupil and the catchlights
A further Curves adjustment layer is now used to darken the pupil only, and lighten any catchlights in the eyes. A simple S curve is sufficient. Again, we select the layer mask, invert it with Ctrl/Apple+I, and paint the effect in with a white brush.

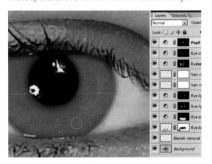

16 Colour change
Finally, we're going to change the eye colour. We start by painting a selection of the iris in Quick Mask mode (so the rest isn't affected and we can concentrate on the eye) then press Q again, invert it with Shift+Ctrl/Apple+I, and add a Hue/Sat layer which comes with a mask based on the selection.

17 And now from brown to blue
We alter the Hue slider until we reach the desired hue, then use a mix of Lightness and Saturation to achieve the colour we're looking for. Brown to blue involves a slight Lightness drop and quite a heavy Saturation drop to achieve a realistic effect.

A digital makeover

Turn a plain Jane into a glamour puss with this comprehensive guide to adding make-up the Photoshop way

Key Photoshop Skills Covered
What you'll learn

CURVES COMMAND

ADJUSTMENT LAYERS

BLUR TOOLS

Essentials

TIME TAKEN
20 minutes

YOUR EXPERT
Matthew Smith

ON THE DISC
Make-up before. psd

You only have to pick up a copy of any of the celebrity magazines to see the stars looking dog-rough without their slap on, to realise just how much make-up can do. And not just for women – this is the era of tinted moisturiser and the metrosexual, after all. It's only a matter of time before the average bloke will be spooning on the foundation as well.

There are, of course, those lucky few who look naturally beautiful, with perfect skin and radiant eyes – but who cares about them? We're interested in the human majority, particularly those subjects who didn't have time to put their make-up on before you snapped them, or aren't particularly adept with their foundation and need a helping hand. And yes, that helping hand can come from Photoshop. It's perfectly easy to apply Photoshop in post-production – which does make you wonder about the future role of make-up artists in magazine shoots.

You might be really surprised to learn what you can achieve the Photoshop way. We've got foundation, concealer, powder, blusher, eyeliner, eyeshadow, mascara, lipstick and lipliner in the retouching armoury, and in more colours than they could physically stock in your average high street shop.

This tutorial covers a relatively conservative make-up look, with some purple eyeshadow, mascara, eyeliner, foundation, concealer, and subtle lipstick and lipliner. But you don't need to be so modest – make-up is a thoroughly creative medium, as any make-up artist in the fashion industry will tell you, so don't be afraid to whack on gold eyeshadow and black lipstick if that's what takes your fancy.

Once you've understood the basics and worked through the steps, you should find pretty much any look is within your capability. Pop into any newsagent and browse through the style mags such as *Vogue* or *Elle* for some really interesting looks. You can even photograph yourself and try different looks before a night on the town!

WORKS WITH | PHOTOSHOP 7.0 AND ABOVE

LONGER LASHES
Get the movie star look

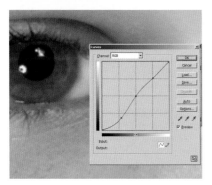

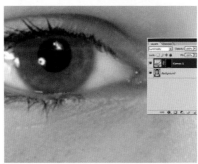

01 Mascara with curves We'll start by adding a little mascara to thicken up the eyelashes top and bottom. The effect is achieved with a darkening Curves adjustment layer, with points plotted to avoid information around the eyelashes being affected.

02 Painting in the curves We invert the mask on the Curves adjustment layer by selecting it and using Ctrl/Apple+I. Then we take a white brush at 50% Hardness and zoom in on the eyelashes, brushing over them one by one. If your Curves layer is spot on, you can brush over them all quite quickly.

03 Eyeliner with Solid Color Next, we're going to add some eyeliner. We do this via a Solid Color adjustment layer, created in the usual way with the Adjustment Layer icon at the bottom of the Layers palette. We chose a dark brown shade, which is usually preferable to black.

04 Painting eyeliner in The layer mask should be highlighted already, so we just use Ctrl/Apple+I to invert it to black. We zoom in with Ctrl/Apple+Plus, and paint a line along the base of the lower eyelid, above the eyelashes, using a white brush on the layer mask at 0% Hardness. You can also use some at the top of the upper lid.

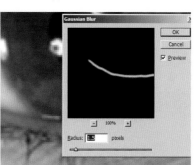

05 Softening the line The line is still going to look a little over-defined, but fortunately we can soften its edges further by using a Gaussian blur directly onto the layer mask, which softens our white line. Go to Filter>Blur>Gaussian Blur and increase the radius until you are satisfied with the result.

Tip

Matching make-up to the eyes

Matching eyeshadow to your eye colour sounds like a good idea, but doesn't work. Your beautiful blues will be lost in a sea of blue eyeshadow. Go for contrast instead. Dark eyes look good in greys, blues, purples and greens. Light eyes need brown, taupe and bronze shades. Darker shades help 'retreat' eyes, while lighter hues, or frosts, 'advance' them. If you want big, beautiful peepers, rely on pale shades.

Tip

Matching make-up to the lips

To make lips appear fuller, pick a lipstick and lipliner in matching shades – go for lighter colours to get this effect. Choose darker shades of both liner and lipstick to make lips appear smaller. To make them look wider, use a liner that perfectly matches your lipstick and line the extreme edges of lips, extending out to corners. Of course, Photoshop's Transform command gives another very efficient method of altering lip shape and size!

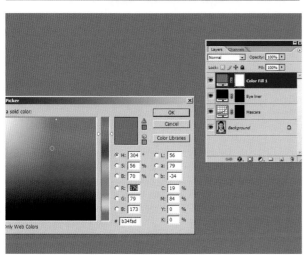

06 Choosing an eyeshadow colour Now we're going to add a little eyeshadow. Add another Solid Color adjustment layer, and pick a colour using the Color Picker. It doesn't matter which colour at the moment, because we can change it later and vary its strength with layer opacity.

07 Applying your eyeshadow Invert the layer mask to turn it black with Ctrl/Apple+I, then take a medium-hardness white brush (around 50%) at 100% Opacity, and paint along the top of the eyelid and into the corner of the eye. Drop to 50% Opacity and paint the colour into the bottom of the eye. Drop the layer opacity to suit.

PRETTY AS A PICTURE
Add sparkle to an image with digital make-up

SKIN CONTROL
Build up a smooth base

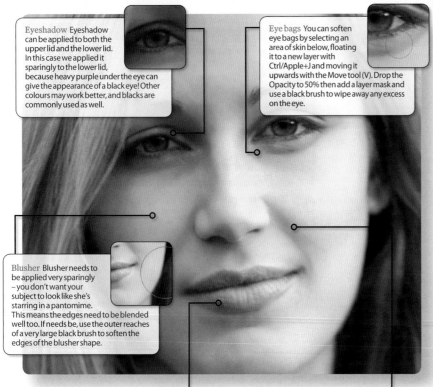

Eyeshadow Eyeshadow can be applied to both the upper lid and the lower lid. In this case we applied it sparingly to the lower lid, because heavy purple under the eye can give the appearance of a black eye! Other colours may work better, and blacks are commonly used as well.

Eye bags You can soften eye bags by selecting an area of skin below, floating it to a new layer with Ctrl/Apple+J and moving it upwards with the Move tool (V). Drop the Opacity to 50% then add a layer mask and use a black brush to wipe away any excess on the eye.

Blusher Blusher needs to be applied very sparingly – you don't want your subject to look like she's starring in a pantomime. This means the edges need to be blended well too. If needs be, use the outer reaches of a very large black brush to soften the edges of the blusher shape.

Lipstick blending mode It's important that the lipstick layer blending mode is set to Color, so the underlying lightness or 'Luminosity' is preserved. With a Normal blending mode, the shade of colour and its opacity can also affect the shadows between the lips – a very light colour would almost neutralise shadows and wouldn't look realistic.

Foundation Don't be tempted to lay on the foundation too thick. Remember that with a Normal blending mode you're affecting the lightness (or Luminosity) as well as colour, so you can destroy all shading detail if you use it too strongly. This is necessary to a degree to reduce specular highlights and darken shadows to even up skin tone, but don't overdo it.

08 Foundation to suit Now we're going to add a little foundation to the face to even up skin tone and give a little sun treatment to pale skin if necessary. Add another Solid Color adjustment layer, selecting a colour that resembles foundation – a warm skin-type colour. You can go a little darker if you're after the fake tan effect.

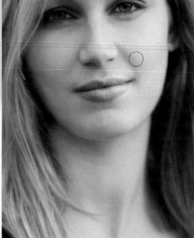

09 Foundation for face and neck Invert the layer mask with Ctrl/Apple+I. Carefully paint the colour back into the skin areas, including the neck, with a white, medium-edged brush, working on the layer mask. Once you've covered areas with precision, you can drop the layer opacity down to something like 20% for a realistic look.

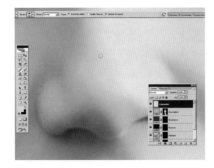

10 Concealer for blemishes Next, we have concealer – commonly used to hide blemishes such as spots. Our concealer comes in the form of the Spot Healing brush (J or Shift+J to cycle through to it) set to Sample All Layers via the Tool Options bar. Use it on a new layer, and simply click on the blemishes and watch them disappear!

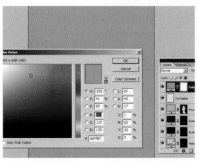

11 A colour for the blusher Now it's time for blusher – applied most often to the cheekbones to add a little colour and give them some definition. You need to add a new layer first, otherwise the Solid Color twins with the previous layer. Then simply add the adjustment layer as usual, picking out a typical blusher colour.

12 Contouring cheekbones Invert the layer mask with Ctrl/Apple+I and paint onto it with a white brush at 50% Opacity and 0% Hardness to bring out the blusher on the cheekbones. Now take a brush at 20% and paint along the underside of the cheekbone colour, darkening that area further to accentuate the cheekbone shape.

GETTING CHEEKY
Bring life to the face with blusher

13 Fine-tuning your blusher
Drop the layer opacity until the blusher is almost unnoticeable – you should be able to tell when you toggle the layer visibility on and off, but not notice directly with the naked eye. You can add a little blusher to the nose bridge, forehead and chin with a 40% Opacity brush as well.

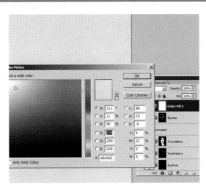

14 Your choice of lipstick Now we're going to apply lipstick with the usual Solid Color adjustment layer technique. Add the layer and pick a colour – doesn't matter which at this stage, as we can alter it later down the line. Use Ctrl/Apple+I afterwards to invert the layer mask to black.

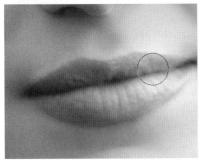

15 Colour mixing Zoom in on the lips with Ctrl/Apple+Plus, and paint onto the mask with a white brush set to 100% Opacity to bring out the colour in the lips. Set the layer blending mode to Color and drop the opacity until the colour is as you wish, double-clicking the Solid Color layer to change the colour again if necessary.

16 Drawing your lipliner Next, add a Curves adjustment layer and drop the curve with a single point to darken things slightly. Now use Ctrl/Apple+I to invert the layer mask. Take a small white brush at 100% Opacity and 0% Hardness, and draw around the very edge of the lips in order to darken them.

UNDER THE MAKE-UP
Building up the effect

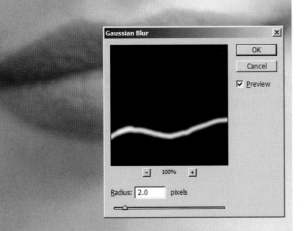

17 Softening the lipliner
The lipliner will probably be too sharp at this point, so make sure the layer mask is still selected and use Filter>Blur> Gaussian Blur to soften the line a little so that it blends in nicely with the lips but doesn't disappear entirely.

Lipliner

Lipstick

Blusher

Concealer

Foundation

Eyeliner

Eyeshadow

Mascara

Background

Cosmetic surgery the Photoshop way

Reshape noses, suck out double chins, stick in cheek implants and create super size lips with cosmetic surgery the Photoshop way

BEFORE

AFTER

Essentials

SKILL LEVEL
Beginner
Intermediate
Expert

TIME TAKEN
One hour

YOUR EXPERT
Matt Henry

If you think removing freckles and spots is a good way to pass the time, wait till you start giving your friends and family liposuction, nose jobs, lip enhancement and cheekbone implants – the hours will just fly by.

Playing plastic surgeon is indeed an addictive pursuit, but before you get too carried away, remember the need to keep it real. 'Real' at least in the sense that it's believable. If your subject is happy shedding three to four stone and you can make it look totally realistic, then there's nothing to stop you performing miracles. However, it's important to

be aware of the sensitivities of your subject. A friend that you might think is in dire need of a nose job may not agree, and you could well find yourself off their Christmas card list for performing surgery without consent!

The good news is there's no rocket science involved here, just some Photoshop trickery. All that's needed is a bit of Transform and Liquify to sort out noses, lips and take a bit of weight off the face, and some careful Dodging and Burning and another bit of Liquify to really emphasise and accentuate those cheekbones.

Of course we've only scratched the surface of professional face retouching here. We haven't covered eye whitening, teeth whitening, roots colouring, skin tanning, eyebrow thinning, eye widening, evening out of skin tone and the rest – but noses, lips, cheekbones and facial slimming are great places to start. Indeed, they're probably the most noticeable aspects of all in terms of facial retouching. You can really transform the shape of someone's face, as the before and after images here will testify. Have fun and look out for future tutorials covering those other important aspects.

NOSE JOB
With a little careful tweaking you can create the perfect nose

Key Photoshop Skills Covered
What you'll learn

LASSO SELECTION
FREE TRANSFORM
LIQUIFY FILTER
CURVES
DODGE AND BURN
HEALING BRUSH

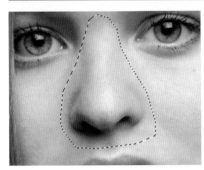

01 Select the nose We'll start with the nose. Reducing the overall size of a nose isn't too difficult. Make a rough selection with the Polygonal Lasso tool, keeping some skin texture around the nose. Float this to a new layer with Ctrl/Cmd+J and then use Ctrl/Cmd+T to initiate Free Transform.

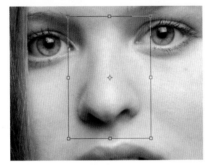

02 Alter the dimensions Reduce either the height or width percentages (or both) in the Tool Options bar. If you've altered the height, the nose may appear too high on the face. Drop Opacity to 30% and press V to initiate the Move tool using up and down cursor keys to align the bottom with the original nose.

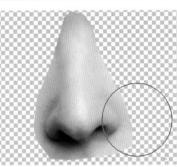

03 Liquify for shape If you're still not happy with the result and want to make more localised changes, you can use the Liquify filter to alter shape, using a suitably sized brush to pull and push certain areas. This is good for thinning a slightly bulbous nose, or straightening a bent one.

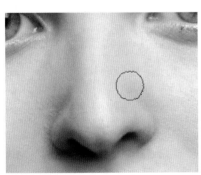

04 Blend the new nose Set Opacity back to 100%. Add a layer mask, take a soft-edged black brush and slowly brush away at the edges of the nose in order to blend the original surrounding skin texture with the new altered texture. Be careful not to erase any of the new nose.

05 Liquify cheekbones Now select the background layer and duplicate it with Ctrl/Cmd+J. Next, go to Filter>Liquify and set the brush to a large size in relation to the cheekbone area. Place the cursor at the point where the cheekbone is most prominent, and drag upwards and outwards slightly. Do the same for the other.

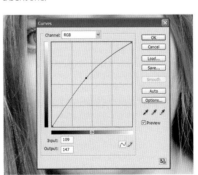

06 Add two Curves layers Now add a Curves adjustment layer and increase the lightness by dragging the curve upwards slightly with a single point. Then select the layer mask and use Ctrl/Cmd+I to invert it to black. Set the blending mode to Luminosity. Do the same again, this time with a darkening Curves layer.

Expert Tip

Cheekbone technique

You'll notice this technique is essentially Dodge and Burn. We're making some areas darker and some lighter. In principle you can use the same technique for males and females, though you have to go a little less hard with males. Women tend to use make-up to accentuate cheekbones anyway, so we're accustomed to seeing darker areas here. Overdo it on a man, and it'll look like he's wearing make-up!

Expert Tip

Female lips

The Cupid's bow lip look is sported by those with genetic good fortune such as Kate Moss, Monica Belluci and Rachel Weiz. It's characterised by a strong double arch in the upper lip that extends quite far upwards towards the nose. The technique shown here will get close, but you might want to shape the central part of the upper lip a little more with Liquify. You may also find it beneficial to increase the width of the lips as well as the height.

CHEEKS AND LIPS
Making the most of them

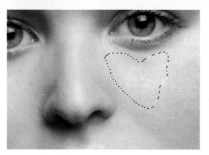

07 Lightening for cheekbones Select the original Curves layer and take a white, soft-edged brush at around 10% Opacity. Now imagine a heart shape that sits below the eye – the selection here gives you an idea. This is roughly the area you need to lighten. Select the layer mask and slowly build up with your brush, being careful not to do overdo things.

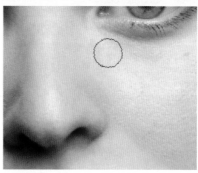

08 Finish the cheekbones Next, switch to the darkening layer, and with the same white 10% brush, start to darken the darker area to the right of the heart area (left for the left cheekbone) with the layer mask selected. Now repeat for the other cheekbone.

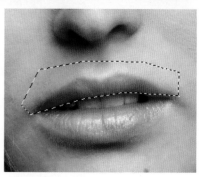

09 Lip selection Zoom in with Ctrl/Cmd and +, and select the Polygonal Lasso tool. Select the background layer and draw a line between the lips and then encircle the top lip, making sure to include a good amount of skin texture in the upper lip.

BEAUTY SECRETS
We share our tricks of the trade

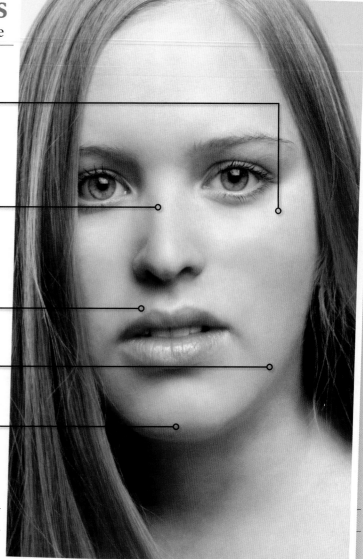

Cheekbones The cheekbones have been lifted slightly and made to look more prominent. We've also added subtle shadows and highlights to create a more sculpted appearance.

Nose The nose has been carefully thinned out in order to produce a less bulbous look in the centre.

Lips The upper lip has been stretched upwards slightly in order to produce the characteristic 'Cupid's bow' shape.

Head and face The head as a whole has been slimmed down a little and the face edges have been brought in.

Chin, neck and shoulders The chin has been tucked upwards and the neck and shoulders slimmed down.

SLIM WITH LIQUIFY
Once the lips are done, we can slim the face

10 Feather the selection Next, press Q to enter Quick Mask mode and apply a Gaussian blur on the mask with Filter>Blur>Gaussian Blur. Don't go too hard on the blur this time around – just enough for a slight feathering so edges don't look too sharp.

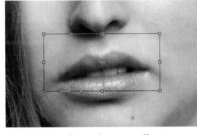

11 Transform the upper lip Press Q to get out of Quick Mask mode and use Ctrl/Cmd+J to float the selection layer. Hit Ctrl/Cmd+T to start a Free Transform, and drag the handle upwards to increase the size of the upper lip. You may need to pull downwards as well to close any potential gaps.

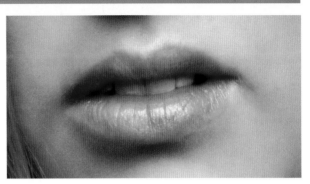

12 Blend the lip Complete your transform and add a layer mask to the new layer with the appropriate Layers palette icon. Take a soft-edged black brush, and brush away at any obvious joins that might be found in the skin section and the lip itself.

13 Face slimming Now we're going to slim the whole face a little. Add a new layer at the top of the stack, then hold down Alt/Option and select Merge Visible from the layer context menu. A new layer will appear that combines everything from below. Next, use Ctrl/Cmd+A to select all and then Ctrl/Cmd+T for Free Transform.

14 Width reduction Next, in the Tool Options bar change the W (Width) setting to a reduced figure such as 97%. Experiment to see what looks best. Press Enter to complete the transform, and then crop the image to the new edges with the Crop tool. Now go to Filter>Liquify. Set the brush to the maximum 600 size.

15 Shape with Liquify Now gradually start pulling inwards from the edges of the face. Start with the outside of the cheekbone area and gradually move downwards, all the time ensuring that you pull in a uniform amount at each point, unless you wish to make shape alterations, such as a round face more square.

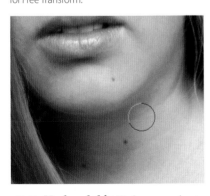

16 Neck and chin Work your way down to the chin area and slim the neck by pulling inwards and downwards. You can drop shoulders a little as well, to suit. Use a smaller brush to push a double chin upwards slightly, then a big brush further into the face to pull the whole chin back down. Repeat as necessary.

17 Healing for blemishes You can accentuate the jawline slightly by selecting a point a little inside and pulling down and away for both sides of the jaw. OK the dialog to finish, add a new layer at the top of the stack, and use the Healing Brush set to Sample All Layers to touch up any blemishes.

LAYER STRUCTURE
More than skin deep

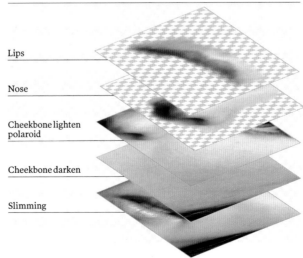

Lips

Nose

Cheekbone lighten polaroid

Cheekbone darken

Slimming

Key
Photoshop
Skills Covered
What you'll learn

CHANNELS
PALETTE

FILTERS

CHANNEL
MIXER

ADDING
SHADOWS

Perfect cutouts

Precise retouching often involves having to select tricky areas, such as hair.
Read on and discover how the Channels makes this job easier

Essentials

TIME TAKEN
20 minutes

YOUR EXPERT
Matthew Henry

ON THE DISC
Hair before.jpg

Cutting out hair can be a task arduous enough to send even the most competent Photoshop user running for the cupboard – and if the conditions aren't favourable, it can be a near impossible job.

The crux of the problem is that wavy strands of hair take an eternity to cut out with tools like the Polygonal Lasso or the Pen – and that's if they can be cut out at all. Particularly at the edges, you're dealing with a complex mass of interweaving strands to sort through and separate from their background. You could easily spend a full

week masking them manually, and we all have better things to be doing!

The other issue is that many of the finer strands are actually semi-translucent, so some of the background is bound to show through – place hair cut out from a black background onto a white background, and there's simply no way you're going to avoid seeing some of the black colouring shining through. You could, of course, lop off large areas of the hair edges that show background colour, but you'll end up with Lego hair that looks like it's been stuck on with superglue.

The technique we have here doesn't perform the sort of major miracles required to detach hair completely from its background colour, but does perform the smaller miracle of cutting out a subject and their hair without the need to get your hands dirty with selection or path tools. As long as you're placing your subject onto a background of roughly similar tone, you'll be able to preserve the finest strands of hair at the edges which are so crucial to making cut and paste jobs of people look realistic. And all without even thinking about the Polygonal Lasso tool…

CHANNEL SURFING
Separate to accumulate

01 **Inspect the channels** Our first step is to select the Channels palette and move through each channel individually to see which offers us the most difference in tone between foreground and background. In this case the red channel picks out the fine strands of hair nicely.

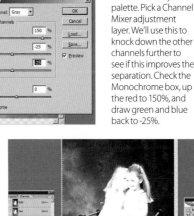

02 **Tweak with Channel Mixer** Click the RGB channel again, and return to the Layers palette. Pick a Channel Mixer adjustment layer. We'll use this to knock down the other channels further to see if this improves the separation. Check the Monochrome box, up the red to 150%, and draw green and blue back to -25%.

Dark subjects, light backgrounds

If your subject was dark and your background light, chances are you will have ended up with a black subject and white background on the mask, rather than the white on black we had for this tutorial. This makes your background into a selection when Ctrl/Cmd are clicked rather than your foreground, so it's best to use Ctrl/Cmd+I to invert first. Or you can use Ctrl/Cmd+Shift+I to invert the actual selection.

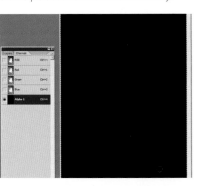

03 **Copy Channel Mixer info** Click on OK and then use Ctrl/Cmd+A to Select All. Next, go to the Edit menu and select Copy Merged (or use Ctrl/Cmd+Shift+C). Now go back to the Channels palette and click the icon at the bottom of the palette that says Create New Channel. A black alpha channel emerges.

04 **Paste into the alpha channel** Next, make sure the new channel is selected and then go back to the Edit menu and select Paste (or use Ctrl/Cmd+V). The changes you made with the Channel Mixer should be replicated into this new alpha channel. You can now discard the Channel Mixer adjustment layer.

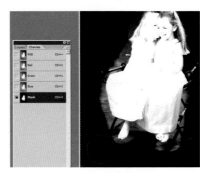

05 **Prepare to modify the mask** The alpha channel is going to be the basis for our mask. As everything black on a mask is concealed and everything white is revealed, we need to work directly onto the channel to turn the subject white and the background black. We can invert the colours at a later stage if needs be.

Using adjustment layers

Add an adjustment layer with the selection active, and that layer will be loaded with a mask based on the selection. Add a Curves adjustment layer, for example, and lighten the curve, and only your subject will be affected. If you want to work on the background instead, perhaps to darken it so the subject really pops out at you, simply select the layer mask and invert it with Ctrl/Cmd+I.

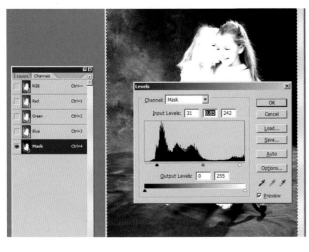

06 **Levels to boost contrast** Our first step is to use a Levels adjustment on the mask. Make sure the channel is selected, and go to Image>Adjustments> Levels. Bring the black slider in slightly to darken the shadows. Don't touch the white slider as we want to preserve detail in the hair highlights.

07 **Burn in the shadows** Now for the fun bit. We're going to darken the background using the Burn tool (O) set to Shadows in the Tool Options bar. Set it to 100% Opacity and about 90% Hardness. Move around the edge of the subject, making sure not to get close – especially to the hair.

SELECT THE HAIR
Pick up as many strands as you can

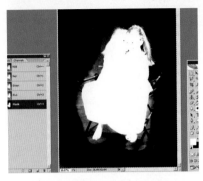
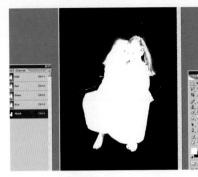
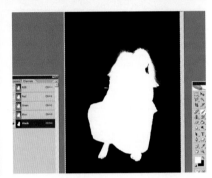

08 Dodge the highlights Next, we're going to select the Dodge tool and set the Range, this time to highlights. Move over the subject with 100% Opacity and 90% Hardness, but leave the edges of the hair alone at this stage. With repeated clicking, we can turn the lighter mid-tones of the clothes into highlights and then into white.

09 Target the edges Even the darker shades of the dress are now white, so it's safe to move in with the Burn tool set to Shadows, as we're not at risk of turning any dress mid-tones into shadows. Work closer to the edges, again avoiding hair edges, and exercising precision near areas still with mid-tones, such as the front foot.

10 Tidy things up We haven't managed to get everything at this stage. Use the Dodge tool set to Highlights to touch up detail, such as the mid-tone on the foot that's now surrounded by shadow, and then zoom in close and paint carefully with a white or black brush set to 90% Hardness to cover anything we've missed.

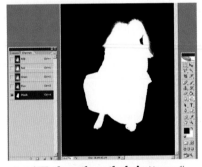

11 Work gently on the hair Now we'll move on to the hair. As we're dealing with some mid-tones, turning everything black and white is going to lose us some of the finer hairs. So we use a Dodge tool set to Highlights at 30% to work over the hair edges, then a Burn tool set to Shadows at 30%.

12 Activate the selection Now we have our mask, and we can do what we choose with it! Before we do anything, we need first to turn the mask it into a selection. To do this, hold down Ctrl/Cmd and click the Mask channel. The selection should now appear. Click the RGB channel to get back to normality, and go back to the Layers palette.

13 New background with hair preserved To add a new background, duplicate the background layer and add a layer mask, which will be based on the selection. Use Ctrl/Cmd+D to deselect, then drag your new background across, making sure the layer sits between the original background layer and its duplicate. We've worked here on the original layer mask to bring back the chair that the girls are sitting on.

LAYER STRUCTURE
The order for flyaway hair

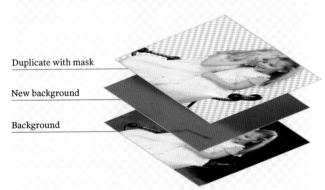

Duplicate with mask

New background

Background

Chapter 5

Creative projects

*Inspiring ways to turn your photos
into digital art, scrapbooks and more*

Tip

Photo start
All of the projects in this section use photos as the start source. This means that you haven't got to worry about having any natural artistic skill – as long as you have a photo you can create some great digital art!

Creative introduction video on the CD

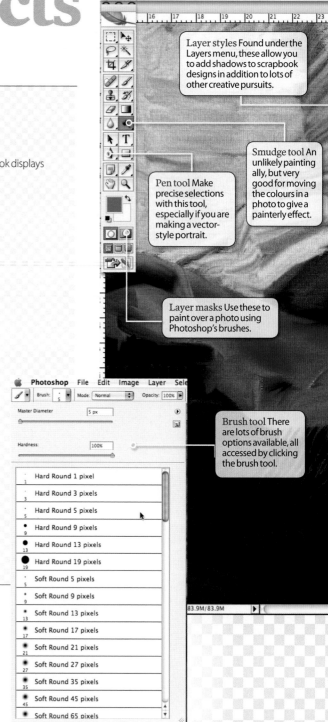

Layer styles Found under the Layers menu, these allow you to add shadows to scrapbook designs in addition to lots of other creative pursuits.

Smudge tool An unlikely painting ally, but very good for moving the colours in a photo to give a painterly effect.

Pen tool Make precise selections with this tool, especially if you are making a vector-style portrait.

Layer masks Use these to paint over a photo using Photoshop's brushes.

Brush tool There are lots of brush options available, all accessed by clicking the brush tool.

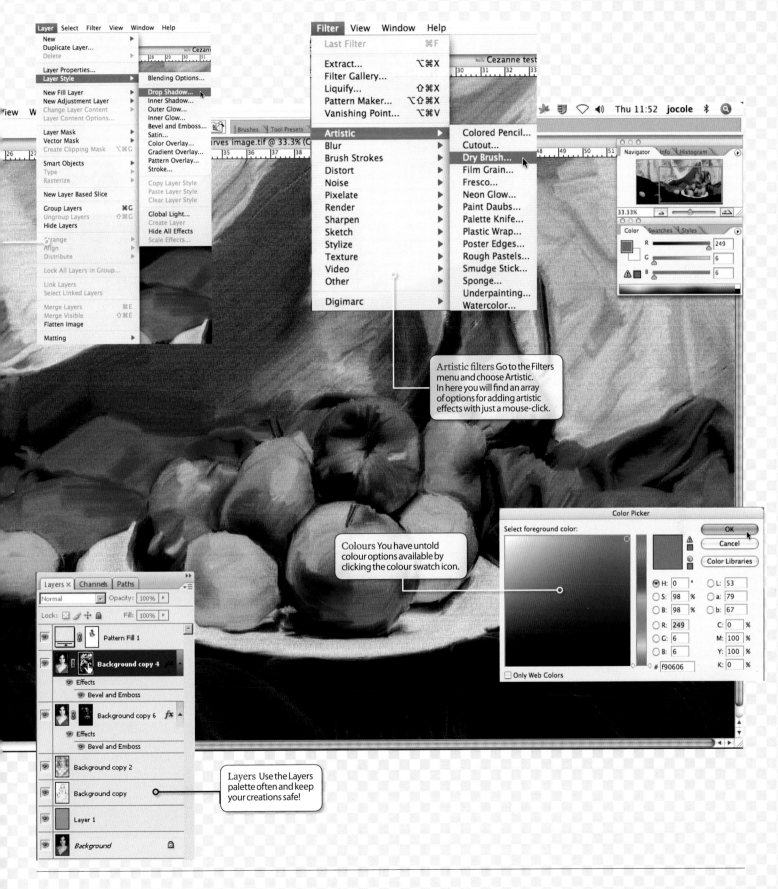

Artistic filters Go to the Filters menu and choose Artistic. In here you will find an array of options for adding artistic effects with just a mouse-click.

Colours You have untold colour options available by clicking the colour swatch icon.

Layers Use the Layers palette often and keep your creations safe!

Creative projects

Unleash the Photoshop artist within you with this range of creative photo-based projects

Essentials

YOUR EXPERT
Jo Cole

ON THE DISC
Check out the creative introduction video on the disc

There's no doubt that Photoshop is a phenomenally powerful image editor, but you may not realise that it is also a dab hand at more artistic endeavours.

Nestled among the tools are all sorts of creative options, from the various brushes through to filters and illustration options. And the best thing is, you don't even have to be able to draw. The beauty of creating art with Photoshop is that you can use photos as the basis of everything. This means that you haven't got to worry about making something look realistic – the photo deals with all that for you. All you have to do is control the tool to get the effect you want.

If it's your first attempt at digital art, we'd recommend using the options in the Filter menu to get started with. From here you can apply paint effects in addition to more imaginative finishes. All it requires you to do is move a slider until you get the look you want. If you are feeling more ambitious, you can use the brushes with layer masks to paint over a photo. The brush will determine the look of the painting, so a chalk brush, for example, will give a chalk effect.

One aspect of creative Photoshop that has arisen relatively recently is that of digital scrapbooking. Photoshop has loads of tools for assembling photos and decorative elements and making them look just like a 'real' scrapbook. We're going to show you how to do all of this over the coming pages and reveal how your photos can be used to make some beautiful art without you having to break a sweat!

Brush choices Photoshop has a really good range of default brushes that can give very realistic results. The Dry Media choices work well here.

BRUSHES
Default and custom

Photoshop ships with a decent amount of brushes that can be further modified using the Brush Dynamics palette. Accessing the brushes is easy – click the Brush tool from the toolbox, head up to the Brush Picker and choose one from the selection. If you want more brushes, click the right-pointed arrow. To alter the shape of a brush, go to Window>Brushes to view the Brush Dynamics. Here you can alter how the brush looks and behaves.

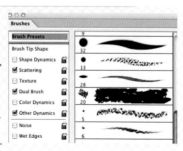

SMUDGE TOOL
Easy digital painting

The Smudge tool might initially look like something that offers limited use, but it is actually a very useful photo painting tool. Select the tool and then you can brush over the photo to blend the colours and detail. This gives a smooth, painterly effect and is even more effective when a texture is also applied. As long as the brushes follow the contours of the object you are painting, you can get great effects.

Layers Building up layers is a necessary aspect of this technique and mimics the way a traditional painter would place layers of paint over each other.

Creative introduction video on the CD

Painting dabs When you are going for a painterly effect, keep your marks short to build up valuable texture and depth.

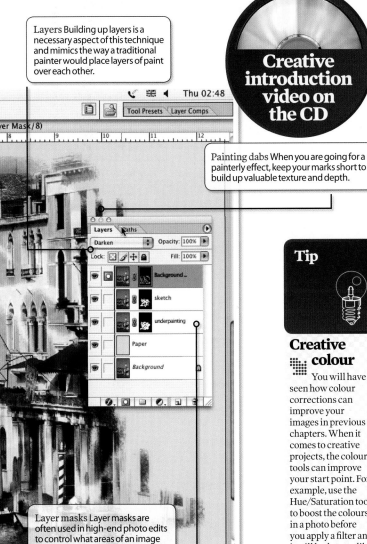

Layer masks Layer masks are often used in high-end photo edits to control what areas of an image is affected. In our case here, they allow us to pull out information from a photo using a stylised brush. The effect is a realistic painting that doesn't cause a headache.

Tip

Creative colour

You will have seen how colour corrections can improve your images in previous chapters. When it comes to creative projects, the colour tools can improve your start point. For example, use the Hue/Saturation tool to boost the colours in a photo before you apply a filter and it will look more like a painting.

Tool of the trade

PEN TOOL
Illustration possibilities

The term 'vector art' is applied to work created in Illustrator and typifies an image that has very flat colour. Pop-art paintings share the same qualities. If you'd like to get a similar effect, it's easy to do using the Pen tool and a photo. Simply use the Pen to work around the photo, selecting areas and then fill with a solid colour. The effect will be very similar to 'proper' vector images and look absolutely great.

Tools of the trade

PHOTOSHOP FILTERS
Filter out the good stuff

The filters (found in the Filter menu) allow you to apply an effect to an image with just a click of the mouse. Each filter allows you to alter its strength using sliders and you can make selections to just alter a certain part of a photo. If you're not sure which one to go for first, here's our pick of the best

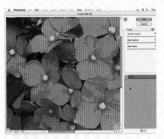

Cutout

Cut it out The Cutout filter is part of the Artistic set of filter options and turns a photo into a flat-looking illustration. A photo is basically simplified, with a reduced number of colours. This is what gives the bold, bright effect and is perfect for creating backgrounds or t-shirt designs, or as a start for comic-book designs for example.

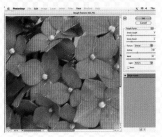

Rough pastels

Real-media solutions A brilliant filter for getting a quick artistic effect (which may be why it's part of the Artistic filters!). Rough diagonal lines will be added to your photo, with a wonderful texture peeping through in some areas. The sliders help you to control the effect, so that you can get it to look exactly as you want, to suit the image you're working from.

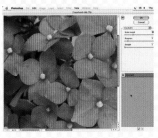

Crosshatch

Lines and crosses Found in the Brush Strokes category of filter effects, the Crosshatch filter looks very painterly without you having to do anything else to it. It applies small, dab-like marks over a photo, which simplifies the shapes and adds a kind of texture effect, which you can leave as it is or combine with other filters to finish it off.

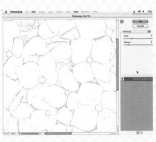

Photocopy

And we don't mean Xerox Nestled in the Sketch collection of filter effects, the Photocopy filter uses the currently selected colours (your foreground and background colours, which are black and white by default) to turn a photo into a copy of itself. You can adjust how much detail is kept, but we like to keep it quite low and suggestive.

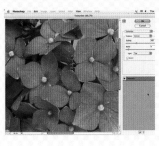

Texturizer

Add some texture Part of the Texture group, the Texturizer lets you apply a texture effect to an image with a simple click and a few slider options for more control over the final look. This is essential if you are trying some digital painting, as you can apply a canvas effect for a traditional look in combination with some of the other filters.

Digital scrapbooking in Photoshop

BONUS
art pack from
Scrap Girls !!

Love scrapbooking with your photos but tired of the actual cutting and pasting? Well, throw out your scissors and glue gun as we show you how to use Photoshop as the scrapper's tool of choice

Who doesn't enjoy turning their family snapshots into fun and creative craft projects? Anyone who doesn't want hand cramps or gluey fingers, and hates cleaning up tiny scraps of paper – that's who!

In today's age of filmless cameras, most photos are digital anyway, so why not keep them that way? In this feature we'll show you the amazing versatility of Photoshop for creating scrapbook layouts that will make you wonder why you ever bothered doing it any other way.

One of the major benefits of digital scrapbooking is the absence of limits. Traditional techniques were bound by the materials available. If you wanted your parchment paper to be a shade darker, or your plaid fabric to be blue instead of red, you were simply out of luck. If there wasn't enough striped ribbon to span the whole page, there wasn't much you could do about it. And what if you and a friend both wanted to use the last piece of stitched leather? That could turn into a very different game of 'Rock Paper Scissors'!

By going digital, you'll never again need to fret over the limitations of physical materials.

Photoshop has pixels aplenty! Resizing papers, changing fabric colours, even duplicating patterns are all simple in Photoshop.

Having your layouts in a digital format also allows you to share them with a larger audience than the guests who pass through your living room. You can present your designs in a whole host of formats for friends and family to enjoy. Email your pages to far-off relatives, post your designs on a web gallery, share them in a forum, create a PDF album or even decorate your own blog. The possibilities are endless. And of course, if you really want to, you can still print out your pages and put them in an album!

Bonus art pack from Scrap Girls!

On this CD you will find a bonus art pack generously provided by the Scrap Girls of **www.scrapgirls.com**. Be sure to check it out for loads of free paper textures, word art, brushes, borders and embellishments. There are even instructions on the best way to use the materials. This art pack is sure to inspire you in

Photoshop creative   **Mac & PC**
Scrapbooking
Photoshop creative
Courtesy of Scrap Girls
Digital scrapbooking resource pack

Includes:
Textures
Brushes
Fonts
Video tutorial

your own layout creations! Much of the artwork on the next few pages uses elements found in this amazing pack. If you like the look of these resources, head along to **scrapgirls.com** to check out the rest of their amazing scrapbook goodies! You'll be inspired.

> "By going digital, you'll never again need to fret over the limitations of physical materials"

Expert tips

Expert: Photoscrapper
Subject: It's all about the photos
As much as I love the creative process of scrapbooking, I have to constantly remind myself that the primary purpose is to enhance the photos. Scrapping can be used to dress up or distract from a so-so photo, but it really shines when you start with a GREAT shot and use it for the central focus of a layout that supports and enhances it.

Expert: mom^5
Subject: To inspire and share
I've found it enormously helpful to connect with other scrappers and share files. I've gotten loads of ideas and inspiration simply from looking at other people's layouts. I've even been able to share some source files so my friends can

use some of the textures that I came up with.

Expert: Pixel_love
Subject: Plan ahead
When I'm out with my family at an event that I know I'll be creating a layout for, I like to think ahead of what the layout might need so I can grab some quick pictures of different things to tie into the theme. For example, at my son's Little League game, I took a close-up shot of a dirt-covered home plate and it made for a great background!

Expert: Wendy Johanson
Subject: Build an archive
I'm constantly collecting textures and images to add to a resource archive I keep on my hard drive. I label each item so I can dip in and out and find whatever I need quickly and for free!

Get your photos ready

Watch for curves

To level out any lighting issues and generally enhance the photo's colour, use the Curves adjustment found under the Image Adjustments menu. Use the Eyedroppers near the bottom to set your white and black points by first selecting the appropriate dropper and then clicking on the darkest or brightest part of your image. Finally, grab a point at the centre of the curve and pull it down ever so slightly until your photo colours are deep and rich.

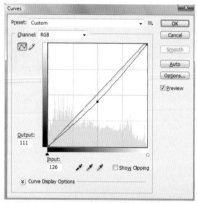

Using a Curves adjustment will help you brighten up the colours in your image

Sharpen up

Most photos taken with consumer grade digital cameras tend to have a slight blur. While it's not overtly noticeable, a touch of sharpening will help make those photos pop on the page. Go to Filter>Sharpen>Unsharpen Mask. Be mindful of the settings, so you don't introduce artefacts into the image. Just a little bit will go a long way.

Sepia tone

Creating a colour cast on an image is a great way to add variation to your layout. To get the same sepia tone we used here, add a Hue/Saturation adjustment layer (Layer>New Adjustment Layer>Hue/Saturation). Make sure to tick the Colorize box, and set Hue to 35 and Saturation to 40.

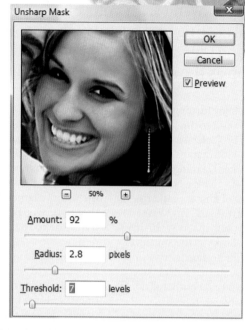

Far left:
Add an interesting look to your image by creating a sepia tone effect

Left:
You'll find that less is more when you add sharpening to your image

Fun with your scanner!

Look around you – our world is filled with different fascinating textures. Your scanner is really just another digital camera specially designed for taking pictures of flat objects. That makes it ideal for capturing the textures and patterns on everyday objects. Use some creativity and try scanning everything from sweaters to firewood. Just don't try to load them through the document feeder! Look below for some inspirational scanning subjects.

This sketchbook page provided a great border element. Bonus texture from the charcoal scribbling too! When we scanned the edge, we put something darker over the paper so it wasn't lost in the white scanner lid.

This child's boot provided several great textures. The red suede, the fur top, the rubber sole and even the stitching are all useful resources. Remember to consider all sides of an object like this. The sole makes a great boot print.

We don't recommend spilling tea on a scanner, but splashing it on parchment can be lots of fun! It also makes great texture scans. Do several of these to build up a library of splats and spills – useful for adding depth!

One of our favourites. Plunking a chunk of firewood down on the scanner will not only mystify your family, but give you some top-notch wood grain textures. Roll the firewood over to get a texture of the bark too.

Idea for a layout

Colour cast Converting the smaller photos to a sepia tone creates additional focus on the primary photo while tying together the colour scheme of the page.

See-through tissue By slightly reducing the layer opacity, the tissue paper becomes semi-transparent while still retaining the texture and effects.

Details Including tiny elements such as this added stitching to the leather, helps give a sense of realism to any digital design.

Tie it together Extra embellishments like this twine and knot can give a layout a more tangible appearance and really make it stand out from other digital projects.

Spill and splash The scans of the splashed tea on paper provide interesting textures that add both warmth and organic shapes to the layout.

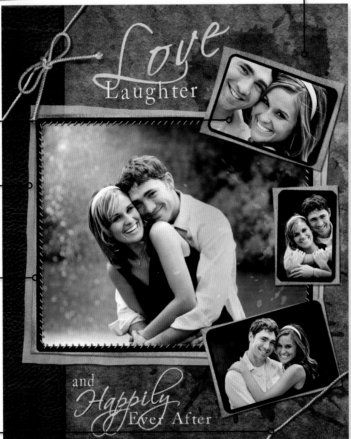

Online resources

The Scrap Girls
URL: scrapgirls.com/index.html
Top of the heap with digital scrapbooking resources. The site offers everything from templates to gallery space, plus an excellent instruction for scrappers. And did we mention the art pack on the CD?

Digital Scrapbooking Magazine
URL: digitalscrapbooking.com
A bi-monthly mag dedicated to digital scrapbooking. Tons of great articles for scrappers of all levels. The site features an 'Ask the Expert' section and sample article from the mag, plus Photoshop tutorials.

Digital Scrapbook Place
URL: digitalscrapbookplace.com
Based around a friendly community of digital scrappers. The site includes a great Scrapbooking 101 primer and several resources for purchase. Its real strength comes from its online community. Check out the extensive gallery and weekly events.

Computer Scrapbook
URL: computerscrapbook.com
A great resource for the time-pressed scrapper. The digital kits are affordable, with elements arranged by theme; no fretting over colour selection or border shapes. Just drop your photos in, arrange the elements and go!

CREATE RICHLY LAYERED BACKGROUNDS

Photoshop makes it so easy to create richness and depth with your custom backgrounds. Here's how we created this wonderfully distressed background for this layout

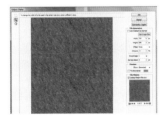

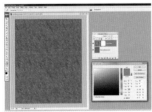

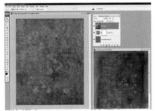

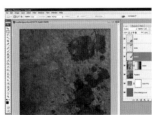

01 Custom pattern First we pulled up the scan with the charcoal scribbling. After selecting a portion we liked, the Pattern Maker under the Filter menu turned that selection into a seamless pattern that filled the background layer.

02 Colour change Next, we added a solid colour adjustment layer using a light brown. Setting this layer's blending mode to Color let the underlying texture show through. Keeping the adjustment as a layer allows for easier editing if required.

03 Tree bark Here we brought in the scan of the tree bark and placed it on a layer over the colour adjustment. The blending mode was changed to Soft Light, and Opacity reduced to 78%. At this point the texture was richly developed and suited for use.

04 Final touch To take the texture further, we brought in the splat and splash scans, set them to Multiply and reduced the opacity. We used a gradient on a layer mask to fade the splash scan into the image from left to right.

Getting a little crafty

Realistic imperfections

One of the great ironies of taking scrapbooking into the digital realm is that the perfection that was nearly impossible to achieve traditionally is now so easy you have to work to avoid it. There's great appeal in letters that are slightly misaligned, paper edges that have some roughness, or shadows that aren't perfectly straight

> ## "One of the ironies of digital scrapbooking is that you have to work to avoid perfection"

lines. Attention to details like these helps break the CG appearance and works towards creating the illusion of being hand crafted.

Consistently solid colours are rarely found anywhere in the real world. Almost everything has at least a slight shift in colour, hue or lighting on one side compared with the other. Lighting is a primary reason for this phenomenon: light decays as it travels and creates subtle changes in the appearance of objects

it illuminates. Photoshop doesn't make allowances for this, so you have to. The best tool to use here is the Gradient tool. Using even a slight gradient instead of a solid colour fill will go a long way towards making your designs appear more realistic.

Create-a-craft

You've probably noticed several amazing digital objects in various scrapbook layouts. Wondering where those came from? Where's the download site? While it's true many

are available for purchase at several scrapbooking sites, at some point somebody had to actually create that element. Unless it's a photograph, it was digitally drawn by a digital artist. It's nothing more than an arrangement of coloured pixels. You happen to be using one of the most powerful pixel arrangers on the planet (Photoshop, if you haven't guessed). So if you need a specific element in your layout, why not have a go at creating it yourself? The key to realistic digital creations

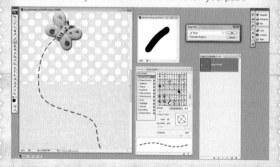

Easy stitching

Stitching makes a great border treatment, or fine detail to increase realism, and Photoshop's custom brush engine makes it easy to do. Start by drawing a shape that looks like a single stitch and define that as a brush tip via Edit>Define Brush Preset. Open the Brushes palette and select the newly defined shape as the brush tip. Adjust the size, angle and spacing until the example line looks like stitching. Go to the Shape Dynamics area and change the Angle control to 'Direction.' Back in the design, use the Pen tool to create a path for the stitching to follow. Change to the Paths palette and select Stroke Path to have your custom stitch brush follow your path.

is observation. Observe the object in reality and take note of shape, colour, texture and how it interacts with light. Now mimic those observations in the digital space. You might be surprised at just how well you can reproduce a real-world object.

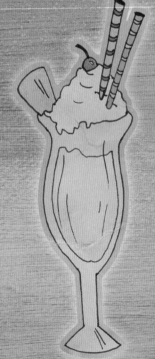

FANCIFUL FLOWERS

Discover how to transform a scan of a simple hair bow into a custom-patterned flower. Our step-by-step will tell you all you need to know...

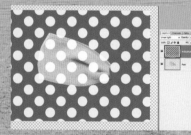

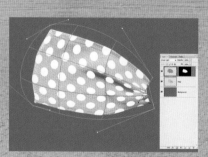

01 **This ordinary bow...** Begin with a scan of a fabric bow with a loop that's of suitable shape and size for a flower petal. Use your favourite selection technique to cut the loop out and copy it to a new file. Go to Image>Adjustment> Desaturate to remove the colour.

02 **With a pretty pattern...** Create a new layer above the petal layer, and a rectangular selection roughly twice as big as the petal. Fill this with your favourite pattern by going to Edit>Fill and selecting Pattern in the Use box. Now change the pattern layer's blending mode to Linear Light.

03 **That fits just right...** Use the Warp tool from the Edit>Transform menu to shape the pattern layer to match the shape and folds of the bow. Don't try to be exact; just get it as close as you can. Then Ctrl/Cmd-click the petal layer and use that selection as a layer mask on the pattern layer.

Shaping your text

Photoshop automatically lays out text perfectly aligned with consistent spacing and kerning. The text, in a word, is perfect. This perfection becomes obvious when placed against a layout that's supposed to look like it was done by hand. By converting the text to a shape layer (Layer>Type>Convert to Shape) the text becomes a vector object with points you can manipulate. This allows you to select and transform individual letters or even portions of letters. A word of warning though – the text will no longer be editable, so it's best to do this on a copy of the text layer while preserving the original.

Ripped edges

If your paper elements have perfect razor sharp edges, they won't look believable. One way to add a rough edge is to combine a layer mask and the Spatter filter. Ctrl/Cmd-click the layer's thumbnail to create a selection in that shape, then click the Add Layer Mask button at the bottom of the Layers palette. With this mask as the active element (not the layer itself), go to Filter>Brush Strokes>Spatter and choose a setting with a high smoothness. This gives your perfect computer-generated edges a more realistic rough paper edge.

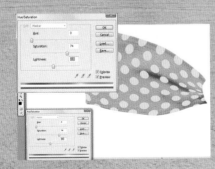

04 **And is the perfect colour...** Select both layers and merge them by pressing Ctrl/Cmd+E. Now go to Image>Adjustments>Hue/ Saturation to change the colour of the new petal. Checking the Colorize box helps to keep the colour consistent throughout the layer.

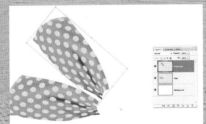

05 **To be transformed...** Hit Ctrl/Cmd+J to make a copy of the petal layer, and sthen elect Edit>Free Transform to get the Transform handles. Drag the pivot point outside the layer's bounding box and place it where the middle of the flower should be. Rotate the copied petal up about 45 degrees.

06 **Into a flower** After committing the transform, press Ctrl/ Cmd+Alt/Opt+Shift+T multiple times to copy the layer and repeat the last transformation until you get enough petals to complete the flower. Now it's ready for a centrepiece and further embellishments!

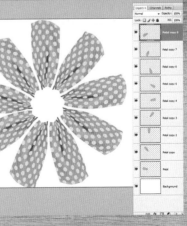

Follow the workflow

1: Photo and inspiration Weddings are often the subject of a scrapbook page. So we started with this photo of a bride. The shot is nice and crisp, and has great motion as she's leaning into her laugh. And the rose petals give us an idea for later.

2: Basic layout plan We now start experimenting with colours and shapes to develop the foundational structure. Having the bride in an oval shape while keeping other angles sharp, keeps the focus on her.

3: Build up textures Texturing is crucial to creating interest in a design. Here we begin to build up textures on the primary elements. Note how the floral pattern fits with the wedding theme. Use the Define Pattern option (Edit menu) to create your own patterns.

4: More textures, shadows and lighting After finishing the layers of textures, we addressed the shadows of the ribbons and the lighting across the design. A layer filled with the Cloud filter and set to Overlay creates great random patches of light and dark areas. Reduce the opacity for a more subtle effect.

5: Primary visual elements The shiny chrome frame was created using Layer Style presets that were adjusted to complement the design. The red bow was hand painted in Photoshop. Watch the video tutorial on the disc to see how this was accomplished.

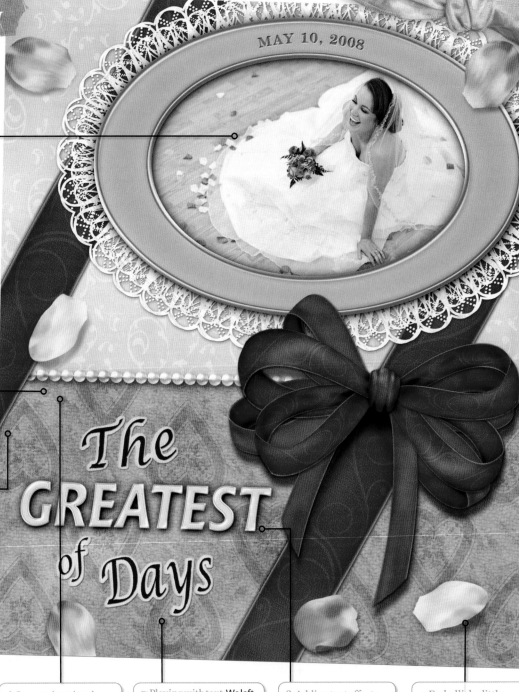

MAY 10, 2008

The GREATEST of Days

Want to see how we created this bow by hand? In the CD, check out the video tutorial as our author, Kirk Nelson, shows just how it's done!

6: Supporting visual elements The string of pearls was created with a layer style on circles of white. The lace around the frame was created with the same flower petal technique shown earlier. Both of these elements bring a splash of white to the design and match the bride's dress.

7: Playing with text We left room for text at the bottom of the page. Here is where we experimented with different typefaces, colours and arrangements. The general design rule for using fonts is if two different fonts are used, they should be very different. Here we used one block style font and one script style font.

8: Adding text effects To tie the text into the design, we gave the word 'greatest' a layer style that reflects the string of pearls and the photo frame. The rest of the text we rendered as layers of cut paper. Remember to treat the edges of the paper text to add realism.

9: Embellish a little Remember those rose petals we mentioned earlier? Well, here we added some of our own hand-painted petals as embellishments. This solidifies the design with the photo and creates a final touch to really finish off the layout.

Tips and tricks

From seamless patterns to realistic shadows, find your favourite scrapping tricks here

Save the pixels

Use adjustment layers to make non-destructive edits such as Curves or Hue/Saturation. This retains the source layer, allows for easy editing later, and comes with a built-in mask!

Dodge and Burn

Need a quick way to add depth and realism to a layer? Try using the Dodge tool to create highlights, and the Burn tool for shaded areas.

Source files

To reduce file size, move some of the complex layered elements into a separate file and then reduce that

element to a single merged layer in the main design.

Watch the lighting

Check Use Global Light in the Drop Shadow layer style to keep shadows aligned, so your layout will appear to have a consistent light source.

Graphics tablet

If you find yourself doing a lot of brush work with your mouse, consider picking up a graphics tablet with a pressure-sensitive stylus. Your hand and wrist will thank you!

Make a template

Once you have a great layout, strip it down to the basic elements and use it as a template for your next layout.

Realistic shadows

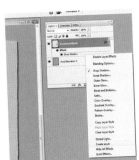

In the real world, it's rare for anything to lie perfectly flat. Typically it'll be a bit uneven due to thickness of the material, a wrinkle or fold, or even the glue that's used will create a distortion of the flat plane. The shadows cast by a non-perfect sheet of paper will also be non-perfect. They will be thicker, lighter and softer where the paper is elevated and tighter, darker and sharper where the material is close to the surface below it. Photoshop's default drop shadow won't do this. Fortunately there's an easy way to accomplish it. First add the regular drop shadow to taste, but then right-click or Cmd-click on the layer style and select Create Layers from the fly-out menu. This creates the drop shadow on its own layer to be manipulated independently of the layer. A favourite trick of ours is to use Filter> Distort>Displace Filter with a pre-made file of a cloud texture to add a nice random warping to the shadow layer.

The Gestalt moment

When it all comes together

So you've taken your photos, created your papers, added your patterns, conjured up embellishments – how do you know when to stop?

That's something we can't answer. You have to decide for yourself when you feel your layout is finally 'done'. Sometimes it simply all comes together like a puzzle and clicks into place. This is what designers refer to as the 'Gestalt moment', when the layout reaches a point where the whole design is more than just the sum of its individual parts. It's an elusive concept – but when you hit it, you'll know.

Making patterns: Respect the Offset filter

Create perfectly seamless patterns with a bit of help from this little-used filter

Frequently you'll need to create textures and patterns that can be repeated or tiled. You will quickly realise that when a pattern tiles, the seams become visible. To create a seamless texture, use the Offset filter (Filter>Other>Offset). Enter values equal to half the document's size, and the seams will be revealed. At this point it's a simple matter to use the Clone Stamp tool to paint away those unsightly lines.

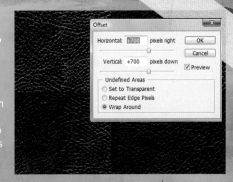

If you have created a scrapbooking layout of your own and perhaps had your own Gestalt moment, don't keep it to yourself. Share it with the world! We'd love to see it on a gallery on you can upload it to

a website, such as at our sister title Photoshop Creative (**www. photoshopcreative.co.uk**). If you join here, maybe visit our forum and invite other readers to join you in a 'collaborative scrap'.

"The design becomes more than the sum of its parts. It's an elusive concept – but when you hit it, you'll know"

Design a holiday montage

Washington DC

Greetings from s...
Hope you are al...
having a fantast...
trip round Amer...
we have been to...
Seattle, seen so...
sites and taken...
to show you all...

Lots of love,
Chris an...

Sights of Seattle

Views of the Space
Needle and downtown
Seattle

Our Trip to America

Design a holiday montage

We show you an innovative way to use your holiday snaps and souvenirs by blending them into a montage of your vacation memories

Rather than hiding your holiday photographs away in an album, why not try a more unusual approach and create a digital pinboard of your trip?

Incorporating photos, postcards, diary entries and Polaroids, it's the ideal way to capture your memories of a fantastic holiday. As an extra step, you could even add real souvenirs and receipts from the holiday to the board by scanning them in.

In this tutorial we'll show you different ways to secure your images to the digital pinboard, such as metal drawing pins, round-headed pins and tape. You've even been given a helping hand – on the disc we've provided a postcard template, handwriting font, metallic drawing-pin style and a selection of images to experiment with. If you want to see how we created the style, simply double-click on it once you've applied it to the layer and you'll see the settings in the Layer Styles window.

In addition to creating a corker of a board texture from scratch instead of photographing a real pinboard, you'll also learn how to make your images look like they are real photos placed on the board. And as if this isn't enough to get your teeth into, we even show how you can make your own postcard complete with personalised stamps, watermark and text in a handwritten style of font.

Follow our steps to begin pinning and taping this year's snaps to your digital board that you can look back on for years to come…

Essentials

TIME TAKEN
One hour

YOUR EXPERT
Zoe Mutter

ON THE DISC
Source photos and styles

Key Photoshop Skills Covered
What you'll learn

COLLAGE AND COMPOSITION TECHNIQUES

CREATING REALISTIC OBJECTS SUCH AS PINS AND TAPE

MAKING A POSTCARD AND STAMPS

Tip

Drag rather than copy

When you are working with layer styles such as the drawing pin, it's easier to use the Move tool to click on the pin and drag it across to the corkboard document rather than copying and pasting the pin layer, as this would mean you then have to click on the layer style and copy and paste this across as well.

CORKY CREATION
Be a pinboard wizard

01 Filter transformation
Create a new document, 29cm high and 38cm wide (300ppi). Set the foreground colour to Red 190, Green 185 and Blue 140, and background colour to Red 87, Green 75 and Blue 50. Fill with the foreground colour. Choose Filter>Noise>Add Noise, check Gaussian and Monochromatic. Enter an Amount of 25. Choose Filter Pixelate>Crystallize at an Amount of 10.

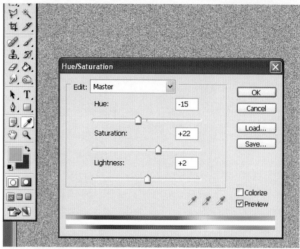

02 Choose your cork colour
Select Image>Adjustments>Levels and move the left and right sliders to meet where the pixels increase. Choose Image>Adjustments>Hue/Saturation and enter a Hue of -15, Saturation of +22 and Brightness of +2. You can blur the cork board and adjust the colour to suit. Add an Inner Shadow layer style as an extra step.

Expert Tip

Don't run into resolution problems

When you're creating many different elements in separate documents and bringing them across to your notice board document, make sure that they are all of the same resolution. Check this by choosing Image>Image Size and looking at the Resolution value. For example, if your notice board is at 300ppi and your postcard is at 72dpi it will appear blurry when you drag it across.

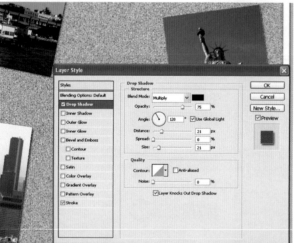

03 Place your photos
Select your photos and copy and paste them into the corkboard document. Rotate and resize using Edit>Free Transform. You'll rearrange your photos later. To make them appear to be on top of the corkboard, double-click the photo layer, bringing up the Layer Styles window. Click Drop Shadow and alter the settings to suit the amount of shadow that you want.

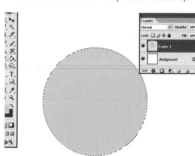

04 Pin it up
Create a new document measuring 8cm by 8cm at 300ppi. Create a new layer, choose the Elliptical Marquee tool and drag out the document while holding Shift to constrain the properties. Pick a foreground colour of Red 230, Green 217 and Blue 105, and fill the marquee using the Paint Bucket tool.

05 Copy our style
Copy the style 'Drawing pin' from the disc to your Styles folder (found in the Presets folder of your Photoshop Applications folder). In Photoshop choose Window>Styles and it appears in the palette. Drag it from the palette onto the drawing pin layer. Delete the background layer. Drag the drawing pin layer across to your corkboard document to secure your photos.

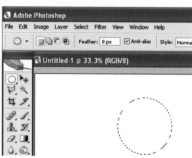

06 Further pin possibilities
To make the second round-headed type of pin, create a new document measuring 15cm wide by 11cm high. You can change the size when it is pasted into the final document. Choose the Elliptical Marquee tool and drag while holding Shift to constrain the selection.

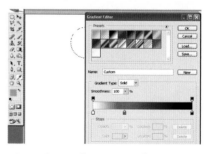

07 Customise your gradient
Choose the Gradient tool. Pick Radial Gradient from the Options bar. Click the Gradient swatch in the Options bar, bringing up the Gradient Editor. Pick a three-coloured preset. Click the colour stop below the gradient's left, click the Color swatch and pick white. Repeat for the middle stop and make it red. Repeat for the right one; make it black.

WORKS WITH | PHOTOSHOP 7 AND ABOVE, PLUS PHOTOSHOP ELEMENTS 3 AND ABOVE (FOR THE MOST PART!)

PIN IT DOWN
Create some shiny new pins

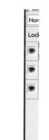

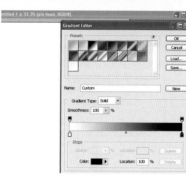

08 Shiny plastic effect Click OK and drag from above and left of the centre towards the bottom right of the pin head. Press Ctrl/Cmd+D to deselect, create a new layer and move it beneath the pin head layer. Call it Pin Base. Choose the Rectangular Marquee tool and make a thin rectangular marquee below the pin head.

09 Pin-point precision Click the Gradient tool and choose Reflected Gradient from the Options bar. Click the Gradient swatch in the Options bar and use the same process as before to make the gradient go from white to black.

Alter your pin colour

If you want to make pins with different coloured heads, before flattening the layers of the pin document select the layer with the pin head on and choose Image>Adjustments>Hue/Saturation. Now move the Hue and Saturation sliders to select a different colour. Flatten as before and save each pin separately.

10 Take a different slant Hold Shift down while dragging the Gradient tool horizontally from the centre of the selection. Press Ctrl/Cmd+D to deselect and Shift-click both the pin head and pin base layers to select them. Now choose Edit>Free Transform and rotate the pin so it is slanting, as we have done above. Delete the background layer.

11 Selective shading Select the pin base layer in the Layers palette. Choose the Burn tool and click just underneath the pin head, creating shading. Create a new layer below the pin base layer and call it 'pin shadow'. Zoom into the end, and with a small black brush draw around the pin end, making it appear to stick in the surface.

12 Cast a shadow Choose a soft black brush the width of the base (Opacity 100% and Flow 35%). On a new layer click the bottom of the pin base, hold Alt and click diagonally. Choose a brush the size of the pin head, click the top of the pin base shadow. Reduce the layer opacity. Choose Layer>Merge Layers and drag the pin to the corkboard document.

Composition class

It helps to organise each area of your board, for example the photo and its corresponding text and pin, into folders. This makes it easier to drag and experiment with compositions. In terms of organisation, ensure that all photographs are not facing the same way, and check that the layer order is correct so they overlap as you want them to.

13 Time-saving template Open 'postcard' from the disc. The lines were created using the Line tool. If you want to create a personal touch, you can add a faint image to the postcard as a watermark. Open your chosen image and use the Move tool to drag it into the postcard document.

14 Watermark of wonder Choose Edit>Free Transform and resize your image to fit the document. Place the layer at the top of the Layers palette. Change the photo layer's blending mode to Overlay and Opacity to 80%. We used the Sun custom shape in the bottom corner, but you can experiment with other custom shapes and designs.

Font Resources

Text time

The text on the postcard was created using the font G-Unit. We have included this on the disc for you to use by placing it in your computer's Fonts folder. To create the text on your postcard, you can also use one of the fonts within Photoshop that is similar to handwriting, or download fonts from the internet. Alternatively, you can write the text by hand and scan it in.

Dear diary

If you want to create the diary entry, open 'paper' from the disc and drag it across to the board. Rotate and resize the paper using Free Transform. Use the same font as for the postcard to write excerpts from a diary entry of the holiday. Choose a dark inky blue colour of low opacity, with a blend mode of Multiply for the text. Create another drawing pin to secure it by dragging the existing pin onto the Create a New Layer icon.

STAMP OF DISTINCTION
Add a global postal feel

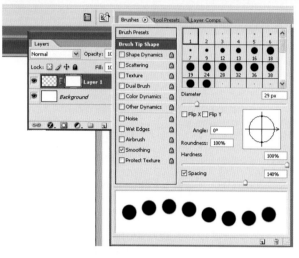

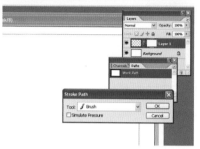

15 Put your stamp on it
Create a document of 6cm wide and 4cm high. Create a new layer. Click the Add Layer Mask icon in the Layers palette. Select the Brush tool, pick Window> Brushes and click the Brush Tip Shape tab. Enter a Diameter of 29px, Hardness of 100% and Spacing of 140. Press D, making the foreground black and background white.

16 The path to stamp success
Choose the Rectangle tool, making sure Paths is selected in the Options bar. Draw a rectangular shape. Make sure the layer mask is active by clicking it in the Layers palette. Choose Window>Paths. In the Paths palette click the small arrow in the top right and choose Stroke Path. Select Brush from the window that appears.

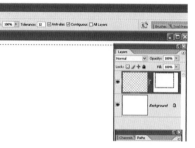

17 Load and fill your selection Click the Load Path as a Selection button in the Paths palette and click on the Layers tab to bring you back to the Layers window. The mask thumbnail will show the path you just created. Click on the layer thumbnail and not the mask thumbnail, and fill the selection with white using the Paintbucket tool.

18 Stampy shadow Delete the background layer. To get rid of the faint black edging, click on the white area with the Magic Wand tool, choose Select>Inverse and hit Delete. Add a Drop Shadow layer style to this edging if you want to make the stamp appear more raised.

19 Incorporate holiday shots Add a photograph to the centre of the stamp edging. We also chose Filter>Distort>Diffuse Glow to add an artistic effect to the image. Select a prominent image from your holiday to add a personal touch, and experiment with filters. We also added text for the price and place of the stamp. Choose Layer>Merge Layers.

20 Custom shape creation Now you have finished your stamp, drag the merged layer across to your postcard. Place and resize it if necessary. To create the wiggly postal stamp, choose the Custom Shape tool and select the Waves shape from the Nature set. Create a new layer, make sure Fill Pixels is selected in the Options bar and drag out the shape.

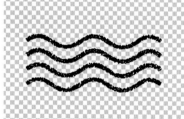

21 Realistic faded stamp effect As an optional extra, copy the shape layer and use the arrow keys to move it down so there are four wavy lines instead of three. Shift-click both layers, right-click them and hit Merge Layers. Choose Filter>Sketch>Torn Edges and enter an Image Balance value of 33, Smoothness of 14 and Contrast of 23. Click OK. Reapply if necessary.

22 Place and perfect the stamp Choose Edit>Free Transform and rotate the stamp slightly. We made ours thinner too. Using the Move tool, place it over the stamp, making sure it's above it in the Layers palette. Fade the layer's Opacity to 55%. Choose the Eraser tool on a 1px setting and cut randomly into the stamp, creating a more worn-away look.

ALERT | MAKE SURE THAT YOUR SHADOWS ALL POINT IN THE SAME DIRECTION FOR A REALISTIC EFFECT

THE AUTHENTIC TOUCH
Building up the pinboard

Produce Polaroids

Create a new document of about 10cm wide and 12cm high, open the photo you want to use and copy and paste it into the document. Pick Filter>Texture> Texturizer and apply it to the white background on a Relief setting of 2. Use the Move tool to position your photo and Free Transform to adjust the size. Add low opacity Drop Shadow and Bevel and Emboss layer styles to the photo layer, and as an optional extra add text. Merge the layers and copy across to the pin board document. Add a Drop Shadow layer style to the Polaroid layer.

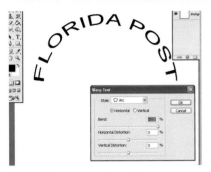

23 Even more stamps! Create a new document measuring 8cm by 8cm. Create a new layer. Pick the Type tool and set the colour to black. Use the font Arial in size 18pt and enter Florida Post. Click the Create Warped Text button in the Options bar, pick Arc from the Style pull-down menu and enter a Bend of +100%.

24 Enclose your text You may need to rotate the text slightly to make it level using Edit>Free Transform. Create a new layer, choose the Elliptical Marquee tool and drag it around the top of the text, holding Shift to form a circle. Choose Edit>Stroke and enter a Width of 10-15 px.

25 Use filters to fade Repeat this to create the bottom 'Florida' text but enter a Bend of -50 in the Warp Text window. Place the text below. Add the date across the centre. Delete the background layer, choose Layer>Merge Visible and apply the Torn Edges filter in the same way as before. Drag the layer to your postcard and reduce the Opacity.

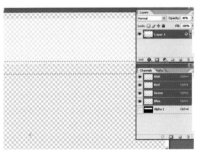

26 Stick it on Create a document 10cm wide, 3cm high. Create a layer and then delete the background. Pick Window>Channels. Click the icon to create a new channel. Create a rectangular selection using the Rectangular Marquee. Fill with white and deselect. Choose Filter>Pixelate> Crystallize, with a Cell Size of 10. Ctrl/Cmd-click the alpha channel in the Layers palette, creating a marquee.

27 Transparent technique Move across to your Layers palette and fill the selection with white. Change the opacity of the layer to 25-40%. Using the Rectangular Marquee tool, drag out a thin selection on the top of your tape and delete it. Repeat this for the bottom. This is because we only want rough edges for the two sides of the tape.

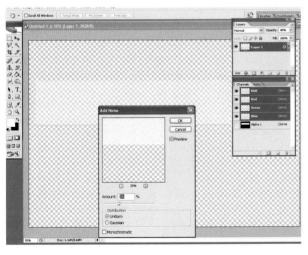

28 Styles and filters Double-click the tape layer, bringing up the Layer Styles window. Choose a Drop Shadow at 60% Opacity, 120 Angle, 11px Distance, 29% Spread and 2px Size. Go to Filter>Noise> Add Noise, check Uniform and uncheck Monochromatic. Enter an Amount of 24. Drag the tape layer to your corkboard document and reduce the Opacity if necessary.

29 Finishing touches Add white titles and borders to your photos, making them look like postcards. We used the same technique as the postcard's postal stamp to create red stamps on the photos of places visited during the holiday. Experiment with different compositions by dragging the elements around and saving the versions to compare.

Magnify your images

Give a montage focus by magnifying and highlighting one image in particular using this simple transparency technique

The problem with photos these days is that with the advent of digital cameras, we have hundreds per occasion rather than the 24 we used to have.

Furthermore, because they're captured and stored digitally, many of us never bother to print them out. It seems a shame – but where would you find space to display 50 photos of 'me on the beach'? One solution is to create a photomontage, incorporating a host of images into one composition. There are many approaches to montage, but a very effective method is to place the photos in a context that makes the montage a piece of art.

When displaying photos in this way, sometimes it can be nice to bring focus to one image in particular. In this tutorial we're going to show you how to achieve this by using a magnifying glass effect to emphasise one image among a pile of photos on a desk. We're going to need to make sure the glass has the appropriate reflections, magnifies the photo a little, and sits realistically on the surface to create a believable composition.

When you're finished, you'll have all the skills that are needed to create an image that uniquely shows off your holiday snaps. You'll learn how to make use of layer styles to build elements that appear 3D, how to hide and reveal layers with masks, and how adjustment layers can help you change the feel of an image quickly and non-destructively.

Essentials

TIME TAKEN
1-2 hours

YOUR EXPERT
Sam Hampton-Smith

ON THE DISC
magnifyingStart

VIDEO
See this video tutorial on the disc

SETTING THE SCENE
Set up your image, ready to receive the focus

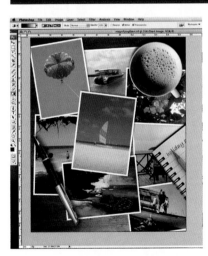

01 Create a new document Open up the starting image 'magnifyingStart. tif' from the CD into Photoshop. We're going to be magnifying the centre postcard image of the boat in this tutorial. First double-click on the background layer to turn it into a normal layer, then name it 'Start Image'.

02 Create a copy This effect will work by having a copy of the original colour image masked over the top of a desaturated version. Create a copy of the Start Image layer by dragging it down onto the New Layer button in the Layers palette. Name the copy 'Masked Image'. Turn off the visibility of the Masked Image layer for the time being.

"This effect will work by having a copy of the original colour image masked over the top of a desaturated version"

MAKING MONTAGES
It's easier than it looks

Making your own montage of holiday snaps isn't as difficult as it may seem. First of all, grab some elements from a stock website such as **http://sxc.hu** – here we've got the wooden desk (#1008244), the cup (#919878), the notepad and pencil (#946153) and the pen (##438254), all from this site. Bring your photos into one document, with the wood set as the background layer. Resize and rotate your images, adding a layer style to add a white stroke for the border and a drop shadow to place the photo in the composition. Mask the other elements and paint in drop shadows for a convincing effect. Hey presto – you have a quick, easy montage.

03 De-emphasise We're going to push back the saturation, contrast and brightness of the original image by applying some adjustment layers. Add a new Hue and Saturation adjustment layer, and tick the Colorize box. Set Hue to 30, Saturation to 25 and leave Lightness at 0.

04 Tone it down We've got a really nice sepia effect here, but it would be a shame to lose all the colour of the original photos, so let's tone it down by setting Opacity in the adjustment layer to 70%. This lets colour seep back in while still reducing the saturation dramatically. Compare before and after by flicking the adjustment layer's visibility on/off.

05 Warm it up This step is optional. If you'd like to warm the image up a little more, apply a further adjustment layer in the same way. Here we've opted for a Photo Filter adjustment layer (only available in CS3 onwards), at 20% Density. This acts in the same fashion as having a gel over the lens when shooting, and accentuates certain colours.

CREATE THE MAGNIFYING GLASS
Use a mask to reveal the full colour image

06 Unleash colour
We'll now create the magnifying glass. Show the Masked Image layer, then make a selection with the Circular Marquee tool; opt for a slightly larger selection than the size you want the glass to be. Ensure the Masked Image layer and selection are active, then add a layer mask by clicking Layer Mask in the Layers palette.

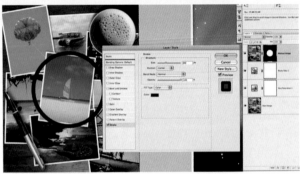

07 Add a frame The colour area isn't terribly well defined just yet, so let's add the frame of the magnifying glass. With the Masked Image layer still active, choose Layer>Layer Style>Stroke. Set Size to 80px, Position to Center and Color to a dark brown. We opted for '#3D2506', but you can choose whatever suits you.

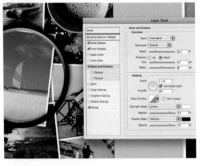

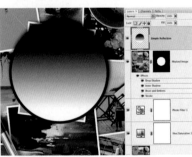

08 Add some depth We've dealt with the definition issue, but it all looks a bit flat, so while the Layer Style dialog is open (if you've closed it, go to Layer>Layer Style>Stroke again) let's add a Drop Shadow by ticking that box. Try to match the shadows in the composition; we opted for Angle -110°, Distance 45px, Spread 40px and Size 100px.

09 Inner depth We need to add an inner shadow to complete the placement, so tick that box in the Layer Style dialog. Set the Distance to 40px, the Choke to 25% and the Size to 80px. Finally, add an Inner Bevel in the same way, using Depth of 221%, Size of 45px and Soften of 8px.

10 Reflections To be convincing, we need to add some reflections to the glass. To start with, let's add a simple gradient. Hold down Ctrl/Cmd and click on the layer mask for the Masked Image layer to load this as a selection. Create a new layer, calling it 'Simple Reflection', and fill it with a black to white gradient using the Gradient tool.

ADD THE HIGHLIGHT
The extra twinkle that makes all the difference

Tip

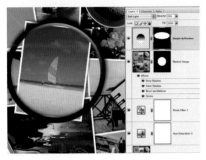

11 Mask and blend Set the blending mode of this layer to Soft Light and reduce Opacity to 50% to get a nice blended effect. Draw a big egg-shaped selection covering the top two thirds of the lens, make sure the Simple Reflection layer is active, then click Add Layer Mask in the Layers palette to add a mask and complete the effect.

12 Highlights We need a stronger light reflection to complement the one we've just created. Ctrl/Cmd-click the layer mask for the Masked Image layer again to load this as a selection. Holding down Alt/Option, draw a circular marquee offset to the left and down from the current selection. This will be removed from your existing selection. Aim for a moon crescent shape.

13 Magnify the picture The glass should be magnifying the picture, so to simulate this, once more Ctrl/Cmd-click on the layer mask of Masked Image. Select the Masked Image layer and then select Filter> Distort>Spherize. Choose an amount of 65% and click OK to add a nice magnification effect to the image.

Different bevels

In this tutorial we've opted for a very simple bevel for the magnifying glass frame, but there are many more possibilities. When adding a Bevel and Emboss layer style, experiment with the different bevel types and positions to get an effect that you're happy with. Pay particular attention to the Gloss Contour and Style attributes in order to get a full range of effects from this versatile style.

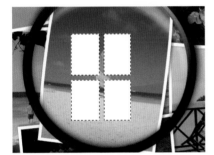

14 Windows Let's add one more reflection to the glass to help sell the distortion. Draw a rectangular selection to represent a window, then using the Alt/Option key to swap to a 'minus' selection, remove the window frame shapes so you end up with a four-pane window selection. Fill this with white onto a new layer called 'Window'.

15 Spherize the window For the last time, Ctrl/Cmd-click on the layer mask of the Masked Image layer. Make sure you have the Window layer active, then select Filter>Distort>Spherize and once again choose an amount of 65%. This will bend the window shape to match the distortion of the underlying image.

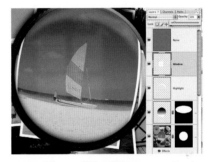

16 Blur and blend This is way too harsh just now, so add a Gaussian Blur with a value of 20px, and set Opacity in this layer to 10%. You might want to go back to the Simple Reflection layer and add a blur to this layer as well. Be careful to blur the layer mask rather than the layer itself, as the mask defines the hard line you might be seeing.

17 Get a handle on it Create a layer called 'Handle'. Using the Rectangular Marquee tool, draw a handle-shaped selection. Use the Shift key to add to your selection, adding extra width where the handle will meet the lens. Fill the selection with the same brown used for the lens frame, then add drop shadow and Bevel/Emboss layer styles to give the handle a 3D appearance. Finally, rotate and position below the lens in the layer stack to complete the magnifying glass.

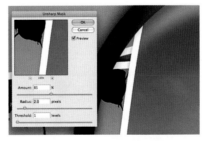

18 Accentuate the detail Zoom in to view your document at 100%. With the Masked Image layer active, go to Filter>Sharpen>Unsharp Mask. Enter values of 85% for Amount, 2.0 for Radius and 1 for Threshold to bring out detail and sharpen the edges of the colour area of the composition.

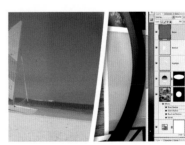

19 Final polish Create a layer at the top of the stack and call it 'Noise'. Go to Edit>Fill and set the Fill Contents to be 50% grey. Go to Filter>Noise>Add Noise, and select an Amount of 1%, Gaussian Distribution, and tick Monochromatic. Click OK, then change the blending mode of the layer to Overlay.

Spring Vacation

Master photo montages

Essentials

TIME TAKEN

2 hours

YOUR EXPERT
Lora Barnes

ON THE DISC

Source files

Looking for a clever way of presenting lots of different photos in one coherent image? Try this montage technique, which is deceptively easy to create

Taking a photo is easy enough, but when it comes to presenting all of your images in the best way, you might end up scratching your head.

A lot of the time it might just be a case of printing out single images and putting them in frames, but if you have a collection of photos from a single event, then it's sometimes nice to have more than one photo displayed at a time. Montages are one solution to this, and involve different elements or photos being used to make up one image. Often people will apply a feather to the edges in an effort to make a seamless whole, but this can sometimes end up looking a bit naff. If you follow this tutorial, though, you can still have more than one image in a file, but achieve a more exciting and fresh result.

The montage here takes its cue from the mosaic effect, where a whole picture is made up of separate squares. In traditional mosaics these would be coloured squares that are used to give form to the image. In our example, the squares are composed of bits of photo, housed within a crisp white frame. The effect work best if you concentrate on a strong subject, and then you can treat background elements with different blending modes or filter effects. This means the viewer's eye still has a main point of focus, but then on closer inspection they realise that there is in fact lots of different photos.

Because this technique manages to incorporate so many different elements, it is perfect for a wide range of uses. It can be used as an cover to a photo album, possibly made into a card, or even used as the menu for a DVD. Why not create a template that can be used in photo book services, such as Blurb books? Of course, there doesn't have to be a reason for doing it apart from the fact that it's an unusual and effective way of presenting a photo. And from a purely educational standpoint, you learn lots of valuable Photoshop tricks, including making selections, working with layer styles and creating a traditional film strip. Once you perfect this technique, we suspect you will start using it on all of your images.

GET INTO POSITION
Prime the elements for the tutorial

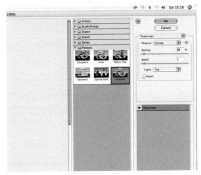

01 **The main photo** Copy the 'holiday photo.jpg' file from the tutorial files on the disc. Create a new layer and then double-click on the foreground colour square in the toolbar. Choose a suitable paper colour – we went for pale blue (Cyan= 11 Yellow= 3) – and then click OK.

02 **Create a canvas** Now go to the Edit menu and pick the Fill option. Select foreground colour and click OK. Pay a visit to the Filter menu and go to Texture>Texturizer. Pick Canvas from the Texture drop-down menu and set Scaling to 59%, Relief to 3 and Light to Top. Click OK.

03 **Move into place** Double-click on the 'holiday photo' layer in the Layers palette to unlock it. You need to do this so you can move it to sit above the paper layer in the Layers palette. Making sure your still on the 'holiday photo' layer, pick the Move tool and move the image up and to the right-hand side. Go to Edit>Transform>Scale to reduce its size a little.

PHOTOSHOP CS AND ABOVE, PHOTOSHOP ELEMENTS 3.0 AND ABOVE (ALTHOUGH SOME STEPS WILL DIFFER) | **WORKS WITH**

Secrets of successful montages

Although this technique can work on pretty much any photo, there are a couple of things you can do to make sure you get optimum results. If you are working on a portrait photo, try not to cut the face up – use one square for the whole face area. Also be careful to keep the square selections reasonable close together. If they're too far apart you won't be able to see what the original photo was!

MAKING SELECTIONS
Start building up the squares

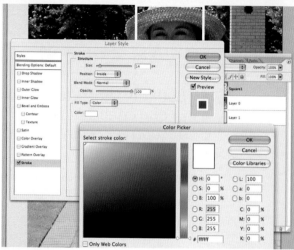

04 **Hip to be square** Go to the toolbar and select the Rectangular Marquee tool. Now make a selection of about 6 x 6cm over the face. Copy and Paste onto a new layer and call it 'Square'.

05 **Stylish addition** Double-click on this newly created layer in the Layers palette to bring up the Layer Style dialog. Click on Stroke at the bottom left-hand side. Change the Size to 14px and set Position to Inside. Click on the colour rectangle at the bottom and choose White.

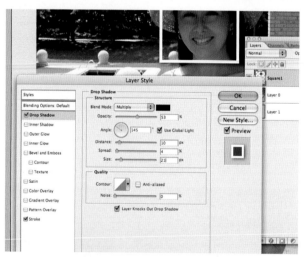

06 **Not finished yet** Still in the Layer Style palette, choose Drop Shadow. Set the Blend Mode to Multiply and change the Opacity to 53%. Move the Angle to 145 and check Global Light. Change the Distance to 10px, Spread to 4% and Size to 21px. Click OK. This layer is now our template for the layer style and we can copy the style into each square layer once they've all been cut out (see step 10, 11).

07 **And again** To get identical selections for the rest of the image, go to Select>Reselect. This brings up your last selection. Click back on the 'holiday photo' layer in the Layers palette. Pick the Rectangular Marquee tool once more and move your mouse over the marching ants of your selection. When you see a white arrow, click and hold your mouse button down and move the selection to a new position. Copy and Paste as you did before.

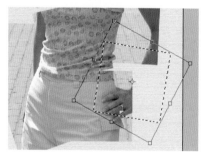

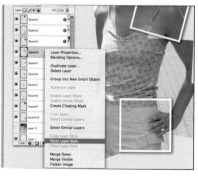

08 **Variety is the spice of life** To keep the montage interesting, you need to vary the angle of the selections. This gives a nice scattered look. After you have brought the selection back by reselecting, go to the Select menu and pick Transform Selection. You can now click and rotate the selection. When you have your angle, hit Return and then Copy and Paste in the same way.

09 **The nifty part** To apply the Stroke and Shadow effects to all of your selections, Ctrl-click (Mac) or right-click (PC) on the first layer that you have already applied the layer style to and select Copy Layer Style. If you're in Elements, go to Layer>Layer Style>Copy Layer Style.

10 **Paste layer style** Now click on each square layer in turn in the Layers palette and Ctrl/right-click to pick Paste Layer Style. Elements users can go to Layer>Layer Style>Paste Layer Style. Keep doing this on each one until all your squares have white frames and shadows.

ADDING VARIATIONS
Mix up finishes for more striking effects

Tip

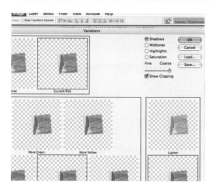

11 Varied finishes You can keep your selections as they are or add some variations in colour. We clicked on random layers and applied some different effects. Go to Image>Adjustments >Variations. Click Shadows and have fun! We chose More Blue and More Yellow for some of our squares.

12 Not just Variations In addition to Variations, you may like to try a quick blast of the Color Balance option (found under Image>Adjustments>Color Balance). You might fancy desaturating some as well. When you've finished adding effects, select all of the square selection layers in the Layers palette and go to Layer>Layer Merge.

13 Photo editing Click on the 'holiday photo' layer and change the blending mode to Luminosity. Reduce the Opacity slider to 44%. With the Rectangular Marquee, draw over the photo, leaving an even border around the outside to neaten things up a bit. Go to Select>Inverse and then delete.

Loading brushes
To alter the current brush set, select the Brush tool and then click the little brush preview square in the options bar. When a window appears with all the brush choices, click the little right-pointing arrow. Select one of the brush sets and then click OK. You'll see the new brushes appear in the window.

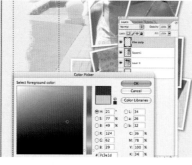

14 Border effect Deselect your selection and then click the Eraser tool. Choose the Large Texture Stroke from the Wet Media brushes set. Make it quite a big brush at around 150 or bigger. Erase around the edges to create a painterly effect. If you're unsure about how to change your brush set, see the side panel on this page.

15 The film strip With the main image kind of finished, it's time to create a film strip. Create a new layer and call it 'film strip'. Use the Rectangular Marquee to select a long rectangular section on the left-hand side. Go from the top to the bottom. Choose a reddy brown for the Foreground colour and fill the selection.

16 On the top Move the film strip layer to the top of the Layers palette. Change the blend mode to Multiply and open the 'jumbo ferry' file from the CD. Go to Image>Image Size and change the Height to 3 and Width to 4.5. Click OK, then select all and copy

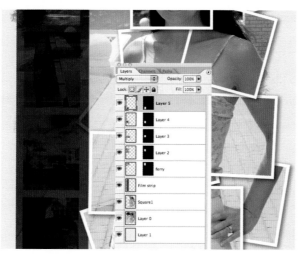

17 Paste it in Go back to the montage document, create a new layer and make a rectangular selection in the shape and position of an image on a negative. Choose Paste Into from the Edit menu. Go to Image>Invert and change the blending mode to Overlay.

18 Next picture Create another new layer, go to Reselect in the Select menu. Move this selection down where you want the next image to sit on the strip and open 'Sailing again' from the CD. Reduce image size to 4 x 5cm. Select All, Copy and Paste into the selection on your new layer as before, invert and set the mode to Overlay. Repeat for all the photos on the disc until your negative strip is complete.

USING THE FILM STRIP
Go for the traditional feel

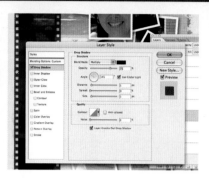

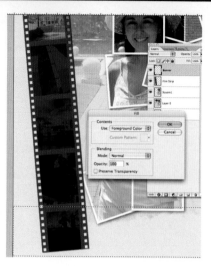

19 Final touches Click on the 'film strip' layer once more and make a small square selection along the side and press Delete. Repeat the process along both sides of the strip to give it that authentic look.

20 Same style You need to apply a drop shadow to the film strip, but the Layer Style command remember the last values so there's no need to change any settings. They will be the same as the montage shadows which is just what we want so just click OK. Select all of the film strip layers in the Layers palette and merge.

21 In position Go to Edit>Transform> Rotate and move to the angle shown here. Create a new layer and call it 'banner'. With the Rectangular Marquee, make a selection across the bottom of the image and then fill with a cream colour.

22 More border Use the same Large Texture Stroke brush eraser as before and erase along the sides of the banner. Go to Filter>Texture>Texturizer. Again you don't need to do anything except click OK as it retains the previous settings you chose for the blue background. Now go to Edit>Transform and rotate to give a slight angle. Go to the Layer Style and select Drop Shadow. Drop the Opacity down to 30% and Size to 12px. Click OK.

23 Type it in Choose a dark blue and select the Type tool. Choose a font you like (we chose Mistral Regular) from the top bar and enter your text. To change the font size or colour, highlight the text and change the value in the top bar.

LAYER STRUCTURE
Building up a montage

24 Nice touch Add some decoration to the banner by choosing the butterfly brush from the Special Effect brush set. Open the Brushes palette, click Scattering and move the Scatter slider up to 1000%. Choose two colours for the foreground and background and then click around the banner and text.

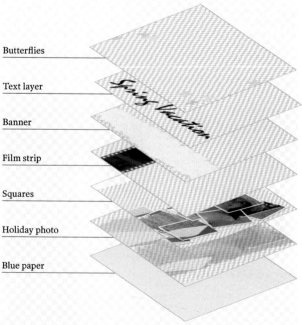

Butterflies

Text layer

Banner

Film strip

Squares

Holiday photo

Blue paper

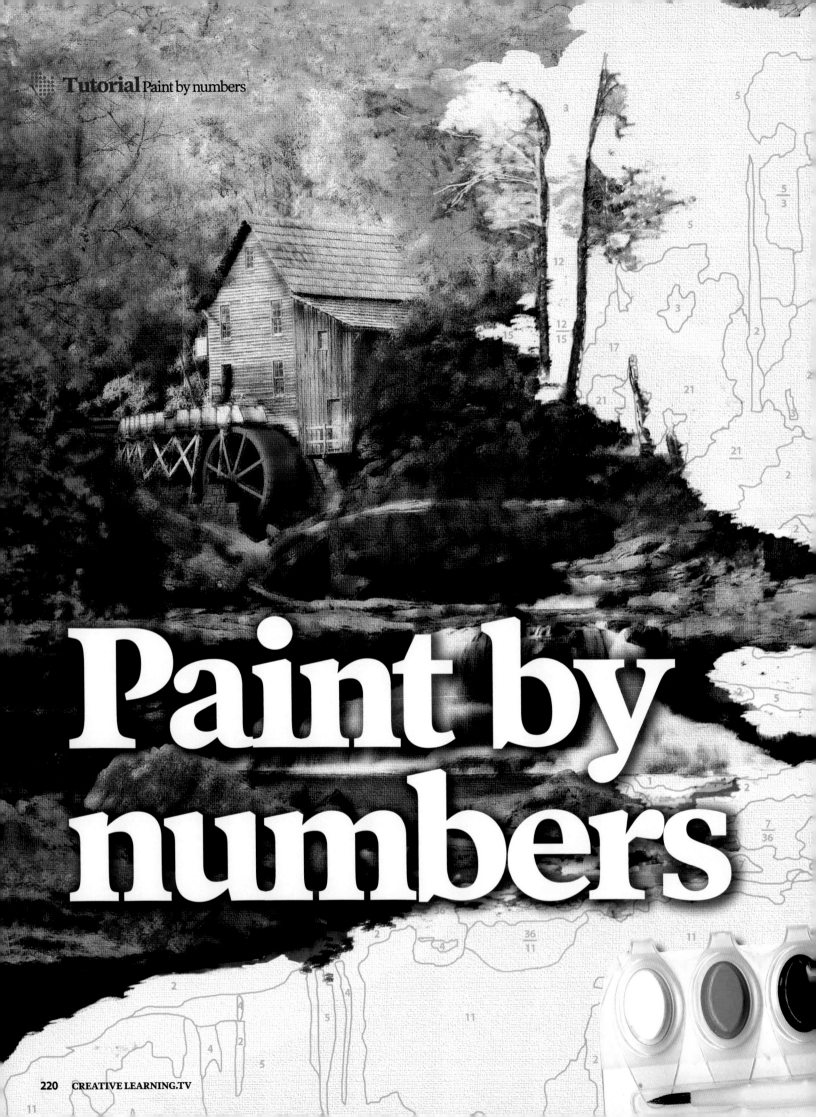

Paint by numbers

You don't need natural artistic talent to create great digital art – filters enable you to produce excellent results. Read on and discover how they can work for you

Anyone who has delved into the Filter menu will know there are many delicious creative-sounding options for making a photo into something much more interesting. So we decided to see just how far you could go with these filters. Assuming no artistic experience or knowledge, we picked three photos, shared them around the Photoshop Creative team and waited to see what would happen. Is it really possible to create a digital painting just by moving a few sliders around? We planned to find out and learn a bit more about filters along the way…

Understanding filters

Over 100 filters ship with Photoshop, all accessible from the, er, Filter menu. Filters are a bit finicky about what kind of images they work on – Bitmap or Indexed Color files are right out, and some will only work on RGB documents. To save mucking about with modes while creating, it's best to work with an RGB file. Once selected, a filter will be applied to the active layer or selection.

Some filters will be applied instantly, and you can repeat the application to build up the effect. Some will open a small dialog window where you can adjust the intensity of the filter, while others will launch the Filter Gallery. This offers a new workspace where you can access and apply multiple filters, preview the effect, and zoom in and out of your burgeoning painting to make sure all is going as it should. Only about half of all filters live in this gallery, but most of those used in artistic creation are found here.

Each filter in the gallery comes with sliders that allow you to alter characteristics for that filter. You can also apply more than one filter to an image – rather like creating new layers. This happens in the bottom right palette of the Filter Gallery, and the icon you need looks like a page with a corner curled over. Click this and a new 'layer' will appear above the first one. As soon as you click on a different filter, it will be applied to the new layer. This means you can build up a rich effect and avoid flat-looking images.

As well as being able to stack up different filters on top of one another, you can also rearrange them to get the

You can just apply one filter (left) but for more realistic effects, build up multiple filters (right)

exact effect you want. Keeping with the layers comparison, you click on the filter you want to move and then drag it to the new position. You can also click an eye

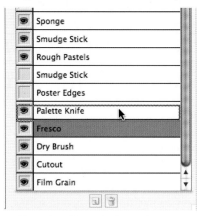

In addition to laying filters on top of one another, you can also move these 'layers' about or turn their visibility on or off

icon to hide/view a filter so you can get an accurate assessment of what needs to be added or removed.

Painting with filters

It's quite a good idea to think of filters as your cooking ingredients. Decide which elements you want for your effect and then pick the correct 'flavours'. For example, in watercolour paintings you can often see sketch marks. If you run a Sketch filter along with the Watercolor filter, you can achieve a similar effect.

You don't have to stick with the obvious filters in order to get painterly results. The Clouds filter, for example, is excellent for giving a smudgy effect that's reminiscent of an Impressionist painting. The Blur filters are also good for softening the harsh edges of a heavily filtered image.

One other tool that deserves your attention is the Fade command. Found under the Edit menu (although it's not in Elements), it controls the opacity or blending mode of any filter. This can be effective in dulling down the sometimes brash results a filter can give and brings you closer to that painting goal!

The best filters for painting

The Filter menu is organised into different sets, the names of which give a pretty clear indication of what result you can expect. You won't need to use all the filters when you're digitally painting, but here's a look at the best ones:

 # Pastel

Pastels generally have a loosely defined style, which means they work well on blurry shots that you might otherwise consign to the bin. The medium also makes great use of textures. Here we've used a nice water and bridge shot to emulate Impressionist painters such as Monet.

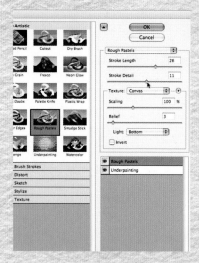

Filter controller: Jo Cole

Time taken: 5 minutes

Why I chose this look: I've tried using pastels in real life, but only manage to produce a dirty, smeary mess and end up getting covered in pastel dust. I love taking photos at twilight, but am too lazy to carry a tripod so my shots are always slightly blurred or noisy. This technique means I can make use of my dodgy shots and even pretend I intentionally made them blurry to get a better painted effect! I love the texture this style produces – have a look at the water, it's all smudgy and lovely!

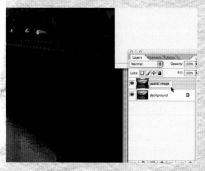
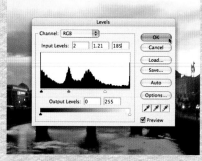

01 **Create a safe copy** Open up the 'impressionist pastel.jpg' file from the disc. You can see how this photo has suffered from a lack of tripod – it's slightly blurry. None of this will matter when it gets some filter treatment! Create a duplicate layer of the photo and name it something suitable like 'pastel image'.

02 **Brighter outlook** Because this look destroys any detail and darkens a photo, take a trip to the Levels dialog and lighten things up. In the Input Levels bit, enter 2, 1.21, 185. The photo will look horrible, but trust us… if you don't do it things will end up all dark and foreboding.

03 **The first filter** We'll start the proceedings with a trip to the Underpainting filter. Go to Filter>Underpainting and the Filter Gallery will open. Set Brush Stroke to 1, Texture Coverage to 11; set Canvas as the texture, Scale to 125, Radius to 9 and Light to Top. Things will suddenly look very painterly!

04 **Rough it up** Click the New Layer icon (looks like a page curling) and then click Rough Pastels. This is where you get to add all the chalky, smudgy goodness. Start by setting Stroke Length to 26 and Stroke Detail to 11.

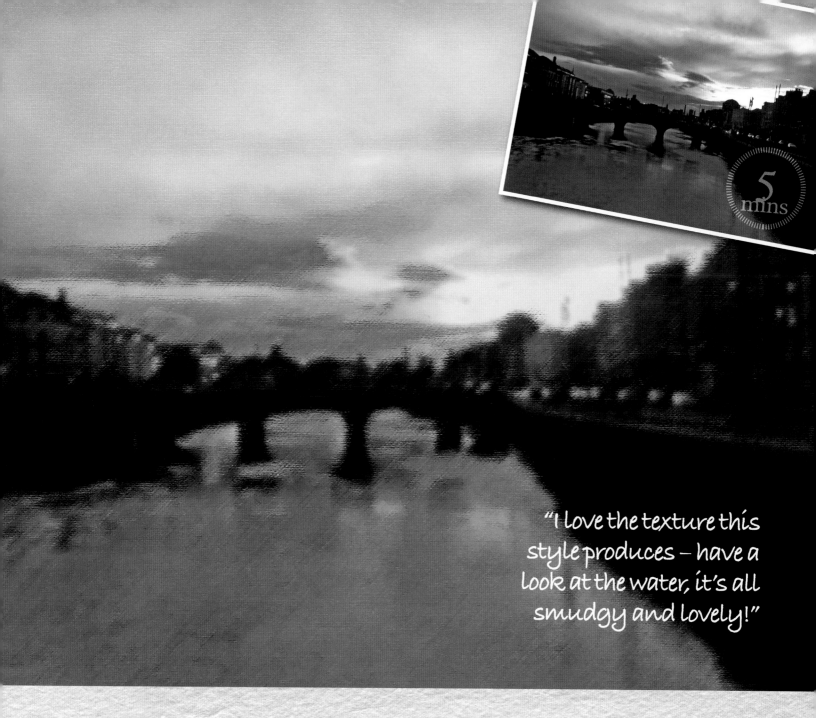

5 mins

"I love the texture this style produces – have a look at the water, it's all smudgy and lovely!"

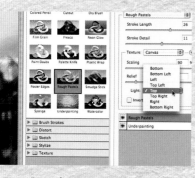

05 **Boost the texture** From the Texture pull-down menu, make sure Canvas is selected and then set Scaling to 90%. Set Relief to 7. If you set Relief too high, you will get lots of diagonal lines that look a little too perfect for a pastel painting. Make sure Light is set to Top and leave Invert unchecked. Now click OK.

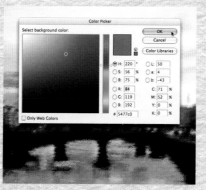

06 **The final touch** Back in the main Photoshop interface, double-click on the Foreground square to access the Color Picker and choose a really dark blue. Double-click on the Background square and pick a mid blue.

07 **Cloudy day** With your colours selected, create a new layer and go to Filer>Clouds. Set the blending mode to Multiply and lower the Opacity slider to 20%. This darkens the whole picture slightly and the cloudy pattern gives the impression of hand smudges.

Tip

When using the Rough Pastels filter, try and hang back on the Relief slider. The higher it goes the more noticeable the pastel 'strokes' will be. You'll end up with uniform diagonal lines, which isn't a trademark of the pastel style!

Artistic filters achieve painterly and artistic effects, and are the obvious first stop for anyone looking to get arty. Colored Pencil gives an, umm, coloured pencil look on a coloured background. It uses your currently selected background for this, so choose wisely. Dry Brush simplifies an image into areas of common colour and then paints the edges. Think of what would happen if you mixed the qualities of watercolours with oils. Fresco is a coarse style with swiftly applied dabs, so it's great for landscapes but won't keep a lot of defined edges. Palette Knife reduces details to give a thinly painted canvas effect. Rough Pastels applies pastel chalk to textured background. Where colours are bright, chalk appears thick. Where they are darker, the texture is revealed a bit, emulating that dusty pastel effect. Smudge Stick softens an image by smudging the darker areas. The Sponge filter gives you textured areas of contrasting colour, but it can sometimes look like your image has loads of water stains. Underpainting

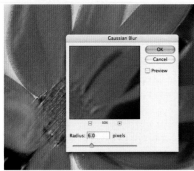

About half of the filters are accessed from the Filter Gallery, but some will bring up their own dialog window

puts your photo on a textured background and then paints on top. You lose a bit of detail, but it's a good place to start when going for a washy paint effect. Watercolor does as you'd expect.

The Blur filters are actually really good for softening areas or smudging things together. Think of them as a digital version of blending paints or merging edges with your thumb. Gaussian Blur is particularly good because it adds low-frequency detail and gives a hazy effect.

The Brush Strokes filter group also gives a painterly or fine-art look. Accented Edges boosts edges of an image. When edge brightness controls

5 mins

"This style works particularly well on portrait shots"

⣿ Colored Pencil

One blast of the Colored Pencil filter will rarely give you the look you want, but all it takes is a couple of layers and you can get a pretty decent result that's the perfect starting point for all sorts of creations. If you wanted to take an image such as this one even further, you could erase a few areas back, have parts of the photo poking through, smudge different parts… there's a lot of choice and potential. This style works particularly well on portrait shots, especially when the subject is against a pale background. Turn a photo of a loved one into a sketch or maybe use it as the basis of a greetings card.

Filter controller: Zoe Mutter

Time taken: 5 minutes

I like this filter because:
I find it really difficult to get good results from coloured pencils – somehow everything seems to end up looking like a child's drawing! But using this filter means I can get the look without getting the stress.

Tip

⣿ If you want to go for more of a sketchy effect, it's a good idea to bump up the contrast a bit before applying the filter. This will remove some of the detail in the photos and give the filter fewer lines to hang on to.

01 **Coloured paper** Open up the 'pencil drawing.jpg' file from the CD. Create a new layer and fill with beige (R = 250, G = 241, B = 217). This will act as our paper colour underneath the Pencil coloured filter layers.

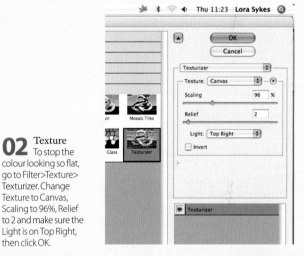

02 **Texture** To stop the colour looking so flat, go to Filter>Texture>Texturizer. Change Texture to Canvas, Scaling to 96%, Relief to 2 and make sure the Light is on Top Right, then click OK.

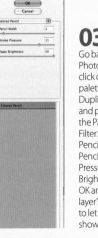

03 **Colour sketching** Go back to the original Photo layer and double-click on it in the Layers palette to unlock it. Duplicate this layer and put it on top of the Paper layer. Go to Filter>Artistic>Colored Pencil. Change the Pencil Width to 3, Stroke Pressure to 11 and Paper Brightness to 50. Click OK and change this layer's mode to Multiply to let the Paper layer show through.

04 **Strengthening tones** And that's basically it. How easy was that! Obviously there's more you could do, but for a great starting point this is perfect. Just to finish it off, I duplicated the Pencil coloured layer and put it on top of all the other layers, and then changed the layer mode to Color Burn and its Opacity to 33% just to strengthen the darker tones in the hair.

are set high, accents resemble white chalk. When low they look more like black ink. Angled Strokes repaints a photo using diagonal strokes. Light and dark areas are painted with strokes going in opposite directions, giving a dynamic, messy effect. Crosshatch retains detail, adds texture and roughens edges. Dark

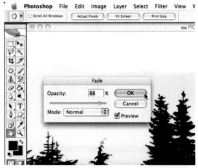

As soon as you apply a filter, the Fade command appears. This lets you reduce the filter Opacity or change the Mode

Strokes paints dark areas with short, dark and tight strokes, and is looser and longer with light areas. Ink Outlines applies fine narrow lines over original details. Spatter re-creates the spatter look of an airbrush. The higher the options, the more simple the effect. Sprayed Strokes repaints using an image's dominant colours and uses angled strokes. Sumi-e gives a kind of Japanese style. Think of a brush loaded with paint applied to absorbent paper.

Distort filters may not be your first stop on your digital painting journey but the Ocean Ripple filter adds random ripples to an image so it looks like it's underwater. If set correctly it also looks like paint and can be a good base layer.

The Pixelate collection of filters gathers together pixels of similar colour values. The best one for painting is Pointillize. This breaks up colour into random dots, using the background colour as canvas area between dots. It's basically your one-click way of emulating the Pointillist style of painters.

Render filters are primarily associated with 3D work, although there is one that comes in handy when making digital painting. Clouds gives a soft cloud pattern that's perfect when layered, and is used to create Impressionist-style effects. Fibers is also worth experimenting with because it uses the foreground and background colours to give the

 # Watercolor

The watercolour style of painting will never go out of fashion, so it's no surprise that Photoshop has a filter to help you get the same effect. By careful adjustment of the sliders you can easily get a good result, and applying a heavy canvas texture will help add to the effect. A photo of flowers makes the perfect subject – look at how the water in the vase has turned out. Perfection!

Filter controller: Lora Barnes

Time taken: 4 minutes

Makes life easier because... I really like painting, but haven't got round to doing any lately. I'd like to say it's because I've been too busy, but basically I've got far too lazy – plus working in Photoshop every day has opened my eyes to the powers of the digital realm. Umm, let me think… a couple of days sat at an easel or five minutes at my Mac. Guess which one I'd choose!

01 Brush strokes Open the 'watercolour. jpg' image from the CD. Unlock the layer by double-clicking on it in the Layers palette, and then duplicate this layer. Go to Filter>Artistic>Paint Daubs and change Brush Size to 8 and Sharpness to 38, and make sure the Brush Type is Simple. Click OK. This gives the image stronger highlights and a touch of texture to kick things off.

02 Ray of sunshine Quite a few of the painting filters tend to dull and darken down the image – so before we do any more, create a new layer, choose a pale yellow as your foreground and change the background colour to white. Select the Gradient tool and click and drag from the top left to bottom right. Change this layer to Overlay and its Opacity to 60%.

03 More painting Duplicate the Paint Daubs layer and place it above the Gradient layer. Go to Filter>Artistic>Watercolor. Change the Brush Detail to 14, Shadow Intensity to 0 and Texture to 1, then click OK. Change the blending mode to Overlay and the Opacity to 70% to let some of that light back in.

04 Spread it about Duplicate the Watercolour layer and place it on top of all the other layers. To reduce the intensity of the yellows, change the blending mode to Hue. To finish it off go to Filter>Blur>Gaussian Blur and move the slider to 40.1. This gives a nice paint bleeding effect especially around the vase, giving it that authentic watercolour look!

4 mins

"Look at how the water in the vase has turned out – perfection!"

impression of woven fibres. This makes a perfect base for the Colored Pencil filter.

Sketch filters are another staple for digital artists. They use the foreground and background colours, so be aware of this. Chalk & Charcoal takes the highlights and midtones of an image and redraws them with a midtone grey colour in chalky effect. Shadow areas get replaced with black diagonal charcoal lines. The foreground colour is used for the charcoal, while the background colour is used for the chalk. Charcoal gives a more smudged effect. The foreground colour is used for the charcoal, while the background colour is used for the paper. Conté Crayon re-creates a look of dark and white conté crayons. The foreground colour is used for dark areas, while the background colour takes care of the light areas. Graphic Pen uses linear ink strokes for redrawing an image. The ink colour is

Adding texture to a digital painting is an instant way of making it look realistic and inviting

dictated by the foreground colour, while the background colour is used for the paper. Water Paper gives the impression of blotchy paint daubs on wet, fibrous paper, giving a heavily blended effect.

Stylize filters are generally a little too harsh or wacky for most artistic effects, but there is a gem. Find Edges will do pretty much as it says, by outlining the edge of an image with dark lines. The background will be white.

Texture filters are perfect for the final flourish to a digital painting. They allow you to give depth to an image. Craquelure can look like embossed wallpaper, but when used small, it gives a pleasing crackly texture. Texturizer is the big daddy, because of the Canvas option. This suddenly makes your filter painting look very realistic.

The best art filters

At a loss where to start on your digital filter painting quest? Here's our pick of the best filters to play with, along with a handy list of which filters are good for certain effects

What filters to use for...

The sketchy look

Crosshatch
Chalk & Charcoal
Charcoal
Conté Crayon
Graphic Pen

A painterly feel

Palette Knife
Dry Brush
Paint Daubs
Smudge Stick
Underpainting
Watercolor
Dark Strokes
Spatter
Sumi-e
Ocean Ripple

A chalky effect

Chalk and Charcoal
Chalk
Rough Pastels

Texture

Film Grain
Rough Pastels
Mezzotint
Mosaic Tiles
Texturizer
Fibers

Texture

Texturizer   Craquelure   Mosaic Tiles

Render

Clouds   Fibers   Lighting Effects

Sketch

Chalk & Charcoal   Charcoal

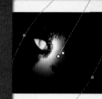 

Conté Crayon   Graphic Pen   Water Paper

Artistic

Colored Pencil   Dry Brush   Fresco   Paint Daubs   Palette Knife   Poster Edges

Rough Pastels   Smudge Stick   Sponge   Underpainting   Watercolor

Brush Strokes

Accented Edges   Angled Strokes   Crosshatch   Dark Strokes

Ink Outlines   Spatter   Sprayed Strokes   Sumi-e

Blur

Gaussian

Noise

Add Noise   Median

Pixelate

Mezzotint   Pointillize

Stylize

Find Edges

Distort

Diffuse Glow   Ocean Ripple

Pop art portraits

Essentials

TIME TAKEN
4+ hours

YOUR EXPERT
Charlene Chua

ON THE DISC
vector-start.jpg

Key Photoshop Skills Covered
What you'll learn

SIMPLIFY A PHOTO
USE THE PEN TOOL
WORK WITH PATHS

Clean, crisp lines and bold flat colours are the trademark of pop art and vector work. But who says you need to learn Illustrator to create your own? Do it here in Photoshop!

Vector art is both a style and a kind of graphic that's often unmistakeable and confusing at the same time.

While the exact definition of the term gets pretty technical, the vector 'look' is unmistakable – sharp crisp lines and even, precise colours reminiscent of the pop art work made famous by artists like Andy Warhol. These days, people who deal mainly with vector-based images generally use vector-drawing programs such as Illustrator and FreeHand. A vector image is made up of mathematical points and can be scaled up and down without any loss of quality. While Photoshop isn't quite so flexible, it still sports enough of the necessary tools for you to create the effect.

In this tutorial we're going to 'vectorise' a photo. We'll cover the basic ideas behind vector art, and

how to go about making photos easier to vectorise. Then we'll construct the artwork from the photo, working mostly with Photoshop's Pen tool. There'll be a lot of talk about paths, since that's really what makes up vector art – so if you're not familiar with the Paths palette, have a quick read through Photoshop's Help file for a quick explanation.

Vector artwork usually consists of lots of shapes layered on top of one another. This can cause your file to become heavy and complex, so take your computer's power into consideration before you start anything. Name your layers and sort them into folders if you can. Lower the file resolution if you don't intend to print it out later. You can also flatten layers as you go, but save an unflattened backup copy in case you want to change anything later.

GET SETTLED DOWN
First steps to vector heaven

01 The starting line Open up the file 'vector-start.jpg'. This lovely lady is going to be the subject of our tutorial. Before doing anything, have a good look at the picture. Sit back and squint your eyes. See how the picture is simplified into globs of colour? That's the basic idea behind the vector look – keeping things down to an elegant minimum.

02 Posterising Choosing colours from a photograph can be tough. To make things a little easier later on, simplify the photograph's colour with a basic filter. Hit Filter> Artistic>Poster Edges, and set Edge Thickness to 4, Edge Intensity to 0 and Posterization to 3. Hit OK and let the filter render itself.

03 Know your tools For this tutorial we'll mostly be making use of the Pen tools to create the illustration. As with Illustrator, the Pen tools are great for creating precise lines and curves that would otherwise be difficult to draw. Unlike a brush, a Pen tool does not actually create a stroke when used; instead it draws an invisible line or path.

WORKS WITH | PHOTOSHOP 7.0 AND ABOVE

From this...

...to this

Tool School

Dragging your paths

In step 4, we tell you to click and drag to get a smooth curve. Here's how you do it. Click to make a starting point. Now position the Pen tool cursor where you want to make your next point and click, BUT DON'T LET GO! With the mouse button still held down, drag up, down and around to get the path line where you want it. When happy, let go of the mouse and repeat for the rest of the object you're tracing!

Tool School

Simply does it

Pens are quite unlike the other drawing and painting tools in Photoshop, and people usually start using them with a fair bit of caution. A common mistake with new users is creating far too many points. With paths, the fewer points there are, the smoother the resultant shape will appear. The trick is to learn how to control direction lines so that you get the curves you want with as few points as possible.

THE DREADED PATHS
Learn this essential technique

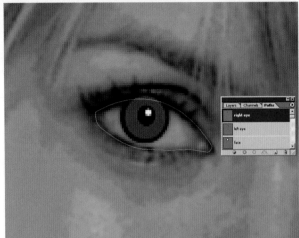

04 **Paths 101** We're going to start on the left eye. Select the Pen tool. In the top Options bar, make sure you are working in Paths (middle icon). Zoom in on the eye, and start to click around it to get a general shape. Click and drag to create a smooth curve for the upper part of the eye. See the left box out for how to do this.

05 **Close and save** When you're done, close your path by clicking back on the first point you created (you'll see the cursor change to a pen with a tiny circle next to it). Now go to your Paths palette. Double-click on Work Path and rename it to save the eye shape. Save your paths to prevent them being overwritten by the new paths you create.

06 **Iris** On a new layer, use the Elliptical marquee to draw circles for the iris. Pick an eye colour from the reference photo with the Eyedropper tool, and hit Edit>Fill. Return to the path palette, Cmd/right-click the eye shape and choose Make Selection. In the Layers palette, click Add Layer Mask to neatly enclose the iris within the eye shape!

07 **Lashes** You're able to create more than one path on the same layer. You can choose how you want multiple paths to interact with one another from the Options bar. Choose Add to Path Area and use the Pen tool to draw a bunch of shapes for the eyelashes. Save this path, select it and fill it with a deep brown.

08 **Finishing the eye** Create another layer and use the eye shape to make a selection, then fill it with a pale yellow for the eye whites. Group all your eye layers together into a set. Rearrange your layers so the lashes are on top, followed by the iris then the eye whites. Repeat the entire process to create the right eye.

09 **Show some face** Start constructing the face as you did the eye. Use the Pen tool to trace a general outline of the face. Don't worry about getting it precise around the edges of the fringe – when we do her hair later, those bits will get covered. Close your face path and name it Face to save.

10 **Picking a base** Use the Eyedropper tool to pick out a base skin colour. It may help to zoom in on the face. Click on the flesh tone that seems to be the most neutral. A suggestion would be the area around the girl's right cheek. Create a new layer, select the face shape and fill it with colour, then hide the layer.

11 **Create contrast** Next, we need to draw out the shadows and highlights. To make it easier, duplicate the posterized photo. Hit Image> Adjustments>Hue/Saturation: set Hue to -180 and Saturation to -100. Now go to Image>Adjustments> Brightness/Contrast and bump Contrast up to 70. You can now clearly see the light and dark areas.

HEAVENLY HAIR
Here comes the science bit...

Making a truly successful vector-style image hinges on the use of shadows and highlights. Although the style is typified by its 'flat' colours, you still need some depth to prevent the image from looking like it's come from a colouring book. Here we take a closer look at how we built up the hair, the most complex part of the image.

You can clearly see in the three pictures below how our model went from a flat, uninteresting beige to a lovely set of luscious locks!

Hair base

Start with shadows

Final touches

Start by creating an overall hair shape. Fill it with a suitable colour – a tip is to pick something with the Eyedropper then turn up its saturation. Note that although she may be blonde, the girl's hair is NOT yellow!

Next, work in the shadows. Dyed hair in particular is quite colourful, and you can mess with a range of shadow colours. Vary the shadow shapes and sizes to create the illusion of depth and volume.

Finish up by adding the highlights and coloured edges. Keep these as thin strips and use them sparingly. A tip here is if you want a more textured look, keep your shadow and highlight shapes small and pointy!

SHADOW DANCER
From flat to fantastica

12 Medium shadows Now you can start tracing the shadows! Trace out the medium shadows first (remember, you can draw more than one shape on the same path layer). The light source is from her left, so include more shadow on her right. Don't worry about matching the face outline exactly – you can use the face shape to create a layer mask later.

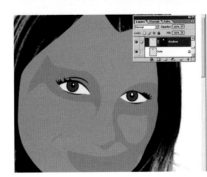

13 Medium shadows 2 When you're happy with your paths, save and select them. You can use the Eyedropper to pick a fill colour, or trust your artistic judgement to select a colour that's similar to the base skin tone, just a tad darker. Either way, fill in the shadows on a new layer, then use the face shape to mask it.

14 Dark shadows Repeat the process, this time drawing out the darker shadows. These are normally reserved for the edges of the face, around the eye and under the lip. Don't draw shadows around the cheeks because that will make the subject look old. Choose a colour, and repeat the fill/mask procedure on a new layer. Move this layer above the medium shadows.

Tool School

Edit paths with the Direct Selection tool

Sometimes a path needs to be tweaked after it's drawn. Editing paths is mostly done with the Direct Selection tool. Click on an anchor point with this, and you'll be able to shift the point around. Click on the little circle at the end of a direction line (the lines that protrude from an anchor point), and you can adjust the length and curvature of the path. Selected points will show as a solid square instead of a transparent one.

BUILD UP DETAIL
It's a long process, but worth it in the end

15 Highlights Create highlights in the same manner – use the Pen tool to draw shapes, only this time select the lightest bits. The shiny bits of a face are usually the cheeks, nose and chin. Keep highlights minimal so they don't overpower the overall skin colour. Fill and mask, and move the layer to the top of the heap.

16 Accents Add detail to the face by using the Pen tool to draw small shapes to form the nose, eyebrows and lips. The thing to note here is to keep things simple and minimal. A little spot of brown is enough to give the idea of a nostril, and a thin brown line suggests the crack of a mouth.

17 Hair While it may look complex, the hair is really just more of the same. Switch back to the colour photograph, use the Pen tool to draw out a general shape for the hair, and pick out a suitable colour with the Eyedropper. The hair layers should be above the face, and the main shape should cover the uneven face bits from before.

18 Building volume Still using the Pen tool, create various little bits for the hair shadows and highlights. It can get tricky because hair is not one even tone, but just keep in mind that you're not trying to duplicate the photograph – you're simplifying it. Add some deep brown and orange-yellow bits to achieve the dyed look a la vector style!

ANATOMY OF A PATH
The power of the Pen tool

Paths can be confusing, but they tend to work like a join-the-dots puzzle. All paths are defined by their anchor points. An anchor point, which looks like a small square, gets created when you click on the canvas while using the Pen tool. If you click and drag, you'll create a smooth point. If you simply click, you'll make a corner point. Smooth points connect to each other with curves, whereas corner points connect via straight lines.

All paths appear in the Paths palette. New paths automatically appear on the Working Path layer,

so it's a good idea to save paths on their own layers. Saved paths can be selected by clicking their respective layers. You can add or remove individual paths on a saved path layer.

Paths can be edited with various tools. The Path Selection tool allows you to select and reposition an entire path, while the Direct Selection tool lets you tweak individual anchor points. The Convert Point tool changes a smooth point to a corner point and vice versa. Points can be added or removed from a path by using the Add Anchor Point and Delete Anchor Point tools.

19 Layer as you go Naturally, the head and hair sit on top of everything, and the same goes for their layers. Using the techniques above, we added, in this order, her neck, sweater and forearms. Keep everything simple from here on, otherwise it will distract attention from the main focus of the picture – the face and hair.

20 In the jeans Use the Pen tool to draw out the general shape of the jeans. To create the somewhat looser shadows and highlights here, try the Freeform Pen tool. This tool is a cross between a pen and a lasso – it lets you draw paths in a more intuitive manner, although it's not nearly as precise as a normal pen.

RESOURCES | IF THE PEN TOOL STILL HAS YOU FLUMMOXED, VISIT **HTTP://GRAPHICSSOFT.ABOUT.COM/OD/PHOTOSHOPTUTORIALSSHAPESPEN/** FOR MORE HELP

FINISH UP
Gradients make all the difference

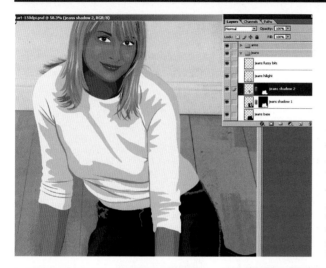

21 Blue jeans
Select the Freeform Pen tool and draw paths for the jeans' shadows and highlights. Fill them with colour and mask them with the general jeans shape. Finish off by drawing in the little fuzzy bits on the sides. You don't need to mask these, since they are supposed to stick out of the jeans anyway.

22 Replace the background Yeah!
Almost done! Hide the photograph layers, and find some funky colours to replace the background. Go ahead and choose something completely different from the pale wall in the photo. We dropped in an orange wall and red floor to create a more dramatic-looking picture. Try various colours or even dropping in a texture to get some wild results.

23 Special effects Before wrapping up,
add some spice by dropping in some subtle gradients in key areas. Zoom in to the eyes, and draw a couple of shapes for her eyeshadow. Select the eyeshadow shapes and fill them with a brown foreground-to-transparent fill on a new layer. Decrease the Opacity to 51% and reposition this layer at the very top of your face group.

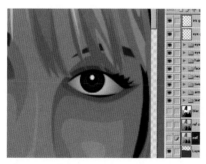

24 Dazzling eyes Still on the eyes – create
a couple more layers and leave them right at the top of the list. On one layer, select your eye shapes and individually fill them with the gradient. Change the mode to Multiply and set it to 80%. To add some colour to the iris, repeat the above but change your foreground colour to blue.

25 Done! That's it! The picture is complete.
If you're a perfectionist, try opening the photo file separately and compare the two. If you think some colours don't quite look right, you can use the colour correction tools to make adjustments now, or add details you may have missed out earlier.

LAYER STRUCTURE
Building up a vector masterpiece

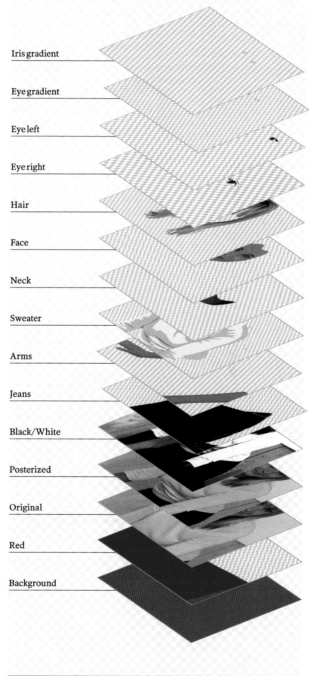

Iris gradient

Eye gradient

Eye left

Eye right

Hair

Face

Neck

Sweater

Arms

Jeans

Black/White

Posterized

Original

Red

Background

Paint like Cézanne

We provide you with all the tools and techniques you need to emulate 'the father of modern art'

Look up Paul Cézanne in any art book and chances are you'll read something along the lines of him being the father of modern art. And there's a very good reason for this – look at his paintings throughout the course of his career and you can see them move from still lifes to Cubist masterpieces.

For this tutorial we're concentrating on his still life period. Starting with a very roughly photographed bowl of fruit, we use the Smudge tool to paint over the photo. The beauty of the Smudge tool is that it picks up colours and shapes from the photo so you don't have to worry about drawing or shading anything. Plus it's a really quick effect. Cézanne used lots of nice big strokes, so you needn't be too precise. It's just a

case of getting used to how the tool works and then having lots of fun with it. Because Cézanne's work was quite dark and expressive, you haven't even got to be that accurate. Keep strokes nice and loose, and you'll end up with a better painting.

Our source photo is quite big, so if you have an older computer or you just want part of the photo, feel free to concentrate on one bit – the bowl of fruit, for example. When you've got to grips with this tutorial, you can apply the effect to other photos. Try giving the Cézanne look to your family pictures.

The Smudge tool is an excellent way of getting realistic paint effects. Be confident in the marks you put down with your imaginary palette knife and have a bit of messy digital painting fun!

Essentials

TIME TAKEN
40 minutes

YOUR EXPERT
Lora Barnes

ON THE DISC
Cezanne starter image.jpg

Beginner's
Photoshop
Creative projects

From this...

...to this

SURPRISE YOURSELF
Discover the artist inside you

01 To start Open the starter image on the CD. Make a copy of this layer and call it 'Base'. To get the look of dry, scratchy paint for the base layer of paint go to Filter>Artistic>Rough Pastels. Change Stroke Length to 21, Stroke Detail to 19, Texture to Canvas, Scaling to 66 and Relief to 19. Lastly, for the Light Direction choose Bottom.

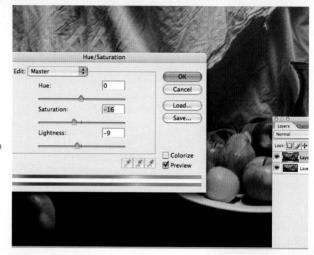

02 Light and dark Cézanne's still life paintings have quite harsh lighting, creating strong shadows and midtones. This image needs dulling a touch so we don't end up with fluorescent yellows. Go to Image> Adjustments>Hue/ Saturation. Leave Hue on 0 but change the Saturation to -16 and Lightness to -9.

Tool School

Snapshot to success

This technique all takes place on one layer, which means you need to protect yourself in case anything goes wrong. The best way is to take snapshots throughout the process, so if something did go wrong you could go back to a happier state. Snapshots record how an image looks at a certain time and are accessed via the History palette. To create a snapshot, click the New Snapshot button in the History palette.

03 Smudge it! Take a look at the next page if you haven't used the Smudge tool, to get an idea of its effect. You'll get to know what size brush to use and what direction to pull or push the paint in, but for now pick a medium to large (say 162 pixels) Thick Pencil brush (in Natural Brushes 2). On the front apple, make quick, short marks from left to right around its centre.

04 Base coat Move across the image looking at the areas that don't have much detail, and start smudging in sections. Remember to keep following the contours of the object you're painting, especially when you come to the folds of the fabric and the fruit. You don't have to reach the edges – you'll do this with the smaller brushes. The next five steps will take the most time.

05 Less is more There are only a few marks, but this gives us some big blocks to work around with medium/small brushes. Now take a snapshot of the image in the Layers palette. The History palette will fill up, and smudging takes place on one layer, so regular snapshots are vital.

06 Medium size Keep the same brush type but downsize to about 104px. Really work around the contours of the fruit and cloth. Don't feel you must complete one area before moving on. Keep the whole painting at the same level.

TIP | THE BEAUTY OF CÉZANNE'S WORK IS ITS ROUGHNESS – DON'T BE TOO PRECIOUS WITH YOUR BRUSH STROKES!

PAINT WITH THE SMUDGE TOOL
Make sure you get perfect strokes every time

The key to this painting is following the natural contours of the photo object. Use smooth strokes and you'll always get good results

UNDERSTANDING THE SMUDGE TOOL

Small brush

Medium brush

Large brush

Right to left pull
The three images here show the effect of the Smudge tool. We kept the Strength at 86% for this painting, but feel free to have a play with this if you want less or more smudge! Basically, wherever you start off is the colour you drag through to where you stop.

Smudge tool

Left to right
As with the right to left example, it doesn't really matter which way you smudge, but just be aware if you start on red and go into a green area, the red will bleed across. This can land you in trouble if you use a big brush close to the edges, because it'll leak out.

Continuous motion
As well as making a series of quick marks in one direction, you can also cover areas quickly by keeping the mouse button held down and making sweeping motions. This merges colour a lot more, so avoid wherever you want to keep detail.

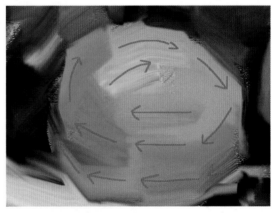

Define the sections
Try and visualise objects as if they were made out of slabs of colour. Treat highlights, midtones and shadows as separate areas.

Smooth direction
The Cézanne effect is achieved by making short strokes and following the direction of the fruit.

Contours
Because you are smudging the detail, you need to keep to the same contours so you can still make out what you're painting.

ATTENTION TO DETAIL
Sorting out the fiddly bits

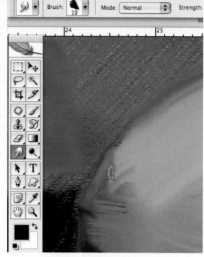

07 A closer look at the background material Reduce the brush size down again to around 65px and start to follow the contours of the cream background fabric. Make sure that you keep the highlights and midtones separate as much as possible – if they blend together too much, the illusion of cloth will degenerate into a muddy mess.

08 Small brush Change the size of your brush to about 19px and start to neaten up the edges of the fruit and the plate, or any other areas that the other brushes were too big for. With a smaller brush the continuous motion is more effective than trying to make little marks, especially when you're using it to smooth between the bigger smudge marks.

09 The navy textured fabric The foreground navy ribbed material may look really scary to do, but it works out quite nicely. Change the Size to about 77 and Smudge across the untextured areas. Now reduce the size of the brush again and start to stroke down the raised lines and stroke up the material in between. Again, don't feel you have to cover every square inch – just accent the material rather than smudging it to a pulp.

WORKING IN CEZANNE'S STYLE
Decide upon the defining qualities

When creating the look of an old master, it's important to incorporate their style. Here's our tribute to Cézanne…

Billowing fabric Cézanne often used fabric in his paintings, either draped over a table or hung in the background. We simply folded up some sheets on a table and hung a couple of bed sheets in the background. The Smudge tool made them look a lot better and captured the bold Cézanne look.

Feeling fruity Cézanne painted a lot of fruit in his time, which is easy enough to replicate. He tended to have the odd piece of fruit tumbling away, which we've done here. Cézanne was a notoriously slow painter and it's been said that he had to use wax fruit because real fruit kept going off!

Lot on your plate The vast majority of Cézanne's still life paintings showed fruit on a plate. The plates were normally white, so we just used a plain dinner plate to arrange the fruit on.

A good pitch(er) Another staple component of a Cézanne still life is jug or vessel of some kind. These were normally placed at the back of the painting. We just used a glass water pitcher, although a ceramic jug would work just as well. You could also try a vase or bottle.

NOTES | APPARENTLY CÉZANNE'S MODELS KEPT QUITTING BECAUSE HE TOOK SO LONG TO PAINT THEM!

POLISH THOSE APPLES
Put the finishing touches to your masterpiece

Tool School

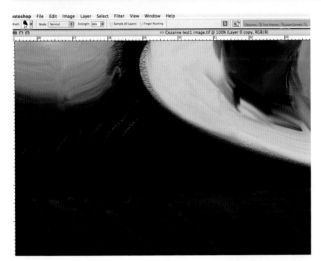

10 Revisit areas
Now's the time to step back and see which areas need more attention. Perhaps you want to introduce some bigger brush marks, now you have a feel for what you're doing. Or perhaps you're not happy with one of the pieces of fruit and want to rework it (see tip on the right). So have a bit of a tidy up around the plate and other bits that need defining.

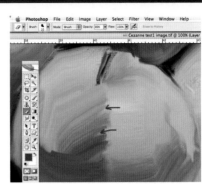

11 Smaller still A great thing to do with a smaller brush is to drag through the edges of the existing bigger smudge marks with short sharp marks in the opposite direction. This enhances the edges, making them look streaked with paint.

Eek! A bad apple

If you're an hour or so through your creation and you have a section or maybe just one piece of fruit you can't rescue and you feel it's ruining the rest of the image, don't despair. Simply duplicate the original layer again, apply the rough pastels and resmudge the areas you're not pleased with. Now place this new layer below the existing fully worked layer. Choose a soft brush as an eraser, click on the top layer and then simply rub out the ugly bits to reveal the new creations lying underneath.

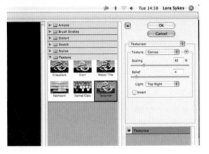

12 Add canvas texture Once you're happy with the painting side of things, it's time to add a canvas texture. Go to Filter>Texture>Texturizer and pick Canvas. Set Scaling to 82%, Relief to 4 and Light to Top Right. Click OK. Remember, once the texture's on you can't smudge on this layer without smudging the texture as well.

13 Lasso the back sheet The back sheet is quite yellow and we want it more bluey white to go with the other fabric, so a quick fix is to lasso around the back sheet with a feather of about 12px. Then go to Image>Adjustments>Color Balance. One by one, click on Shadows, Midtones and Highlights in the Tone Balance and pull the slider right until the yellow tone starts to go more blue.

14 Levels Without deselecting, go to the Image>Adjustments>Levels menu and click on the white triangle on the right. Move it towards the centre a touch (as in the screenshot). Click on the grey triangle in the middle and move this along to the left until it looks similar to the screenshot above.

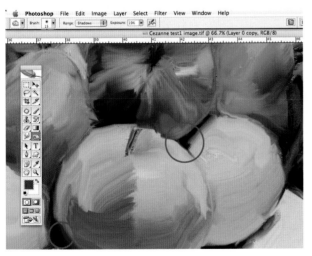

15 Burn shadows
Back to the foreground. Cézanne used deep shadows and midtones on and around his fruit, so we need to burn ours in a bit more. Choose the Burn tool in the toolbar. Load the Basic brush set and pick the Soft Mechanical brush at 16px. Set Range on the top bar to Shadows and Exposure to 19%. Start burning in all the shadow areas on the fruit and the light blue material.

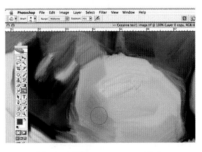

16 Burn midtones Keep with the same Burn brush but up the size to between 40 and 95%. Change Range to Midtones and up Exposure to 46%. Brush quickly over a few of the midtone areas on the apples, lemons and a few bits of the fabric. If you want less of a contrast, just drop the exposure percentage. And that's it… your masterpiece is complete!

BEFORE

Paint a portrait in oils!

If you've always wanted to paint a portrait of a loved one in oils but lack the painting ability, we have the answer!

Essentials

TIME TAKEN
1 hour

YOUR EXPERT
Tim Shelbourne

ON THE DISC
Start image courtesy of Priscila Elizondo – find more of her images at www.sxc.hu

When it comes to traditional painting, perhaps the most fundamental difference between one painting medium and another is that of the surface quality.

You only have to run your fingers over an oil painting to appreciate its unique properties, and that's what we're going to recreate here thanks, as usual, to a little Photoshop magic. One of the mantras of the traditional artist in oils is 'Darks thin, lights thick'. In practical terms this means that darker areas in the painting are painted with thin, liquid paint, and lighter areas are applied thickly, allowing the paint to stand proud of the surface and creating an effect known as 'impasto'. This is one of the most difficult effects to replicate in Photoshop, but vital to achieve a convincing appearance.

We're going to achieve this impasto effect here by using a simple layer style.

If you have little or no traditional painting ability, then this Photoshop method is just for you, because all that it involves to create the finished painting is some simple mark-making with a couple of special Photoshop brushes.

We'll use the initial start image via a couple of layer masks to supply all the colour and shading, but we'll use it in a way that creates a truly unique and spontaneous looking oil painting. Photoshop even provides us with the facility to apply a super-realistic canvas texture. So, if you've always wanted to create a portrait masterpiece in oils, here's your chance. Fire up Photoshop and get painting!

ALL ABOUT LAYERS
Set the scene by preparing your layers

Key Photoshop Skills Covered
What you'll learn

HOW TO USE LAYER MASKS

HOW TO CREATE AN IMPASTO EFFECT

HOW TO USE TEXTURES

01 Filled layer Open the start image and add a new layer (Ctrl/Cmd+Shift+N). Choose a midtone warm grey colour for the Foreground swatch and go to Edit>Fill, choosing Foreground Color for Contents. Click on the background layer and duplicate it (Ctrl/Cmd+J).

02 Glowing Edges filter In the Layers palette, grab the background copy layer and drag it up the layer stack, dropping it above the filled layer. Now go to Filter>Stylise>Glowing Edges. Use these settings: Edge Width 4, Edge Brightness 12, Smoothness 11. Click OK to apply the filter.

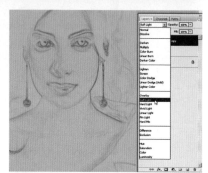

03 Sketch layer Go to Image> Adjustments>Desaturate. Now invert this image via Image>Adjustments>Invert. In the Layers palette, set the blending mode for this layer to Soft Light. Now click on the background layer and duplicate it again. Drag this layer to the top of the layer stack.

WORKS WITH | PHOTOSHOP 7.0 AND ABOVE

04 Simplify the detail To simplify the detail in the image, go to Filter>Artistic>Palette Knife. Use these settings: Stroke Size 25, Stroke Detail 3, Softness 9. Click OK. Now go to Image>Adjustments>Curves. With two points on the curve, create a shallow 'S' shape as shown in the screenshot above to increase the contrast a little.

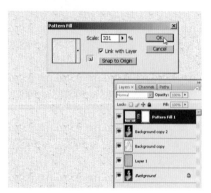

05 Canvas Texture Go to Layer>New Fill Layer>Pattern. Click in the Pattern swatch and hit the small right-pointing arrow, choosing Artists Surfaces. From the Pattern swatches choose Canvas. Set the Scale slider to 330% and click OK. In the Layers palette, set the blending mode for this layer to Linear Burn.

 # THE TECHNIQUE BEHIND THE ART
How we got that authentic oil painting look

Impasto effect The effect of heavy paint, or impasto, is created by the use of a Bevel And Emboss layer style. This gives the colour on this layer a degree of relief, with raised edges to the marks made on the layer mask, giving the effect of the paint standing proud of the surface.

Canvas texture For added realism we've applied a canvas texture to the whole image via a simple Pattern layer. This layer sits at the top of the layer stack so that it has an effect on every layer below it. You can adjust the visibility of this pattern simply by adjusting the layer's Opacity.

Brush dabs As you work, it's important to think about the size and direction of your brush strokes. Use the brush at a smaller size and with shorter strokes in more detailed areas, and use broader, more spontaneous strokes in less detailed areas around the centre of interest.

Outline The simple outline layer serves as a guide for painting, just like an artist's initial sketch would do. Also, by leaving areas of the 'sketch' visible in the finished image, you can add an authentic feel to the painting.

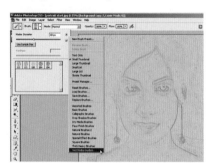

06 Layer mask and choose a brush Return to the image layer below and add a layer mask via Layer>Layer Mask>Hide All. Now choose the Brush tool. Click in the Brush Picker and hit the small right-pointing arrow, choosing Wet Media Brushes. From the brush thumbnails choose Brush With Thick Flow Medium Tip. Hit F5 to display the Brush options.

07 Modify the brush In the Brush options click on the Texture category. Click in the Texture swatch and choose Weave. Increase the Scale slider to 125%. Click on Other Dynamics and set the Opacity Control to Pen Pressure. Make sure that Color Dynamics is NOT checked. Finally, click on Brush Tip Shape. For Roundness enter 50%. Enter 30 for Angle. In Shape Dynamics, set Minimum Size to 75%.

08 Paint onto the mask Click directly on the layer mask thumbnail on this layer and ensure that the Foreground swatch is white. In the Options bar reduce the brush Opacity to 50%. Now, using the brush at around 180 pixels, start to paint over the face.

BUILD UP YOUR PAINTING
Follow these techniques to create the right effect

09 Varied strokes Use short, loose strokes at various angles to start revealing some colour in the image. Make sure to leave plenty of canvas showing through. In the outer areas such as the hair, background and the woman's jacket, use broad sketchy strokes, again leaving plenty of canvas visible. When you're happy, Ctrl/right-click the layer mask thumbnail and choose Apply Layer Mask.

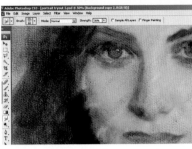

10 A little smudging Choose the Smudge tool, and from the Brush Picker choose the Large Texture Stroke brush. In the Options bar set the Strength to around 30%. Now use this tool to smudge areas here and there. You can confuse some of the outlines by pulling and pushing them with this tool, adding realism to the brushed effect.

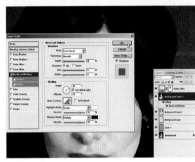

11 Add a layer style Click on the original background layer and duplicate it (Ctrl/Cmd+J). Drag this layer to the top of the layer stack. Go to Layer>Layer Style>Bevel and Emboss. In the Layer Style dialog, enter 3 for Depth and set Size and Soften to zero. Choose Inner Bevel for Style and Smooth for Technique. Click OK.

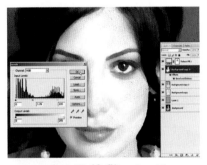

12 Palette Knife filter Go to Filter> Artistic>Palette Knife and use these settings: Stroke Size 26, Stroke Detail 3, Softness 10. Click OK to apply the filter. Now go to Image>Adjustments>Levels. Enter 1.29 in the central box and 220 in the right-hand box. Add a layer mask to this layer via Layer>Layer Mask>Hide All.

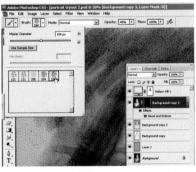

13 Another brush Choose the Brush tool and hit the right-pointing arrow in the Brush Picker, choosing Thick Heavy Brushes. From the brush thumbnails choose the Rough Round Bristle brush. In the Brush options use the same settings as you used for the previous brush.

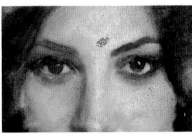

14 Impasto brush marks Click directly on the layer mask thumbnail attached to this layer. Now use this brush at around 100 pixel size, with white as the foreground colour, to start adding detail and impasto to the face. Use short strokes at different angles here, following the contours of the face. Make sure to use the brush at a small size over the key facial features in order to add detail here.

15 Darks thin, lights thick It's best to use this brush at low opacity in the darker areas and higher opacity in the light areas, so that the paint appears thin in the darks and thicker in the lights as it would in a traditional oil painting. The more you work with the brush on this layer mask, the more the painting will build up.

16 Build up the paint Vary the size of the brush as you work over the rest of the image, still using the brush at partial opacity so that you can slowly build up the thickness of the paint by overlaying strokes in different directions. It's important to use plenty of movement in your strokes, especially around the outer areas of the painting.

17 Duplicate and hide Once your painting looks similar to the screenshot, with partially opaque colour over the majority of the subject but plenty of bare canvas still showing through, duplicate this layer (Ctrl/Cmd+J). Click directly on the layer mask thumbnail for this duplicate layer and go to Edit>Fill, choosing Black for Contents.

Painting with layer masks

Although, technically speaking, we are painting here, we're not actually applying any colour. The vast majority of the painting is taking place directly on layer masks, and it's important to understand precisely how they work. Here we apply a black-filled mask to each image layer which completely hides it. The colour from the associated image layer is revealed through the brush strokes by painting onto the black layer mask with white. In layer masking terms, black conceals and white reveals the associated image layer. Shades of grey reveal the associate image layer at partial opacity. It's vitally important during this project that you paint on the layer mask and not on the associated image layer, so before you start to paint, make sure to click directly on the thumbnail for the black mask in the Layers palette. You can actually view the layer mask in isolation by holding down the Alt key and clicking the mask thumbnail. Alt/Option-click the mask again to return to normal view.

THE FINAL MASTERPIECE
Add the finishing touches

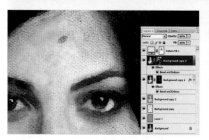

18 Smaller marks Hit F5 to show the Brush Properties and uncheck the Texture category. Close the Options palette and in the Options bar set the brush Opacity to 100%. This is the layer where we'll add most of the detail, so reduce the brush's size to between 80 and 100 pixels and start carefully painting over the face with short strokes.

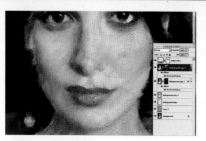

19 Adding detail We want a broken feel here, so don't paint solid areas of colour but use lots of strokes in different directions. It's important to use the brush at a small size over the eyes, nose and mouth, as this is where the detail needs to be concentrated. Use the finished image as a reference, so you can make your strokes roughly follow the contours of the face.

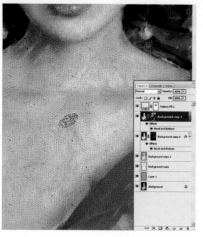

20 Broken colour We want the majority of the most opaque paint concentrated within the face, so in the chest area you can increase the size of the brush and use less pressure on your stylus, or reduce the brush Opacity in the Options bar so the paint is more broken and less opaque here.

21 Gestural strokes When painting over the hair and the woman's jacket, use the brush at 100% Opacity again and use more energetic, gestural strokes. It works well here to overlay strokes in opposite directions to one another. Here you can see the layer mask in isolation, which will give an indication of the brush strokes applied to this layer mask.

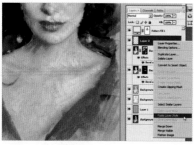

22 Paint layer When you're happy, right-click the Layer Style entry for this layer and choose Copy Layer Style. Now add a new layer (Ctrl/Cmd+Shift+N), right-click this layer in the Layers palette and choose Paste Layer Style. Reduce the brush to a very small size and choose a mid gold colour for the foreground swatch.

23 Finishing touches With this, and lighter tones of the same colour, add a few marks to define the earrings a little. Don't worry, you don't have to draw here – just a few simple marks as in the finished image will give the effect of detail. Also add a couple of white ticks in the eyes to intensify the catchlights.

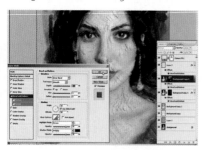

24 Layer Style Depth setting We're done now, but before flattening and saving the image, double-click the Layer Style entry for the layer below and increase the Depth value to around 200%. This will not look good in the PSD file, but needs to be increased now as the flattening process vastly reduces the impasto effect. After Photoshop flattens the image, you'll notice that your impasto brush marks look incredibly realistic and the paint really does appear to stand proud of the canvas surface.

LAYER STRUCTURE
The making of an oil painting

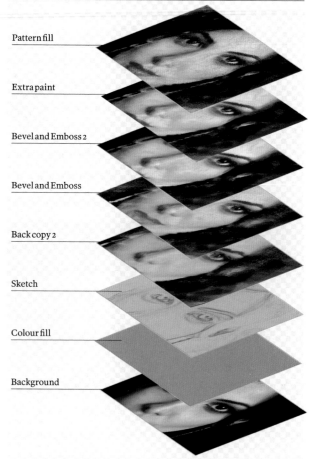

Pattern fill

Extra paint

Bevel and Emboss 2

Bevel and Emboss

Back copy 2

Sketch

Colour fill

Background

Paint the four seasons

A tree can be beautiful no matter the time of year, but why settle for just one season

Essentials

TIME TAKEN
4-5 hours

YOUR EXPERT
Sam Hampton-Smith

ON THE DISC
Original tree from sxc.hu:© micromoth, Sketch, Leaf brush, Blossom brush, Final image

Have you ever taken a photo of a scene but wished it had been a different time of year, or yearned for that little bit of 'je ne sais quoi' in your images?

Yearn no more! In this tutorial we'll take an average photograph of a tree and turn it into a work of art, creating four distinct seasons and colour correcting the image to reflect the four different times of year. You'll learn how to use the Select Color function in Photoshop to create convincing snow coverage, create brushes and paint in leaves, fake a sunset and create a painted moon.

These techniques will not only be useful in creating this project, but will also be adaptable to many others – whether you simply want to make the sky seem more blue, or accentuate all the colours in a sunset. As with anything worth

doing, it's going to take some practice and a lot of patience to get a convincing result, but persevere, and you'll add an arsenal of useful tricks and techniques to your armoury to help give your images that extra sparkle and take them from

> ## "You'll add an arsenal of useful tricks to your armoury to help give images that extra sparkle"

ordinary to extraordinary. So, without further ado, let's begin by opening up the starting image of a tree (on the disc) and diving in…

PREPARE YOUR PHOTOGRAPH
Make the most of what you already have in your image

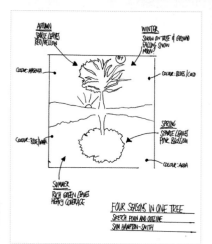

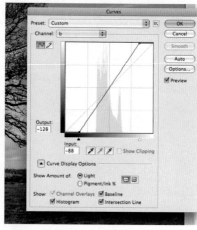

Key Photoshop Skills Covered
What you'll learn

CURVES AND COLOUR ADJUSTMENTS

LAB COLOUR CORRECTION

CREATING BRUSHES

USING BRUSH DYNAMICS

01 Plan your image For this kind of image, you're going to want to have a fairly clear idea of where you're going right from the start. We recommend that you draw a quick plan you can refer to, in order to help you remember which season goes where. This needn't be accurate, and can literally take 30 seconds – but you'll find it will prove invaluable.

02 Convert to Lab The image we have as a starting point is great, but it looks a little washed-out. Let's make the most of it by ramping up the colour. Select Image>Mode>Lab Color. This converts the image into a different colour model, where the luminance information is stored separately from the colour information – great for making non-destructive colour enhancements.

03 Make levels adjustments Create a Curves adjustment layer, and create a graph as in the screenshot above for both the A and B channels. It's important to be symmetrical with your curves, or you will introduce colour casts. Finally, select the Lightness channel and add a slight S curve to increase the contrast. Select Layer>Merge Visible, then Image>Mode>RGB.

WORKS WITH | PHOTOSHOP CS AND ABOVE

PLANNING YOUR PICTURE
Put everything in its rightful place

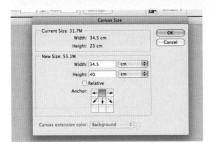

04 Increase the canvas size Our canvas needs to be about twice the height of the current image, but needn't be exact. You might want to create a slightly different crop once you see the tree growing in two directions. Double-click the background to convert it to a normal layer, then select Image>Canvas Size and click the top middle anchor button. Set Height to 40cm and hit OK.

05 Duplicate and mirror Drag the tree layer to the New Layer button to create a duplicate. Go to Edit>Transform> Flip Vertical to reflect the image along the X axis. Using the Move tool (if it's not selected, hold down Ctrl/Cmd to temporarily switch), drag the reflected layer down so that the bottom of the trees intersect nicely.

06 Add layer masks You can now see how the image will fit together, but the two layers meet badly. It would be nice to maintain some of the extra grass at the bottom left of the upright tree. Add a layer mask to the inverted tree, and paint out the horizon on the lower left quadrant to let extra grass show through. Repeat where necessary.

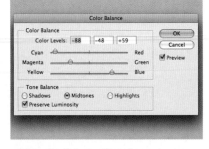

07 Clone in differences The bottom tree could now be a reflection in a lake, and if that's the effect you want, keep it that way. However, it can be a little jarring on the eye to see the same element reflected along an axis, and may interfere with the effect. Use your Clone tool to add some subtle variation to the landscape, top and bottom.

08 Add colour correction Using the Rectangular Marquee tool, draw a selection covering the winter quadrant. Make sure you have about half the tree within your selection. Add a Color Balance adjustment layer with the selection active. The adjustment layer will automatically be masked to the selection area, so your corrections will be limited to the winter quadrant.

09 Cool down the colours In winter the sun is lower in the sky. The colour temperature of light is generally more blue, as the sun refracts through more of our atmosphere. Move the sliders to introduce more Cyan, Magenta and Blue in the Midtones, and a lot more Blue in the Highlights.

10 Repeat for the other seasons Repeat this process for each of the other seasons, noting that spring is generally a little warmer, with more green, summer is warm with oranges and yellows, and autumn is moving back towards magenta and reds. Use your own artistic judgement to get an effect you like. We've gone for an extreme version of autumn here.

11 Good structure This composition is going to require quite a few different layers, so start naming and organising them now before it's too late. Create a layer group (like a folder) for each season and make sure each relevant layer sits inside the appropriate group.

MAKING YOUR OWN BRUSH
Create the right tool for the job

Tip

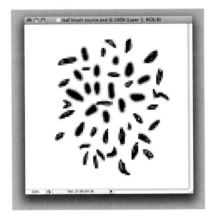

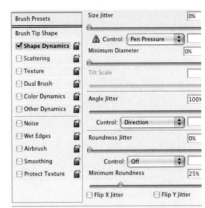

12 **Create a leaf pattern** Create a new document 100px square, and using a 1 or 2px hard-edged brush, draw a pattern of random leaf shapes in black. The leaves should be moving in different directions to be realistic, and should vary in size, but try to keep the overall size fairly small. (Find the example 'leaf brush source.psd' on the disc.)

13 **Convert your drawing into a brush** Once you're happy with your pattern of leaves, you can convert it into a brush that you'll use for a lot of the remaining steps. To define a brush from a document, simply select Edit>Define Brush Preset. Give your brush a name (such as 'leaves') and click OK. Return to your main document.

14 **Set up your brush dynamics** Select the Brush tool and open the Brush Palette options to get access to all the dynamic settings. The key setting here is to enable Angle Jitter under Shape Dynamics. This will randomly rotate your brush as you paint. Set the Control drop-down to Direction, and you'll be ready to start painting in leaves.

Details

To be convincing, work at the right level of detail to match surrounding areas. Taking the leaves on our tree as an example, it's tempting to grab one of Photoshop's default brushes and size it up to give quick coverage. It will look great when you're zoomed out, but when you view at 100% or print the image, it'll look awful: blobs of paint instead of crisp little details. To avoid this, pick or create a brush with the right level of detail for the image. Try to work at 100% Zoom, and if the leaves look wrong, change your brush.

SPRING, SUMMER, AUTUMN, WINTER
How to season-hop in a few swift steps

Colour The secret to convincing leaves is to use many colours, different sizes and varying levels of opacity. Start with the darkest colours and work to the lighter tones to get nice depth to your image.

Adjustment layers Don't be afraid of using multiple adjustment layers to get the right look. If one isn't precise enough, add a second and isolate specific areas to apply the adjustment using the layer mask.

Wash it You can also add colour washes directly by using gradients set to go from your colour choice to 50% Grey. Set the layer to use the Overlay blending mode. The grey will disappear and your colour will blend in.

Blending modes Fill a layer with 50% Grey and set the blending mode to Overlay. It will be transparent, but you can now add effects and filters such as the Lens Flare effect you see here.

Tip

Reference materials

We all know what a tree looks like in spring, but there's no substitute for looking at images. Get a feel for spring colours and how the blossom sits on the branches. Compare how light and shadow interact in the sun, and note the way snow falls in waves. Use Google Image Search, Flickr or iStockphoto to search for 'spring blossom', 'tree in summer' and 'snow falling'.

Tip

Brushes

You can define a brush from any image. If it's in colour, when you define the brush Photoshop converts it to greyscale. But it can be hard to read tonal values in a colour image, so convert it to greyscale ahead of defining the brush, via Image>Mode>Grayscale. When you're ready to define your brush, go to Edit>Define Brush Preset and give it a name.

MAKE LIKE A TREE
Paint leaves onto the tree to sell the season

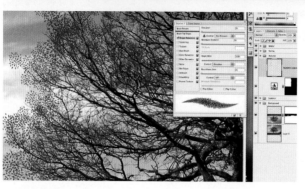

15 Autumn leaves Select a warm red-brown colour and create a new layer in the autumn layer set. Using your brush, single-click repeatedly over the autumn quadrant of the tree. This is going to take some patience to get right. Work all over the tree with single clicks until you have a nice coverage of red-brown leaves. Don't click and drag, or the effect will be less convincing.

16 And more leaves Select a richer red colour and repeat the process. When painting, it's also worth increasing and decreasing the size of your brush as you click to paint. Use the square bracket keys ([and]) to do this quickly. Cover the quadrant again, then repeat with a warmer yellow. You may find this takes five or six different colours before it looks suitably realistic.

17 Use the blending modes Set your layer to use the Multiply blending mode, then create another layer (Normal, 60% Opacity) and add yet more leaves to give coverage to some of the branches, and fill in details where necessary. By using the blending modes you can help anchor the leaves you've painted into the image, and thus fool the eye a little more successfully.

18 Spring and summer The process for spring and summer is the same. In each case, add a layer to the appropriate layer set and work in the detail starting with the darkest/tonally dullest colours first. Set to Multiply and work in extra details on a separate layer. Summer will take the longest, as you'll need to fill in a lot of different colours around the rich dark green tonal range. Spring should be more sparse and lighter in colour.

19 Snowy branches Turn off the winter adjustment layer and draw a rectangular marquee over the winter quadrant. With the selection active, go Select> Color Range. Pick a light brown from the tree trunk using the Eyedropper, and set Fuzziness to 130. Hit OK. On a new layer fill with white, then turn the adjustment layer back on.

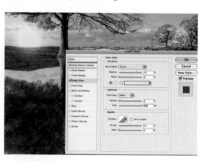

20 Setting sun in autumn On a new layer, draw a circular marquee and fill it with a pale yellow. Select Filter>Blur> Gaussian Blur and select 24px. Add a layer style by choosing Layer>Layer Style>Outer Glow, and select the Lighten blending mode and then a Size of 250px. Position your sun low on the horizon.

FLOURISHES AND DETAILS
Add the finishing touches to create interest and sell the image

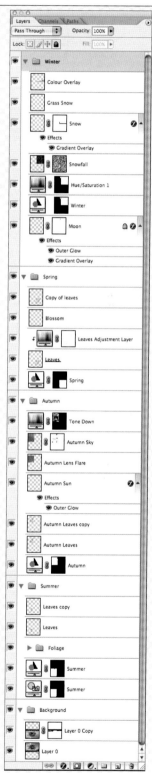

21 Winter moon Let's add a winter moon. On a new layer draw a circular marquee and fill with pale blue-grey. Pick a darker colour (not too dark), and with smaller selections fill in some craters. Add a Gaussian Blur, 3px, and go Layer>Layer Style>Gradient Overlay. Use Multiply blending mode, 10% Opacity and 135° Angle. Add an Outer Glow if desired.

22 Blossom in spring To add blossom we'll use pretty much the same technique that we did for the leaves, but paint with pinks and whites instead of greens. It's worth your while creating a new brush for this task, with a few nice petal shapes quite close together. Blossom will normally appear at the ends of branches. Don't forget to enable the Brush Dynamics to rotate the brush and add randomness.

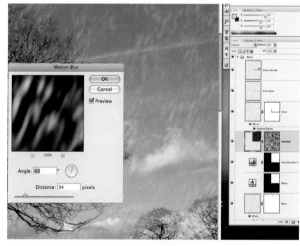

23 Instant snowfall Create a new layer, make a selection covering the winter quadrant, and choose Edit>Fill> Contents. Use 50% grey. Hit 'D' on your keyboard to return to the default colours, then select Filter>Noise>Add Noise. Give the layer a Gaussian Blur at 6 pixels, then compress the levels using Image> Adjustments>Levels. Bring the sliders in to the middle so they practically touch. Finally, add a motion blur (Filter>Blur>Motion Blur), and set the layer to Screen.

24 Blending colour corrections It's time to get working on the way the different colour adjustment layers blend into one another. Using a big soft brush, work on the adjustment layer masks to provide a nice gradual blend. Remember, you can paint with white to reveal the adjustment – so don't feel limited to the hard edge that you created earlier.

25 Look upside down! It's worth tilting your head upside down to get a view of the picture the other way up, or simply choose Image>Rotate Canvas>180°. By doing this you'll see the image in a new light, and may pick up on bits that need extra attention simply by changing your perspective on the image.

Create a ripped paper collage – Photoshop style!

BEFORE

Essentials

TIME TAKEN
2 hours

YOUR EXPERT
Kirk Nelson

ON THE DISC
Original image: 'StatueLiberty. jpg'; Colour swatches 'LibertySwatches. aco'

Turn a photo into a ripped paper collage without destroying a piece of parchment

You may have seen masterful works created by artists with an amazing ability to produce dramatic shapes and inspiring compositions with the most basic of mediums, ripped pieces of paper.

Perhaps you've been inspired enough to try your hand at this art form. So you gathered together multiple colours of construction paper and a bottle of glue and set at it… Now let's be honest, raise your hand if all you ended up with was a pile of confetti and your hands covered in sticky, dried glue. Or perhaps you actually managed to glue the paper down, but the result looked like it could have been done by

a six-year-old… Yeah, us too. It wasn't pretty. Well, fortunately for us, the same effect is easy enough to accomplish in Photoshop. A few filters, adjustment layers and clever use of layer masks will restore your ripped-paper confidence in no time.

You'll want to start with a subject which has an easily recognisable shape that's large and interesting. Try to avoid subjects that rely on a lot of details, because they will quickly drop out with this medium. We chose the Statue of Liberty as a source, due to the remarkable contour lines and familiar dramatic shape. Plus the picture is public domain. Bonus!

Key Photoshop Skills Covered
What you'll learn

FILTER COMBINATIONS
LAYER MASKS
ADJUSTMENT LAYERS

LOOK, MA – CLEAN HANDS!
Create a cut paper collage without the mess

01 Getting started Create a new file that is 25cm wide and 29.5cm tall at 300dpi with a white background. Open the 'StatueLiberty.jpg' file from the CD and drag it onto the centre of your new file. Now use the Polygonal Lasso tool to make a selection around the statue itself and hit Ctrl/Cmd+J to copy this to a new layer. Name the new layer 'Statue.' Use the same technique to create a 'Pedestal' layer.

02 That's one smart blur To help visualise the solid shapes of colour needed for the cut paper look, we need to remove much of the minor details from the image. A good way to start is with the Smart Blur. Select the Statue layer and go to Filter>Blur>Smart Blur. Set the Radius to 25, Threshold to 50 and Quality to high, then hit OK.

03 Cut that out! The blur removed the detail, now let's define the shapes. Go to Filter>Artistic>Cutout. Adjust the settings until you get a good balance of shape complexity and simplified detail. Here we set the Number of Levels to 4, Edge Simplicity to 5 and Edge Fidelity to 3.

PHOTOSHOP CS AND ABOVE | **WORKS WITH**

Using the colour swatches

The Color Swatch palette is a great way to keep your colours organised. Instead of trying to remember the RGB values of the colour you want or fumbling with the Eyedropper, use a colour swatch. Clicking a swatch sets your foreground to that colour; Ctrl/Cmd-click sets the background colour. To load the colours we used in this tutorial, use the fly-out menu by clicking the triangle on the right, then hit Load Swatches. Select Large List in this menu to see the colours and their names more easily.

DIGITAL PAPER
Create the look of ripped paper with some Photoshop filters

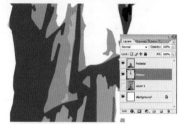

04 Touch-ups The Cutout filter left small islands of colour and intricate lines that wouldn't be believable as ripped pieces of paper. So select a round, hard-edged brush, hold down Alt/Option to select the paint colour and paint over those troublesome areas until you have smooth shapes of a medium level complexity.

07 Create dark green paper Click the StatueDark layer, then the StatueDark colour swatch to set your foreground colour. Hit Alt+Backspace (or Opt+Delete) to fill with colour. For a papery feel, go to Noise>Add Noise and adjust to around 5%, Monochromatic. Follow with Filter>Blur>Gaussian Blur set to 1 pixel.

05 Colour layers The statue will use four colours and a white backing. Open the Swatches palette; load 'LibertySwatches. aco' from the CD. This adds the colours we used to your Swatches list. Now add five layers on top of the Statue layer: 'StatueWhite', 'StatueDark', 'StatueMidDark', 'StatueMidLight', 'StatueLight'.

08 Paper shapes Hide the StatueDark and StatueWhite layers so you can see the basic Statue layer. Grab the Magic Wand, set the option for Add to Mask, Tolerance 10 and Contiguous Off. Select the darkest parts of the layer, then reveal the StatueDark layer. Make sure the layer is active; hit Add Layer Mask in the Layers palette. This creates a layer mask to give shape.

06 White out Before we layer on the coloured shapes, let's create a white backing. Ctrl/Cmd-click the Statue thumbnail to create a selection in that shape. Expand it by 5 pixels (Select> Modify>Expand), click the StatueWhite layer and go to Edit>Fill to fill the selection. Now deselect using Ctrl/Cmd+D.

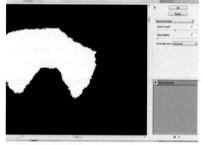

09 Rip it up! The shapes are working well, but the edges are too smooth to be believable as ripped paper. They need to have a jagged feel. Click the thumbnail of the mask you just created and go to Filter>Brush Strokes> Sprayed Strokes. Adjust the settings until the edge has a ripped feel. A Stroke Length of 9, Spray Radius of 0 and Horizontal Direction works well.

TROUBLESHOOTING DISPLACEMENT MAPS

You might notice that the Displacement Map step at the default settings appears to ignore some of the diagonal lines. What's going on here? Is Photoshop malfunctioning? Not at all. It just looks that way. What's happening is that the Displacement filter is shifting pixels according to the Horizontal and Vertical Scale settings. Essentially, it's moving pixels up and left. If this happens to fall along the same line that you've drawn, the shift is imperceptible and appears to be doing nothing to those edges.

So how do we fix this? Simply run the Displacement filter a second time (Filter>Distort>Displace), but change one of the settings to a negative value and a few pixels more or less than before. That should do the trick!

10 Cloud displacement The edges appear ripped but still have smooth lines. 'Cloud displacement' will fix this. Create a document of 25cm x 29.5cm, hit 'D' to set the colours to black/white. Go to Filter>Render> Clouds. Save the file as 'clouds.psd'. In your working file make sure the layer mask is the active layer and go to Filter>Distort>Displace. Use the defaults, hit OK and select the clouds file to use as a displacement to break up the smooth lines.

11 Drop shadow Now we need to make the shapes look like they are separate pieces that were pasted onto plain white paper. A subtle shadow can help accomplish this illusion. Add a Drop Shadow layer style and set Distance to 1 pixel and Size to 3 pixels. This creates a soft, subtle shadow that sets the shapes off from the white background.

'PAPERLESS' RIPPED PAPER ART
Making paper art from pixels

12 **More ripped effects** We noticed when ripping up actual paper that the layers tended to separate along the ripped edge. This is evident by a slightly lighter colour along the rip. To simulate this, go to Layer>New Adjustment Layer>Hue/Saturation. Check the Use Previous Layer to Create Clipping Mask box. Set Saturation to -19 and Lightness to 23. Now click the adjustment layer's mask thumbnail and hit Ctrl/Cmd+I to invert the mask and hide the adjustment. Set your paint colour to white and use a small scatter brush on the mask to paint in the adjustment along the edges. Don't just outline the shape – the less uniform the app, the more realistic the illusion.

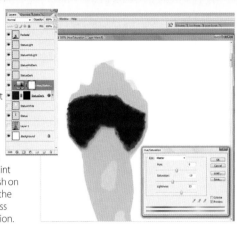

13 **Look! It's Lady Liberty in paper!** Repeat steps 7-12 for the rest of the statue, matching the swatch colours with the layers of the same name. You may want to adjust the numbers on the displacement step to create more variation between the pieces of paper.

LAYER STRUCTURE
How we created our paper world

14 **Put her on a pedestal** Move on to the Pedestal layer, using the same Smart Blur settings and Cutout filter as you used on the statue. Create new layers: 'PedestalWhite', 'PedestalDark', 'PedestalMid' and 'PedestalLight.' Notice your swatches have colours already set up for these layers as well. Using the same techniques as before, create the paper pieces for the pedestal.

15 **Shine on!** Just above the background add two layers, 'Halo' and 'Burst.' Set your foreground to the SunYellow1 colour and background to SunYellow3. On the Halo layer select a circle around the torch and use the Gradient tool to create a radial gradient going from the light yellow to the dark yellow. Similarly, on the Burst layer use the Polygonal Lasso tool to create the shape of light rays shining out. Fill this selection with the same radial gradient.

16 **Shining happy paper** Guess what's next? Yep, turn those light rays into paper! You can skip the Smart Blur and go straight to the Cutout filter with these. Three layers should work out nicely: 'SunYellow1', 'SunYellow2' and 'SunYellow3.' Check the sidebar for tips on how to get to those diagonal lines that the displacement step seems to ignore.

17 **Blue skies ahead** Finish off the piece by adding some blue geometric shapes in the background. Run them through the same technique you should have mastered by now. Then sit back and rejoice in the fact that your hands aren't sticky and you don't have to clean up hundreds of tiny pieces of ripped paper!

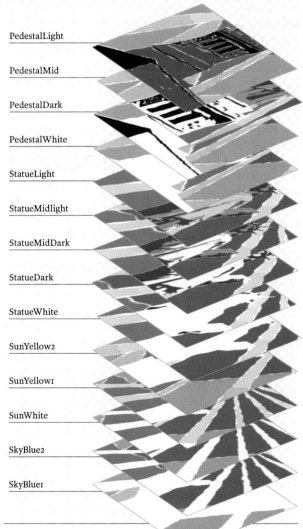

PedestalLight

PedestalMid

PedestalDark

PedestalWhite

StatueLight

StatueMidlight

StatueMidDark

StatueDark

StatueWhite

SunYellow2

SunYellow1

SunWhite

SkyBlue2

SkyBlue1

CD contents

Follow the tutorial and learn new skills with these files

Latest Magazines & Back Issues, Books, eMags, Binders & Merchandise

imagine**shop**.co.uk

Buy Online

Advertisement

Beginner's Photoshop

www.creativelearning.tv

Please Select | **Photo editing** | **Restoring photos** | **Photo manipulation** | **Retouching photos** | **Creative projects**

Welcome

Photoshop is festooned with tools that allow anybody to create the images they want. It doesn't matter if you are completely new to the program or if you have only used it in a limited way; this book teaches you essential Photoshop skills and this disc holds all the resource files you need to try the tutorials for yourself. As a bonus, we also have a special quick start video tutorial for each chapter. These walk you through the tools and techniques you will be using in each chapter, giving you an overview of how they work and how to get the best from them.

By using the resources found on this disc, together with the guides in the book, you will not only be able to edit your photos to perfection, you will also have the skills to turn them into whatever you choose!

CREATIVE LEARNING .TV

Jo Cole, Editor in Chief

Home | www.creativelearning.tv | www.imagineshop.co.uk | **Quit**

Photoshop® is a registered trademark or trademark of Adobe Systems Incorporated in the United States and/or other countries and is used with express permission.

Essential content

Tutorial files

Follow all of the tutorials in this book using these files. You'll find starter images in addition to extras such as actions, swatches and everything else you need to complete the tutorials

Video tutorials

If you are completely new to Photoshop, these video tutorials are essential viewing. They walk you through the basics of each chapter, explaining the tools and techniques you will be using